1952

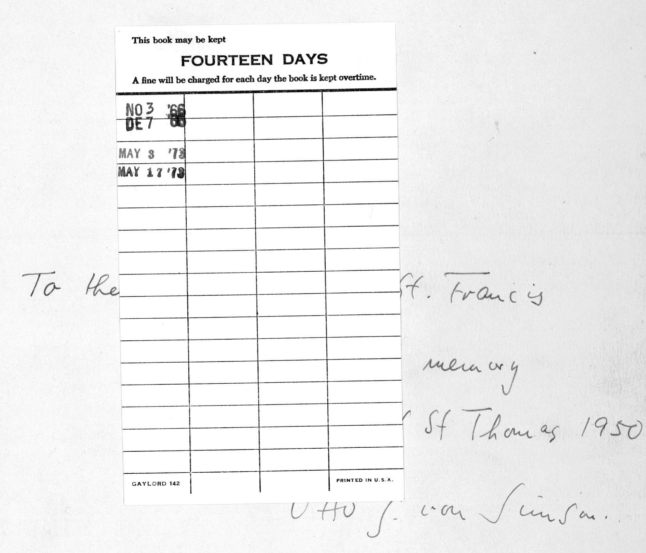

This book may be kept

FOURTEEN DAYS

A fine will be charged for each day the book is kept overtime.

NO 3 '66			
DE 7 66			
MAY 3 '73			
MAY 17 '73			
GAYLORD 142			PRINTED IN U.S.A.

To the ... St. Francis

memory

St Thomas 1950

Otto G. von Simson.

SACRED FORTRESS

Byzantine Art and Statecraft in Ravenna

THE EMPEROR JUSTINIAN. MOSAIC IN SANT' APOLLINARE NUOVO

SACRED FORTRESS

Byzantine Art and Statecraft in Ravenna

By

OTTO G. VON SIMSON

THE UNIVERSITY OF CHICAGO PRESS · CHICAGO

THE UNIVERSITY OF CHICAGO PRESS, CHICAGO 37
Cambridge University Press, London, N.W. 1, England
W. J. Gage & Co., Limited, Toronto 2B, Canada

To

MY WIFE

PREFACE

THIS essay is devoted to three churches in ancient Ravenna that were built during the reign of the Emperor Justinian in the decisive period of his administration and, at least partly, at his command. These sanctuaries, with their architecture and their famous mosaics largely intact, are perhaps the greatest surviving monuments of the early period of Christian art, which not only culminates but ends with them. I have here attempted to see them against the entire panorama of the age in which they were executed and in the political atmosphere of which they were a part. No work of art is fully intelligible without such knowledge of its background; and the greater the work of art is, the more universal must be the historical setting in which it is to be seen and which is reflected in it. All this is true in a specific sense for the monuments of Ravenna. Here the imaginative creations of the architect and the mosaicist were designed to mirror the decisive political issues of the age and, indeed, to inspire them. This art is "propaganda" in the grand sense, called into being in a moment of historical emergency and intended to sway the minds of a generation by the power of intuitive vision. In historical perspective these monuments have thus become clues of unrivaled significance to the ideals and aspirations of a century which, dividing Christian antiquity and the Middle Ages, has shaped the history of our civilization.

The group of works which I am going to discuss are not altogether easy to understand. It has taken me well over a hundred pages to explain them. They were not—as nearly all art since the Renaissance has been—created as graceful pastime and are not meant to entertain. They embody the idea under which a great civilization subsumed its entire existence—the idea upon which the life of everyone, no matter what his social station and education, was ordered and which gave cohesion and strength to the complex structure of an empire.

Works of art which express such a normative idea must assume the most solemn character. Their imagery invokes the inexorable deeds of power, the sublime visions of faith. The monuments of Ravenna had this function; hence our task is rendered at once more difficult and more rewarding, for, if we try to lift their message, we shall find the entire epoch clinging to it.

Above all, the art of Ravenna appears somewhat forbidding to us because of the idea which it conveys. Today the concerns of what we call "Byzantine civilization" appear as fancy and fable. We find it strange or even repulsive to see the actions of a powerful state motivated by dreams. And many a reader will weigh the sumptuous and magical irridescence of Byzantine culture against the sacrifice in blood and tears exacted by the Emperor Justinian for its completion and will find the price too high. With such a viewpoint we have no quarrel. Byzantium offers us the spectacle of a civilization not primitive but highly sophisticated, and yet altogether molded by the power of the imagination. The influence of this power upon the lives of individuals and of society appears in the monuments that we are going to study.

Interest in Byzantine art has markedly increased within recent years. This phenomenon is not without significance, since it is but part of a much wider pattern of intellectual experience. Twenty years ago, a great poet, W. B. Yeats, set out on his imaginary voyage to Byzantium. He left behind him the civilization of the nineteenth century—to him "no country for old men"—and turned to "the sages standing in God's holy fire as in the gold mosaic of a wall." These he invoked to be "singing masters" of his soul, to

> Consume my heart away; sick with desire
> And fastened to a dying animal
> It knows not what it is; and gather me
> Into the artifice of eternity.[1]

The "artifice of eternity" is a treasure of the Byzantine emperor of which the poet had read somewhere, "a tree made of gold and silver and artificial birds that sang." The wonderful contrivance has here become a symbol. And we sense the nostalgia which moved the poet to turn from the perpetual and sterile adolescence of his (and our) civilization to that of Byzantium, absorbed in the childlike wisdom of play. Yeats was not alone. An entire generation has set out to explore the sub-rational and supra-rational strata of the mind. This interest is reflected even in the historical investigations of our time. Instinct and intuition and their manifestations in art, religion, and lore, which the historians of the eighteenth century ridiculed and those of the nineteenth century explained as the results of malady or repression, are more and more attracting the attention and the critical sensibility of students of history. Bergson saw in the mythopoetic power of the imagination, in the *faculté fabulatrice,* the instinct to which the race owes its survival and its eternal justification. The historian is inclined to see in it the energy which molds civilizations.

Yeats's golden tree reflects the yearnings of our age; but at the same time the poet has intuitively seized upon an image which epitomizes the spirit of Byzantine culture. The "artifice of eternity," an object of pure contemplation, serene in itself and setting the mind free as does a play, is at once sacred symbol and precious toy. Byzantine man was a *Homo ludens.* To him the world was a theater, created and directed by the Divine Poet. And he perceived the conquests and catastrophes of history, and his personal destiny in their midst, with the detach-

ment which is at once the detachment of contemplation and of play. Hence his untiring labors, as theologian, artist, and legislator, to crystallize the riotous carnival of the world in an austere pattern, to see the abstract in the concrete, and to distil symbol, metaphor, and dream from the reality of things. It is this manifold activity to which we refer when we speak of the "Byzantine style."

Every historical epoch reflects itself in documents peculiar to itself. "Sociological" statistics are the documents germane to a generation which has surrendered almost entirely to the contingencies of material existence. By the same token, it is a play—solemn, awesome, sublime, but still a play—which to posterity embodies the genius of Byzantine civilization. I refer to the liturgical drama of the eucharistic rite. The significance of this drama transcended the sphere of worship. It embraced the political world and mirrored man's existence on earth and in the life to come. And upon closer investigation we shall discern in this sacred play the contours of an epoch of Christian civilization patterned after what, for that generation, was the reality beyond realities. This is the spectacle to which we now turn.

As the curtain rises, we behold a vast panorama. The time is the sixth century, the Golden Age of Byzantine civilization. "Within the girdle of these walls," we might say, echoing Shakespeare,

> are now confin'd two mighty monarchies
> Whose high upreared and abutting fronts
> The perilous narrow ocean parts asunder.

In our drama the ocean is the Adriatic Sea. The two powers opposing each other are the Roman emperor, who had made Constantinople or Byzantium his capital after ceding Italy to her invaders; and the Ostrogothic kingdom in Italy, which, under Theodoric, the greatest ruler of Germanic antiquity, had become an almost autonomous territory, in which Latins and Teutons lived peacefully together. The Emperor Justinian's decision to wrest Italy from Theodoric's heirs led to the Gothic War, in the midst of which the sanctuaries were built to which this essay is devoted. Between the two enemies stood the power which was eventually to seize the prize—the papacy. The great struggle, in which the opponents realized their individual character and their irreconcilable missions, centered around Ravenna. This city is also the scene of our drama.

We can no longer witness the liturgical pageant of the sixth century in which these great events were reflected. As we try to reconstruct it, we are assisted not only by the liturgical texts but also by the sanctuaries in which it was enacted. Here the mosaics are of special importance. If we may consider San Vitale or Sant' Apollinare Nuovo sacred stages for the enactment of the drama, the mosaics which adorn them are stage decorations and settings eloquent enough to make us visualize the twofold vision of history and eternity which the actual drama unfolded. To understand this language, we must leave behind us many of the concepts and conventions of the present day and must transport ourselves into a world in which such concepts as "image" or "imitation" or "representation" or even "prayer" have retained their original, strong, and pristine meaning, which differs widely from our own. The attempt to understand this ancient world will be eminently rewarding. In these symbols of stone and color a great civilization submits its legacy.

O. G. v. S.

CHICAGO
Feast of St. Apollinaris of Ravenna
July 23, 1948

ACKNOWLEDGMENTS

THE following pages have grown out of a series of public lectures on the interrelation of religion and art in the early Middle Ages delivered during the autumn of 1945 at the University of Chicago under the auspices of the Committee on Social Thought. I am indebted to my colleagues and students in this true community of scholars, above all to its chairman, Professor John U. Nef, whose encouragement and advice have sustained me through the entire work. Two grants by the Social Science Research Committee, under the Rockefeller Foundation, and by the Division of the Humanities of the University have enabled me to prepare the volume for publication.

Dom Anselm Strittmatter, O.S.B., has bestowed upon the work his great erudition and insight with a generosity and patience which few eminent scholars have to spare for the work of others. To his knowledge of the liturgy the book owes innumerable improvements; but I must claim its shortcomings for myself. Dr. Ernst Kitzinger, of the Dumbarton Oaks Research Library, was good enough to read the entire manuscript. I have benefited much from his critique. Ursula von Eckardt prepared the index.

The essay was already completed when M. André Grabar's magisterial *Martyrium* appeared. This work has confirmed and deepened some of my own interpretations, even though to me the author's main thesis, that of the influence of the cult of relics upon early Christian art, seems occasionally to be carried too far. Luckily, I was able to enrich my own manuscript before it went to press by references to this work, perhaps the most important contribution to Christian archeology in our generation.

Without my wife's help, devotion, and encouragement, this book could not have been written. To her it is dedicated.

TABLE OF CONTENTS

[xiii]

LIST OF ILLUSTRATIONS

CHAPTER ONE

Dramatis Personae: Justinian · Julianus Argentarius · Maximian

THREE times Western civilization has been shaped in the city of Ravenna. Here, in 49 B.C., Caesar gathered his followers before crossing the Rubicon. He thus tied the city to the fortunes of the Roman Empire; and, under Augustus, Ravenna became, like Misenum, a principal base of the Italian fleet and one of the important cities of Italy. Today Ravenna preserves hardly a trace of that period of political, economic, and cultural prosperity.

In 1321 the greatest Christian poet died in Ravenna. Dante had come to the city at the invitation of its lord, Guido Novello da Polenta; within its walls he completed the *Divine Comedy*. The eyes which had been the last to behold the vision of the imperium in its glory closed where Caesar had prepared its foundation. The storms of time which have swept through Ravenna have effaced the vestiges of Dante's visit to Ravenna, as they have those of Caesar.

But between the visits of Caesar and Dante, almost in the middle of the span of fourteen hundred years, lies the epoch which not only linked Ravenna indissolubly to the history of the Roman Empire but made the city its political and spiritual heart. Early in the fifth century Emperor Honorius transferred his residence from Rome to Ravenna. From that time on and until the death of Justinian in 565, Ravenna played a political role often hardly less important than that of Byzantium and often more important than that of Rome.

History placed Ravenna between these two cities. An Italian town with a great Roman past, a port looking toward Byzantium, a natural fortress between impenetrable swamps and the sea,[1] Ravenna seemed predestined to become the setting for the great struggle in which the universal Empire sought to maintain itself against the centrifugal tendencies that threatened it from within and attracted its enemies from without. During this century and a half the traditions of East and West, enemies elsewhere in the Empire, still appeared to embrace each other in Ravenna. Pressed by the onslaught of heterogeneous forces—Arian Goths in Italy and Monophysite Greeks in the East—the sphere of the imperial idea gradually contracted until Ravenna became, culturally no less than militarily, the embattled outpost of the Christian Empire. Within the walls of that Adriatic city the ideas which had once permeated the entire civilized world eventually appeared curiously compressed and entangled, but with an intensity which seizes the visitor even today.

Through a unique stroke of good luck the scene of this historical drama has not been dissolved by the forces of time. According to contemporary standards, Ravenna is no more than a sleepy country town; grass grows between the cobblestones of its quiet streets. But it is hardly an exaggeration to say that no other city in the world has preserved the life and the breath of the past as completely as has Ravenna. Athens has been transfigured by the ravages of time. The Acropolis no longer bespeaks the historical life of Periclean Attica but the soul of Hellas. In Rome the layers of history have grown one into the other: of the city of the Caesars, of Peter and Paul, of Rienzo, of the Counter Reformation, there exist but fragments; they have destroyed one another. That the life, the continuity, and the unity of history consist of such destructions—such is the message of the Eternal City. Not the life but the dream of medieval Islam has survived in Granada; the spirit of the Christian Middle Ages reached beyond itself in Chartres. What German cities had preserved the character of an epoch are now in ashes. Only Florence can compare with Ravenna in the integrity and purity with which it embodies a great period of the past. But, unlike Ravenna, Florence never was the scene of the decisive political movements of an age. It is the birthplace of, and a monument to, an intellectual and artistic era unsurpassed in the history of the West, whereas Ravenna has been the setting for one of the crises in the history of the world. Within its walls antiquity and the Middle Ages, Orient and Occident, have met and parted. The great tombs of Ravenna are also the gravestones of the Roman Empire.

It is a truism to say that works of art are historical documents, that their serene faces reveal and conceal the intellectual and political life in which they originated. But this truism assumes a special significance in Ravenna. Here the works of the architect and the maker of mosaics are not accidental and unconscious witnesses of past history. In studying the architecture and mosaics of Ravenna, one gradually becomes aware of the fact that they were conceived as instruments of political power, that they plead the great political issues of the time. More important, those issues become completely intelligible only if seen through the rhetorical medium in which they were presented—the art of Ravenna. In its great

symbols there becomes palpable, even for us, the distant spiritual realm from which Byzantine legislation and statecraft derived their inspiration.

I

The "Byzantine" monuments of Ravenna may be assigned to three distinct epochs. The first is associated with the name of Galla Placidia, the second with that of Theodoric, the third with that of Justinian. The present work is devoted to the last and most important of them. But it is noteworthy that we find a common characteristic in all three: political concepts are conveyed in terms of religion. We may be inclined to see in this tendency no more than a rhetorical device—an error which makes an understanding of the age impossible. Since we can overcome our preconceptions only gradually, we may start here with no more than a simple observation: the three greatest rulers that resided in, or governed, Ravenna left only religious monuments to their rule and to the political concepts which guided them.

Galla Placidia lived in Ravenna from 424 onward. It was from here that since 425 the daughter of Theodosius governed the West Roman Empire as its last great ruler. A generation after Galla Placidia's death the Empire collapsed. Of the great works of architecture she commissioned, few have survived. But, of these, two have been wonderfully well preserved: the baptistry of San Giovanni in Fonte (the so-called "Baptistry of the Orthodox") and the mausoleum of the empress. Both will briefly concern us later.

The Gothic period of Ravenna begins with Theodoric's triumphant entry into the city in 493. The event was marked by the murder of Odoacer—a crime as hideous as the execution of Boethius, more than thirty years later. But the monuments of Ravenna reveal the Gothic king's mind to have been as profoundly occupied with religious matters as was that of Galla Placidia. The one building in Ravenna which is the king's work, in the most characteristic and personal sense, is his mausoleum. It has long been recognized that this structure is not an isolated example of early Germanic art but, on the contrary, a magnificent adaptation of Italic funerary architecture. But the great king was not satisfied with expressing in this building his understanding of, and admiration for, classical art. He placed the latter in the service of the Christian cult. The lower story of the mausoleum evidently contained Theodoric's tomb, while the room above served as a chapel. The cult significance of this combination is a theme that will be more fully discussed in a later chapter.

But the many splendid works of ecclesiastical architecture commissioned by Theodoric have strangely disappeared. Some, like the great church of San Andrea de'Goti, have vanished altogether. Others, like Sant' Apollinare Nuovo, the palace chapel of the Gothic king, underwent radical and significant changes when Justinian, after his victory over the Arian Goths, turned their ecclesiastical property over to the Orthodox church of Ravenna. Even more puzzling is the relation of some of the other churches, among them San Vitale and Sant' Apollinare in Classe, to the Gothic rulers of Ravenna.

Both churches, the most magnificent sanctuaries extant in that city, were begun under Gothic rule, many years before Belisarius' entry into the city (540). They are, nevertheless, Byzantine, not Gothic, enterprises; and in this fact lies the secret political mission which the style, as well as the imagery, of these first "Byzantine" buildings of Ravenna conveys even today. They were commissioned by, and remained under the jurisdiction of, the Orthodox see of the city, which for many years had enjoyed that complete freedom which Theodoric's policy of toleration had secured for it almost to the end of his life. Only the king's last measures, while not amounting to an actual reversal of his earlier position, indicate an unmistakable stiffening of his attitude toward the Catholic church. This change finds at least part of its explanation in the extraordinary position which the see of Ravenna assumed immediately upon Theodoric's death.[2]

This event and the circumstances surrounding it were recounted around the middle of the sixth century by an anonymous chronicler, in all probability an Orthodox cleric of Ravenna. According to him, Theodoric died, suddenly and providentially, only three days after he had issued an edict suppressing the Catholic church. The accuracy of this story is more than dubious.[3] But, written at a time when some witnesses of the events recorded were still alive, the story of Theodoric's hostility against the church would not have received the wide credence of which we have evidence, had it been devoid of all truth. What are the facts behind it?

Immediately after Theodoric's death, the Orthodox church of Ravenna became not only an outpost of Catholic doctrine in a still largely Arian city but the most important instrument of imperial policy in Italy. Such close co-operation with Byzantium was not improvised suddenly; it is far less likely that it was the result of Theodoric's "persecution" of the church (as Catholics were soon to call it) than that it was its cause. It is now generally agreed that dogmatic differences between Arians and Catholics had ceased to be a political issue under Theodoric; that even the king's most savage acts—the execution of Boethius and Symmachus and the imprisonment of Pope John—were not directed against the faith of these men but against their political convictions.[4] If, toward the end of his life, Theodoric considered restrictive measures against the see of Ravenna, he was likewise prompted by political considerations.

Theodoric's relations to Italian Catholicism were quite different from those with the Orthodoxy of Byzantium. Here he was faced with a wide and unbridgeable chasm. Imperial policy conceived political and religious issues as inextricably entwined. Orthodox doctrine spearheaded the moves of political, as well as of military, strategy; and nowhere is this fact more apparent than in the great campaign that was designed to wrest the western parts of the Empire from their Arian conquerors. The aging Theodoric knew this scheme; and he was not blind to the role which had been assigned to the Orthodox see of Ravenna. This proud institution in his own capital, housed only a few blocks from his palace, must have appeared to him as a menace to the very marrow of Gothic rule. If he struck a blow against it, he aimed at his greatest enemy, the emperor, and at the formidable weapon which religion became in the emperor's hands. Theodoric died as the struggle was just taking shape. Barely two decades after his death Gothic rule had ended in Ravenna; and the Catholic archbishop, whose power Theodoric had vainly sought to contain, had been installed by Justinian as the city's supreme lord.

The Byzantine strategy which triumphed in this event was, in some of its decisive aspects, not one of diplomatic intrigue or of military operations. It was waged, above all, in the realm of religious imagination and included the legend, composed and circulated in Ravenna, of Theodoric the tyrant and fearful enemy of the Orthodox faith; it included, above all, the magnificent program of ecclesiastical architecture which even today bears witness to the Byzantine phase of Ravenna's history. Unrivaled as monuments to the age of Justinian and to the spirit of the Gothic War, these works have not received an adequate interpretation. In their proud and fervent language we may discover the cause for which Boethius suffered execution and which triumphed, nevertheless, in the collapse of Theodoric's state.

II

Justinian ascended the imperial throne in 527— one year after Theodoric's death. In the policies of Byzantium the event marked hardly a change; Justinian had long been directing the administration of the Empire, and his plans for Ravenna were ready. But, at the moment that he assumed supreme authority, chance granted him the means for their execution.

It is impossible to say what might have happened if Theodoric had either succeeded in retaining the loyalty of the Catholic clergy of his capital or if he had actually destroyed the church. His death after a brief and ineffective period of hostility on his part left his supporters among the clergy of Ravenna helpless and enabled his enemies to drive the see completely into the arms of Byzantium. They could now present his splendid record of religious tolerance as a fiction. The Catholic church owed her existence not to his benevolence but to imperial might. Upon the tyrant's death she had miraculously, like Christ on Easter morn, emerged to triumphant life after three days of deadly peril. The same year, 526, the foundations were laid for the church of San Vitale. Do we not have to regard this temple as a monument of victory, as the radiant counterpart of the dark and ghastly shadow under which the legend of the church cast the memory of Theodoric, her vanquished rival? (Pl. 1.)

By the originality of its structure alone, San Vitale marks an epoch in the artistic history of Ravenna. In Christian architecture the octagonal plan is an image of the Easter sepulcher. Liturgically and mystically, a martyr's sanctuary is both his tomb and Christ's sepulcher; and early Christian theology conceived the dignity of martyrdom as the martyr's mystical transfiguration into Christ. The architecture of San Vitale, evoking this relation of the death and resurrection of the titular saint to the death and resurrection of Christ, is a significant tribute to the Christ-like dignity of St. Vitalis. But the function of the church cannot be explained in terms of the cult only.[5]

In the early years of the seventh century, Pope Boniface IV dedicated the Roman Pantheon to the memory of all Christian martyrs.[6] The act was an illustration of that Christian philosophy for which history was focused around the mystery of redemption; Augustine's *City of God* is the greatest expression of this view. As the sepulcher of Christ had become the scene of his triumphant resurrection, so the Pantheon, the structure of which recalls funerary architecture, now appeared to Christian vision as the Easter sepulcher of the Christian church. The sanctuary became the stational church for the Friday after Easter. Linked to the day of Christ's death by the mystical octave, the liturgy of the Friday after Easter is an echo of the death on Calvary. As the sacred stage for the celebration of this liturgy, the Pantheon lifted the Easter drama into the realm of universal history: the Christian community of Rome was reminded that the death of her martyrs had vanquished the gods of the pagan world.

Was not the church of San Vitale of Ravenna to convey a similar thought, with this difference only, that the enemy whose defeat the building celebrated was not the pagan Roman but the Arian Goth? The church is only the first building in a vast program of ecclesiastical architecture in which the see of Ravenna proclaimed its new power after Theodoric's death; and we may ask if its sepulchral shape was not deliberately conceived as a response to the king's mausoleum. That the church should have been dedicated to St. Vitalis is not surprising. Only a few years earlier a document had appeared in Ravenna which was to have a profound influence upon the ecclesiatical history of this city. Claiming the authorship of St. Ambrose, it established St. Vitalis as the head of a veritable clan of martyrs, making him the husband of St. Valeria and the father of SS. Gervase and Protase. The work, moreover, declared that Vitalis as well as Ursicinus had suffered martyrdom in Ravenna. In addition to vindicating these martyrs as *genii loci* of Ravenna, the *Passio beatorum martyrum Gervasii et Protasii* indicates the exact place which the martyrs had hallowed with their blood.[7] Upon this very spot, which has aptly been called a "little Colosseum," San Vitale rose, and other great churches followed soon after. As if destined to become the Pantheon of Ravenna, San Vitale was dedicated not only to St. Vitalis but to his two sons as well.[8]

The glorification of local martyrs in a number of great sanctuaries is understandable as an expression of local patriotism. The see of Ravenna seemed to have been saved through the intervention of her martyrs. As the Church rose from her persecution, she celebrated again the triumph of her martyrs over death. Yet even at this juncture we are faced with a fact which transfers this homage to a number of saints from the narrow confines of ecclesiastical policy to the realm of universal history: the sacred ground occupied by San Vitale was the property of the imperial fisc.[9] Even during the time of Ravenna's occupation by the Goths, it could not have been used without the explicit permission of Byzantium. Moreover, the circumstances which surround the building of the church make it certain that the architectural program was carried out not merely with the permission but at the command of Justinian.

III

In the twenty-fourth chapter of his *Liber pontificalis ecclesiae Ravennatis*, Agnellus opens that long account of prodigious building activities in sixth-century Ravenna which has made his work a capital source of our knowledge of the art of that period. The first work that Agnellus mentions is San Vitale, the construction of which, as he points out, was begun under Bishop Ecclesius. But the chronicler makes it clear that Ecclesius was not the spiritus rector of the enterprise: "Ipsius temporibus ecclesia beati Vitalis Martiris a Juliano Argentario, una cum ipso presule, fundata est." The bishop is named only after Julianus Argentarius as founder of the great church.

The churches of Ravenna have much to tell us about Julianus Argentarius. His name has been associated with five new churches[10] which rose in his lifetime, four of them in Ravenna (San Vitale, Santa Maria Maggiore, San Michele, Santo Stefano), one in Classe (Sant' Apollinare). No other individual has been more closely identified with the execution of the great architectural program to which these pages are devoted. Three hundred years later, Agnellus was still struck by the fact that the metropolitans of Ravenna, generally so jealous of their dignity and authority, had found Julianus Argentarius worthy of being remembered, together with themselves, as *dedicator* of some of the most splendid churches ever erected. In San Vitale, as well as in Sant' Apollinare in Classe, the dedicatory inscription mentions three names: those of the two bishops who commissioned and consecrated the churches and that of Julianus Argentarius. In San Vitale, moreover, we find Julianus' monogram next to that of Bishop Victor. And in the same church the capsula with relics, deposited when the sanctuary was consecrated, bears only one name, that of Julianus. "Julianus Argentarius servus vester precibus vestris basilicam a fundamentis perfecit." The inscription, like a prayer, invokes the intercession of the saints, as if the donor had built the church for the salvation of his own soul only. But the proudest memorial to Julianus is found in the great dedicatory mosaic in San Vitale. Here he is portrayed between the archbishop and the emperor, an altogether astonishing tribute to a a man whose name otherwise has vanished from historical record[11] (Pls. 2 and 3).

Who was he? In all probability a Byzantine and a layman. His apparent share in the artistic activities of sixth-century Ravenna is such that one has thought of him as a great architect who brought to the Adriatic city the new art which emerged in Byzantium during the reign of Justinian. It appears, indeed, certain that Julianus was responsible for the formal aspects of the artistic works he commissioned during Ravenna's Golden Age. But he cannot have been an architect in the modern sense of the word. The political and social hierarchy of Byzantium conceded little initiative and little dignity to the creative individual. One has only to look at works of art of that period to realize how rigorously personal talent was subordinated to the impersonal motives of a higher will. Procopius insists that Justinian himself interfered twice in the construction of Hagia Sophia.[12] The memorable words with which the emperor entered the newly completed cathedral are well known: "Solomon, I have surpassed thee." He considered the wonderful structure his own creation. To him and to his age, the artist was no more than a craftsman.

But this very fact demanded an architect in another sense, a master-mind able to direct and to inspire the co-ordinated efforts of many. And such a man Julianus Argentarius seems to have been. The architectural program which he directed in Ravenna after Theodoric's death represents an individual effort, unsurpassed in the history of Christian art. Yet the initiative cannot have been entirely his or even, as the wording of Agnellus' remark shows, that of the bishop of Ravenna. The property upon which the churches rose was, as we have seen, donated by the imperial fisc. We must assume that Julianus was a great functionary of the Empire, employed in Ravenna, to use a felicitous phrase of Mgr Testi-Rasponi, as the "long arm" of Justinian himself.[13]

Julianus Argentarius had the authority, the means, even the technical competence, of the "architect." But he was no Maecenas who commissioned and inspired works of art for the sake of beauty and enjoyment only. The magnificent works of architecture which he founded announced, and, in fact, initiated, a great political enterprise. They opened the campaign which the armies of Narses brought to a conclusion. The Gothic War in Italy began not with the death of Theodoric's daughter, Amalasuntha, as Procopius believed, but with the architectural projects of Julianus Argentarius. Amalasuntha herself was unable to defeat a move of such subtlety and ingenuity.

IV

Nothing, perhaps, shows more strikingly the methods, as well as the spirit, of Justinian's policies than the way in which the emperor prepared the eventual downfall of his Gothic enemy. We find it difficult to conceive of the use of religion in politics for other than Machiavellian motives; hence Justinian's statesmanship appears to us cynical and hypocritical. But such an interpretation cannot explain either this statesmanship or its momentary success. We may recall here the remarkable interrelation which, at an earlier age, had linked the mystery religions to the Hellenistic and Roman monarchies. These popular cults followed the establishment of absolute rule and prospered under it. The Christian church is no exception.[14] After the age of persecution, Christianity became the actual link between the ruler and his subjects. It is hardly an exaggeration to say that, in an absolute monarchy, religion assumes the role of a constitution, defending, defining, and limiting the authority of the ruler and shaping the political concepts of the people.

Neither Justinian's diplomatic shrewdness nor his military might could have secured his political position. This could be done only by the general conviction that the Christian faith had in him its true champion, that God himself had ordained him for this holy cause. This belief the emperor shared with his subjects. The stern and terrible measures with which Justinian later sought to bend the church of Rome to his will have caused her to see in him a tyrant who used religious pretexts for political motives. But, however we may judge the emperor's personality, we cannot doubt the intensity and the sincerity of his religious convictions. Nor can we doubt that his subjects, as well as the vast majority of the hierarchy, were convinced of Justinian's theological vocation, that in it even his political authority seemed to originate. In 533 the emperor invited six Monophysite and six Orthodox bishops to that colloquy on the Council of Chalcedon which was later to have such unexpected consequences.[15] On the third and last day Justinian himself appeared among the prelates. As he delivered a long theological discourse, he seemed to the Orthodox bishops like another David or Paul. "If I had not heard with my own ears the words which, by the grace of God, flow from the blessed mouth of this prince [writes a prelate on another occasion] I could hardly believe it." To the pious listener the emperor seemed to unite the fortitude of David with the patience of Moses and the piety of the apostles themselves.[16] The affinities between Benedict's Holy Rule and the Justinian Code have convinced a distinguished historian that the emperor conceived his great legislative work under the inspiration of the ascetical thought of his age.[17]

Of Justinian's great enterprises, none had in his own eyes a more manifestly religious purpose than did his war against the Goths. To him the Germanic invaders and rulers of vast tracts of the Roman Empire were, above all, heretics—it was this fact, not their political tendencies, their race, or their native culture, which made them in the emperor's eyes detestable aliens and natural enemies of his realm. Their defeat was to restore not only the political unity of the Empire but, as he put it, the true unity of peoples united in one orthodox faith. To that age such spiritual union was the prerequisite of political peace.

Justinian's Gothic War has justly been called a crusade in which both contending parties put their faith to the test of arms. In 546, after his conquest of Rome, Totila addressed his armies with words which have justly become immortal.[18] The Gothic king called his soldiers' attention to the sudden change in the fortunes of the war. A few years ago, he said, a large, well-equipped army of Goths had been defeated by a small band of Greeks. "Now, from more than 30,000 of the same enemies, a scanty remnant of the nation, poor, despised, utterly devoid of experience, has wrested the great prize of the war."

"Why," the king exclaimed, "this difference? Because aforetime the Goths, putting justice last in their thoughts, committed, against the subject Romans and one another, all sorts of unholy deeds: but now they have been striving to act righteously towards all men." Even at the risk of wearying them, Totila besought his soldiers to continue in this resolution; for, if they changed, assuredly God's favor toward them would change likewise, "since it is not this race or that nation, as such, on whose side God fights, but He assists all men everywhere who honour the precepts of eternal righteousness."

Totila's words indicate the spirit in which the great war was being fought. He could not envisage victory unless he succeeded in kindling in his armies the faith which animated himself. Justinian's belief in a transcendental cause of military victory was no different. After his victory over the Vandals, the emperor issued a solemn proclamation. As a token of God's mercy, the glorious event seems to him to

[7]

surpass all the other successes of his career. But he views the liberation of Africa after ninety-five years of alien servitude, above all, in the light of religion. He recalls the forced conversions to Arianism, the desecration of churches perpetrated by the Vandals. The vanquished enemy is for him pre-eminently a heretic, an enemy of the soul. The proclamation terminates in a fervent prayer that God may further protect the liberated provinces, that he may enable the emperor to govern in such a way that the whole of Africa may know the mercy of God Almighty.[19]

This attitude of mind must be remembered if we are to understand the great architectural enterprise into which the emperor poured the treasures of his realm, even while his ill-equipped armies met the Goths in the field of battle. Ravenna was the bastion of the enemy's strength. The martyrs of the city, as her *genii loci,* must be won over to the Orthodox side, if Justinian was to rule Italy again.

Two hundred years before, Constantine the Great had given solemn expression to the role that he had assigned to the Christian cult in the political fabric of his empire by a vast program of ecclesiastical architecture executed at his command in the great centers of his realm. These Constantinian churches in Rome, Constantinople, Antioch, and Jerusalem reflected the religious ideas of the age both by the homage paid to the cult of martyrs and by the notable approximation of Christian worship to what has aptly been called the *culte impérial.*[20] The great basilica of St. Peter's in Rome was actually a *martyrion,* the sepulchral shrine of the city's first bishop, erected on the ancient site of the Vatican cemetery. Where such hallowed ground was not available, the sanctuaries were built on imperial property and in close vicinity to the imperial palace. But the relation between the political and the religious spheres, between the worship of Christ and that of the emperor, was indicated by other means as well.

In 326 or 327, on the morrow of his victory over Licinius, which established him as the sole head of the Empire, Constantine laid the foundations to the "royal octagon" of Antioch. This sanctuary, the splendor of which filled the emperor's contemporaries with awe, was dedicated to Christ. But it was known by another title, i.e., "the church of Concord."[21] Grabar has shown how eloquent and how eminently fitting this title was. *Concordia* or ὁμόνοια was a symbol of the Roman monarchy, denoting the peaceful unity of the realm safeguarded by the emperor, in analogy to the divine harmony established throughout the cosmos. Like so many other concepts of emperor-worship, this idea of concord was taken over by Christianity. Christ himself had brought it to the world; his reign insured its eternal duration. It was eminently fitting that the first Christian emperor, after the defeat of Licinius had at once restored unity to the Empire and destroyed the enemy of Christianity, dedicated a great sanctuary to the Concord of Christ—a concept which vividly conveyed the relation of imperial government to the divine economy. We may even ask if the octagonal plan of the building does not have to be regarded as an image of this idea, if the number eight, through the musical symbolism of the octave, was not meant to refer to the "consonance" of universal peace.[22]

It appears certain that both the religious views of Constantine and their architectural expression inspired Justinian's plans for Ravenna. Like his great predecessor, he donated imperial property as building ground for his churches; and, like him, he paid extraordinary tribute to the veneration of martyrs. The great basilica of Sant' Apollinare in Classe, like St. Peter's in Rome, was dedicated to the first bishop of the city, while San Vitale, a *martyrion* even in form, honored several martyrs whom Ravenna claimed as her *genii loci.* In regard to the octagonal plan of this church, the possibility of a symbolic ambivalence is perhaps not entirely to be excluded. In Ravenna itself the idea of the Concord of Christ had been expressed, only a century before, in Galla Placidia's dedicatory inscription on the façade of the church of the Holy Cross.[23] And no other symbol could have better conveyed the abiding political aspiration of Justinian, i.e., the reunion of all parts of the imperium under his scepter through the elimination of heresy and the restoration of one undivided Christian faith. Nowhere could the monumental evocation of this idea be more appropriate than in Ravenna. In San Vitale, moreover, as we shall see in chapter ii, even the mosaics alluded to the relation between the divine and the imperial governments, blending emperor-worship into the mysteries of the Christian rite.

In one respect Justinian's architectural projects for Ravenna differed profoundly from those of Constantine. The latter's churches confirmed a political program which had already become reality. The sanctuaries of Ravenna served a political vision which was not to be realized until many years after their foundations had been laid. When Julianus Argentarius was commanded to begin the construction of San Vitale, his most alert contemporaries could have anticipated the emperor's ultimate designs, though the prospect of their realization must have appeared less than dubious. Barely two decades later, Ravenna had become a capital, not inferior to the great political and ecclesiastical centers of Constantine's empire. Her sanctuaries now gave solemn notice of this fact, as they had earlier helped bring about its realization. Justinian had foreseen both.

In its abstract consistency, which disregards all apparent difficulties of the moment, in its curious blend of political realism and religious fantasy, the project is characteristic of the emperor. Hidden from the world in the vast seclusion of the Sacred Palace, he conceived his political designs like the philosophical moves in a vast game of chess. The role which his strategy had assigned to the see of Ravenna was wonderfully consistent. But as a program of political action it was unreal enough. Neither Julianus Argentarius nor the aging philosopher-king in Byzantium was able to translate this program into the reality of ecclesiastical policies. This task required the masterful hand of another.

V

In the great dedicatory mosaic in San Vitale there appears, more conspicuous than Julianus and on a level of complete equality with the emperor himself, the archbishop who consecrated the church, Maximian. The dedicatory inscriptions in San Vitale, as well as those in Sant' Apollinare in Classe, link his name again to that of Julianus Argentarius. In the rendering of Agnellus, they read: "Beati Apolenaris Sacerdotis Basilica Mandante Vero Beatissimo Ursicino Episcopo A Fundamentis Iulianus Argentarius Edificavit Ornavit Atque Dedicavit Consecrante Vero Reverendissimo Maximiano Episcopo . . ."; "Beati Martiris Vitalis Basilica Mandante Eclesio Vero Beatissimo Episcopo A Fundamentis Iulianus Argentarius Edificavit Ornavit Et Dedicavit Consecrante Vero Reverendissimo Maximiano Episcopo. . . ."[24]

In both architectural projects the two men must have co-operated closely. Since Julianus' share is so emphatically acknowledged, the greater credit for the artistic planning and execution of the churches must go to him. He may even have had his part in the formulation of the political and theological concepts which were illustrated by the mosaics in these churches (and in others that have perished). But these concepts are abstract phantoms unless and until they have been translated into the reality of living experience. And only then can they be expressed in the narrative imagery of art. The mosaics of Ravenna express the great theological and political motives of the sixth century with a force that has perhaps no parallel in Christian art. In this, their decisive aesthetic aspect, these works reflect the genius of the man who translated the projects of Justinian into political reality rather than that of the Byzantine functionary who may have taken part in their rhetorical formulation. The art of sixth-century Ravenna owes its existence not only to Justinian and Julianus Argentarius, but, and perhaps above all, to Archbishop Maximian.

Agnellus' *Liber pontificalis* tells us too little about

Maximian. Agnellus was a medieval chronicler, not a historian. In his work historical and biographical facts appear curiously distorted, dissolved into the cloudlike contours of legend, as in the imagination of a child. It is not impossible, however, to reduce these fables to their historical essence. In the chapter which Agnellus devotes to Maximian, two facts stand out which are of considerable importance. Maximian was not a native of Ravenna but a stranger; and he ruled that see during the decisive period of its history.

Maximian was, according to Agnellus, a native of Pola in Istria. When the newly appointed bishop sought to take possession of his see, he ran into formidable opposition. The people and clergy of Ravenna barred his entrance into the city. From Agnellus' account, the reasons appear fairly clear. In appointing Maximian bishop of Ravenna, Justinian must have passed over the candidate which the city itself had selected for this position. The emperor's procedure was hardly unusual. We shall have reason to inquire into his motives. The shrewdness of his choice soon became evident by the manner in which the new bishop dealt with his hostile flock. Agnellus gives a fairly humorous account of how Maximian was for some time compelled to take up lodgings outside Ravenna and tells how he succeeded, by astute diplomacy, kind words, and lavish gifts, in winning the friendship, first, of the emissaries from Ravenna and, second, of its populace as well.[25]

The substance of this story is undoubtedly authentic. The masterful subtlety and efficiency of Maximian's statesmanship are amply attested by his subsequent career. The fact that in Agnellus' work this career appears only in a series of childlike anecdotes is evidence of that general intellectual decline which prevented the chronicler of the ninth century from comprehending the statesman of the sixth. It must have been, nevertheless, Maximian's political genius which called him to the attention of Justinian and which led the emperor to appoint the obscure Istrian deacon to what, from the political viewpoint,

was the most important ecclesiastical dignity he could confer at the time.

Maximian was appointed in 546. At that moment the great enterprises in which Justinian's statesmanship was engaged had reached a crisis.

The Gothic War in Italy seemed to be going against the imperial armies. It was in 546 that Totila entered Rome. When Maximian assumed control, Ravenna had become the most important Italian city still in the hands of Byzantium.

Belisarius had wrested Ravenna from the Goths in 540. Unable to obtain the necessary funds and supplies from Byzantium, he had often been barely able to hold the city as the last major toehold of the Byzantine armies in Italy. In 548 Belisarius was at last recalled, ignominiously and unjustly. The situation did not improve after his departure. The following year the imperial armies attempted that abortive and pitiful sortie from Ravenna in the course of which the Byzantine general himself, Verus, remained dead on the field of battle.[26]

It is not without interest to compare this commander of the fortress of Ravenna—a habitual drunkard, who was deservedly the target of Gothic contempt and derision—with Maximian, the bishop who just then controlled the political destinies of the city. It is even more interesting to compare the underpaid and underequipped imperial garrison with the host of craftsmen which just then was completing work on the two sumptuous churches into which the imperial court, as well as the see of Ravenna, had poured its treasures: San Vitale and Sant' Apollinare in Classe were solemnly consecrated in the very years of military catastrophe, the first in 548,[27] the second in 549.

Justinian's conduct of the Italian War has been interpreted in various ways. Scholars have attributed his apparent neglect of the campaign to court intrigues against Belisarius. But one does not subsidize a vast architectural program in order to starve an unpopular general, and one does not starve an unpopular general in a moment of military crisis. Other historians have suggested that in these disastrous years the emperor's sole attention was focused on the theological controversy over the so-called "Three Chapters"; they have seen in this pre-occupation with theological problems at the expense of military questions conclusive evidence of the growing senility of Justinian's mind.

In our opinion the opposite is true. To that age the Three Chapters controversy was as important as the Gothic War. It endangered the political structure of the Empire no less than did the Goths. More important: both the theological discussions in Byzantium and the military operations in Italy were integral and indispensable parts of that grand strategy by which Justinian aimed at the restoration of the Empire. But there is only one place in which the interdependence of the two issues or, rather, their intrinsic unity is manifest; this place is Ravenna. This unique position the city owed to ecclesiastical, rather than to economic or military, geography. Neither her great harbor nor her impregnable location predestined Ravenna for the historical role she was to play in the sixth century but rather the singular position which the see of Ravenna occupied in Italy—above all, in regard to the see of Rome.[28]

The bishop of Ravenna, since the fifth century, had wielded metropolitan powers over the Province of Aemilia. In effecting this establishment, Pope Celestine I had acceded to the wishes, and in all likelihood to the pressure, of Emperor Valentinian III, who wanted the see of Ravenna raised to a position commensurate with the importance of the city as capital of the Empire. At the same time, however, the pope had sought to guard against such dangers to his supremacy as had threatened the papacy from the powerful see of Milan: in his own see, the bishop of Ravenna was to remain simply the suffragan of Rome. It had been one of those shortsighted measures which in retrospect are almost incomprehensible.

Her geographic position alone isolated Ravenna somewhat from Italy and drove her economically, politically, and culturally into the arms of Byzantium. At a time when this power was at war with the rest of Italy this fact must assume a peculiar significance. It could not fail to reflect upon the position of the bishop on whom Byzantine administration, as a matter of general principle, bestowed the greatest political powers. The importance to which the bishop of Ravenna thus rose during the Gothic War made him necessarily all the more impatient of his subordination to Rome, under which he had been chafing ever since the Celestine settlement. But what would be the result if Byzantine policies should turn against the papacy? In that event the see of Ravenna must become the spearhead of such policies. This situation arose in the course of the controversy over the Three Chapters, the second great crisis of the 540's.

The dissensions which the Three Chapters brought to a head had been long festering in the Empire. In our context we must confine ourselves to a brief explanation of their nature.[29] In 542 Emperor Justinian had formally condemned the writings of Origen, largely at the instigation of a Roman, the future Pope Pelagius. But Neo-Platonism, which was to be crushed in this fashion, had powerful adherents among the bishops and monks of the Christian East. It remained to be seen what repercussions the unfortunate attempt at legislation in matters of theology was to have—especially when instigated by a stranger like Pelagius.

One year later the struggle broke out. Duchesne has suggested that the personal and regional element loomed large in it, that the leader of the opposition—Theodore Askidas, metropolitan of Caesarea in Cappadocia—was determined to strike a blow against Pelagius, the spokesman of the Roman faction at the imperial court. The great historian is surely right, but it also seems plausible that doctrinal ties may have existed between the Origenists and the far more powerful faction of the Monophysites, which now struck in retaliation. It was this latter party that precipitated the struggle over the Three Chapters, and its eventual victory was a victory not only over Pelagius and his friends but over a pope who had been dead for a century; not only over the

Roman theologians of the sixth century but over Leo the Great and his theology, which had triumphed at the Council of Chalcedon.

The issue was masterfully chosen. The Council of Chalcedon had examined the writings, subsequently referred to as the "Three Chapters," of three Eastern bishops—Ibas of Edessa, Theodore of Mopsuesta, and Theodoretus of Cyrus. All three had been suspected of Nestorian leanings but were eventually cleared of these charges—the Council of Chalcedon formally absolved them from the taint of heterodoxy.[30] The decision was a momentous one. Theodore had disagreed with Origen, and Theodoretus and Ibas had attacked the great Cyril of Alexandria, whose memory and writings the Roman church, much to the grief and resentment of the East, had buried in eloquent silence. An attack upon the writings of the three men was a cautious, but infallible, means of questioning the Chalcedonian settlement itself. A century after the death of their authors, the Three Chapters proved to be an explosive that shook the Empire to its foundations.

In 544, after long deliberations in the library of his palace, the emperor issued the famous edict in condemnation of the Three Chapters. As usual, he secured the adherence of most of the Eastern bishops by threats. It remained to be seen how the successor to Leo the Great would react to the challenge to Chalcedon.

In 545 Pope Vigilius was spirited away from Rome. Virtually a captive of Byzantium, he arrived in that city in 547. Thus, when Maximian of Ravenna took possession of his see, his ecclesiastical overlord, the first of the Italian bishops, had been abducted from Rome. The conclusion is not altogether unwarranted that Maximian, when the great theological struggle opened, was chosen to take the pope's place as spiritual ruler of Italy, perhaps of the West.

The Three Chapters controversy is the background of Maximian's appointment; it is also the reason for the opposition that he encountered in Ravenna. This opposition[31] was composed of anti-Monophysites, of the defenders of the Three Chapters who, throughout Maximian's episcopate, comprised the great majority of the Catholic hierarchy of the West. From the viewpoint of Byzantium this faction resembled a many-headed Hydra; it was Maximian's mission to contain and to destroy it. As a result of the old emperor's clumsiness and cruelty, however, the odds were weighted against Byzantium as heavily in the theological struggle as they were just then in the military one. Nothing attests the political abilities of the metropolitan more conclusively than the way in which he held Ravenna as the ecclesiastical and theological rampart of Byzantium. In his own city the opposition which had once tried to block his entrance did not stir as long as he was in office; only when Maximian was lying on his deathbed did it raise its head again.[32]

In regard to Italy and the Orthodox West in general, Maximian's position was far more difficult. During the ten years of his episcopate the pope remained absent from Rome, a captive of the emperor. The metropolitan of Milan also was in Constantinople. As Mgr Testi-Rasponi has rightly said, the bishop of Ravenna thus became in fact, if not in name, the primate of Italy.

But if this situation vastly extended his powers, it increased even more the difficulties of his task. The situation which confronted him was created by events that took place in Byzantium. Here the emperor, through threats and acts of outrageous violence, was endeavoring to bend the pope to his will. After seven years he at last succeeded. In 554 Vigilius, broken in health and spirit, issued a solemn declaration in favor of the condemnation of the Three Chapters. He died the following year. Justinian had been able to browbeat the bishop of Rome into accepting the dictates of his despotic will; but this victory was a Pyrrhic one. The emperor's goal had been the unification of the East and West under a dogma formulated by himself. The pope's submission was to have been a step in this direction. Instead, the ancient churches of the West now declared their readiness to secede from Byzantium and

Rome rather than follow the pope into what they considered a heresy imposed by the throne.

The possibility of a schism had already appeared in the first years of Maximian's episcopate. In 548 Vigilius had issued his *Judicatum*, which, while seeking to maintain the authority of Chalcedon, conformed completely with the views expressed in the imperial edict of 543.[33] But if Vigilius or Justinian had thought that the pope's submission would be followed by that of the West, they were soon disabused. The churches of Dalmatia and Illyria, even the distant province of Scythia (Dobroudja) rose in protest. Africa went still further: the bishop of Carthage, Reparatus, declared Vigilius excommunicated unless he retracted. At the same time Facundus composed his *Pro defensione trium capitolorum,* a masterpiece which has rightly been called the last flower of the great polemical literature of the African church.[34] In Italy the opposition was no weaker. From all we know about the clergy of Italy, so sadly depopulated by the miseries of war, it was solidly opposed to the condemnation of the Three Chapters.[35]

The danger of an outright schism must have been grave indeed. For a moment even the emperor was frightened. He authorized the pope to withdraw his *Judicatum,* agreed to submit the whole issue of the Three Chapters to an ecumenical council, and forbade the Greek bishops to make any declaration on the dangerous subject until that council had met. Soon, however, the issue took another dangerous turn when Justinian, in violation of his own pledges, published a new edict, the *Confessio fidei,* purporting to settle the dogmatic dispute once and for all and formally condemning the authors of the Three Chapters who, nevertheless, had died in communion with the church.

It is impossible to say what had prompted the emperor to take this step. When his emissaries informed Vigilius of the edict, the pope declared that any bishop who accepted it would *ipso facto* be severed from the Catholic church. With him at this moment was the archbishop of Milan. To his own condemnation of the *Confessio fidei,* he added those of the churches of Gaul, Burgundy, Spain, Liguria, Venetia, and Aemilia, the last-named being the metropolitan province of the bishop of Ravenna.[36]

We need not dwell on the events which followed. The facts recalled here shed adequate light on the effect that this situation must have had on the position of Maximian. As the appointee and instrument of Byzantium, he stood, at this moment, alone against the united churches of the West. If the archbishop of Milan was empowered to speak for the Province of Aemilia—and there is no reason to doubt that he was—the bishop of Ravenna was indeed threatened by a most serious defection within his own metropolitan see. In Illyria a similar situation led the bishops of that province to depose their head, Benenatus, the bishop of Justiniana Prima (Scupi).[37]

VI

How did Maximian meet the crisis?

Agnellus does not answer this important question, but some facts recorded in his chronicle enable us to do it for him. They prove, above all, that the Metropolitan did not waver in his loyalty to the emperor.

Maximian was very well informed of the Monophysite point of view. As a young man he had journeyed to Alexandria. Agnellus has copied some excerpts from a book in which Maximian seems to have given his impressions of the political and theological struggles which led up to the Three Chapters controversy. His reference to Dioscurus II, patriarch of Alexandria, as a "faithful shepherd of his flock," and to his successor, Timotheus, as a good administrator may betray not so much "objectivity of judgment" (as one historian believes) as the ability subtly to intimate sympathy with the Monophysite cause which both prelates championed.[38] Did Maximian, apart from such expressions of opinion in literary form, interfere actively in the struggle over the Three Chapters? A curiously garbled passage in the *Historia Langobardorum* suggests that he did.[39]

Paul the Deacon refers to the bishop of Ravenna as an opponent of the Three Chapters who "at the time of Popes Vigilius or Pelagius" seceded from communion with Rome. This can refer only to Maximian. The facts which confirm this hypothesis we owe to Agnellus.

He mentions two journeys of Maximian to Constantinople. The second of these can only be conjectured to have taken place around 554, the time of Pope Vigilius' final surrender to the emperor. The first journey, on the other hand, can be dated with considerable accuracy. While in Byzantium, the archbishop procured building material for Santo Stefano; according to an inscription, this church was built in less than a year; it was consecrated in December, 550. On May 17, 548, Maximian was still in Ravenna: on that date he consecrated San Vitale.[40] He seems to have arrived in Constantinople in the late summer; and he had returned to Ravenna by May 9, 549, the day he dedicated the basilica of Sant' Apollinare in Classe, an event we may assume to have taken place very soon after his return. Maximian's journey, then, took place between May 17, 548, and May 9, 549. His visit in Constantinople thus coincided with what was perhaps the most critical year in Justinian's reign. On April 11, 548, Pope Vigilius had issued the *Judicatum;* Empress Theodora died late in June, and Belisarius was recalled the same year. When Maximian arrived in the imperial capital, the revolt against the *Judicatum,* fostered by the defeat of the imperial armies in Italy and by the death of the woman who had been the unfailing protectress of the Monophysites, was in full swing. The archbishop of Ravenna cannot have remained aloof from the great struggle; and the position of his see was such that his stand was bound to assume major significance.

What was the purpose, what the outcome, of that journey? Agnellus' answer appears, at first sight, tantalizingly inadequate. The one reason for Maximian's two visits to Constantinople on which he insists—in fact, he calls it *the* reason—was a litigation over the possession of a *silva* near Vistrum in Istria,

in which the see of Ravenna was engaged just then. As a result of the archbishop's journey, Agnellus tells us, the emperor confirmed his old friend in the perpetual possession of the disputed area.[41]

In itself, this issue was hardly of sufficient importance to warrant Maximian's absence from Ravenna at a critical period. On the other hand, it seems to have been much more than a diplomatic pretext for political consultations with Justinian. If, in 548, the emperor found time to settle a territorial dispute, he knew why.

The area in question was part of the *patrimonium histrianum* of the church of Ravenna. The port of Vistrum (Vestre) is not far from Pola, the town where Maximian had been born and where he had been a deacon before Justinian selected him for the see of Ravenna. If the community of this city had once rejected him because he was *aliena ovis,*[42] it now found this same fact a political asset, for Maximian returned to Pola as archbishop of Ravenna; and, as the instrument of the emperor's ecclesiastical strategy, he tied the town to Ravenna, a task for which no one could be better equipped. Upon his return from Constantinople, Maximian built, or at least magnificently enlarged and embellished, the church of Santa Maria Formosa in Pola, as if the humble sanctuary he had served in his youth should now bespeak the dignity to which he had risen. But this architectural project had a much wider significance.

The city of Ravenna had, for a long time, been economically dependent upon the rich province of Istria. Cassiodorus calls Istria *Ravennae campania,* the storehouse of the city (*urbis regiae cella plenaria*).[43] Agnellus' remarks seem to indicate an imperial donation, possibly of vast tracts of land in this district, to the see of Ravenna. If, moreover, the archbishop of Ravenna now solemnly took possession of Pola, this act could not fail to have its political repercussions. Both the territory of Vistrum and the town of Pola belonged nominally to the metropolitan Province of Aquileia.

Among the defenders of the Three Chapters, the archbishop of Aquileia was perhaps the most violent. Rather than give in to the wishes of Byzantium, he eventually led his province into the schism that bears the name of his see.[44] Justinian must have been as anxious to weaken his power as to increase that of his supporter on the episcopal throne of Ravenna. As the two were neighbors, he could not do the one without doing the other. The settlement of the dispute over the district of Vistrum was thus part of a much greater project. So was Maximian's building of Santa Maria Formosa of Pola. As owner of this church, the archbishop of Ravenna wielded both spiritual and political authority in Pola, which remained part of the Province of Aquileia only in name. In fact, the town moved into the orbit of Ravenna; even during the schism of Aquileia the bishop of Pola seems to have been an Orthodox.[45] With the acquisition of the district of Vistrum, as with his entrance into Pola, the archbishop of Ravenna set foot upon the ecclesiastical Province of Aquileia.

If the building of Santa Maria Formosa was a political demonstration, as well as the implementation of an ecclesiastical program, this is true even more of the construction of the churches of Ravenna. It is remarkable that the first of Ravenna's new sanctuaries should have been dedicated to SS. Vitalis, Gervase, and Protase, whom the ancient see of Milan, since the days of St. Ambrose, had considered as its *genii loci,* but whom the *Passio SS. martyrum Gervasii et Protasii,* only a few years before the building of San Vitale, had claimed for Ravenna. It is perhaps an exaggeration to say that the church would not have been built without that treatise.[46] But the magnificent structure, deliberately suggesting the form of a tomb, was like a monumental seal of confirmation placed upon the allegations of the document. The church was the sepulcher of the three saints, and those who marveled at the beauty and audacity of its design were reminded that the martyrs had actually died in Ravenna and belonged to this city rather than to Milan.

This evidence of rivalry between Ravenna and the great metropolitan province of northern Italy is noteworthy but by no means surprising. Ravenna's elevation to a metropolitan see originated (as far as the popes were concerned) in their desire to create a rival to the overbearing aspirations of Milan. The six cities of the Aemilia which, already in the fifth century, had been placed under the jurisdiction of the bishop of Ravenna—Voghenza, Imola, Forlì, Faenza, Bologna, and Modena—had all belonged to the Province of Milan.[47]

But that earlier settlement was a halfhearted one. We have seen how Celestine I had thought it wise not to bestow full metropolitan powers upon the bishop of Ravenna; similar reasons had made him and his immediate successors reluctant to place the entire Province of Aemilia under the jurisdiction of the Italian Byzantium. However, the development was irresistible. The city of Reggio, eloquently enough, dedicated its cathedral to St. Apollinaris of Ravenna; Piacenza, whose bishop had been consecrated by the archbishop of Milan as late as 456, later regarded—equally significantly, as we shall see—St. Apollinaris as its apostle.[48] By the end of the sixth century Byzantium had succeeded in making the metropolitan province of Ravenna coterminous with the exarchate of Ravenna. The decisive step in this direction was the wresting of the whole of Aemilia from the Province of Milan.[49]

This event took place during Maximian's episcopate. Among the bishops of Ravenna, he was the first to use the title of "archbishop," which at that time was synonymous with that of "metropolitan."[50] This marks not only the end of the ambiguous relations of his see to the papacy but also an epoch in Ravenna's relations with Milan: Maximian extended his jurisdictional powers over the entire province of Aemilia. If we ask when, during his comparatively brief term of office, that momentous event may have occurred, the answer can hardly be in doubt. When Maximian assumed office, his position in Ravenna itself was too precarious, his abilities too untried, to recommend a measure which could not fail to incur the bitter hostility of the ancient ecclesiastical lord of Aemilia, the metropolitan of Milan. Two years later, in 548, the step became at once feasible and inevitable.

We have seen that Maximian was in Constantinople at the moment when the great theological struggle had reached its crisis. The formidable opposition on the part of the entire hierarchy of the West which Justinian's dogmatic schemes encountered must have made it seem imperative to him to invest his sole supporter with all the powers at his disposal; all the more so if these powers could be gained by withdrawing them from the emperor's chief enemies. Of these, none were more powerful and none more dangerous to Justinian's political and theological strategy than the three great metropolitans who were also neighbors of Ravenna: the pope and the archbishops of Milan and Aquileia.

Justinian dealt with Aquileia by his Istrian donations. The elevation of Maximian to the rank of archbishop with metropolitan powers over all of Aemilia was a blow struck at Milan. In supporting the pope's condemnation of the emperor's *Confessio fidei*, Archbishop Datius had professed to speak not only for his own Province of Milan but for several others as well, including that of Aemilia. That he acted as spokesman for that province is worth noting. We have, indeed, other evidence to show that the Aemilian bishops, or at least some of them, were active supporters of the Three Chapters,[51] and Datius was sufficiently cautious to stress that he was entitled to speak for only a part of the provinces which he mentioned. But to name Aemilia in this delicate connection and in such sweeping fashion was, for the archbishop of Milan, neither diplomatically tactful nor politically wise; for the man who already ruled part of Aemilia and who was meant to succeed Milan as head of the province was also in Constantinople; and he stood on the side not of Milan but of the emperor.

Datius may have thought that his declaration in behalf of Aemilia would prompt the emperor to suspend a decision in favor of Ravenna which at that moment had not taken effect; or he may have hoped that, even if he came too late, his stand might kindle a revolt in Aemilia which would eventually drive its episcopal sees back into the ancient fold of Milan. If Datius entertained such hopes, he was sorely deceived. Maximian returned from Constantinople as metropolitan of Aemilia, fully the equal of Milan in dignity, in power, in aspirations, and determined to effect the settlement which the emperor had at heart. Of his designs in regard to Milan, the sanctuary of San Vitale, consecrated on the very eve of his fateful journey to Constantinople, is a declaration as impressive as Santa Maria Formosa in Pola is of the struggle with Aquileia.

The political function of the architecture of Ravenna is almost a vindication of Agnellus' merits as a historian. He knows and dutifully records the fact that Maximian, besides obtaining the donation of his *silva*, procured while in Constantinople the building material for the church of Santo Stefano in Ravenna, as well as the relics of St. Stephen and other saints.[52] These facts are all that Agnellus knows or cares to record concerning the archbishop's visit to Constantinople. In the light of what we may assume actually to have taken place on that occasion, the chronicler's information is less inadequate than may be apparent. That Maximian should have procured, while in the Byzantine capital, material for the building of a new church is interesting evidence for the source of the great art of Ravenna, as regards both its style and its material. But what is noteworthy above all is the fact that, in the midst of the most crucial deliberations and decisions of his career, the metropolitan should have found the time for such preoccupations.

"In Honore Sancti et Beatissimi Primi Martiris Stephani Servus Christi Maximianus Episcopus Hanc Basilicam, Ipso Adjuvante, A Fundamentis Construxit . . . ," Agnellus read in the sanctuary of St. Stephen. And in a longer metrical inscription the bishop referred again to the direct and miraculous help that the martyr had bestowed upon the building of his church.[53] Both inscriptions stress the exalted dignity of the protomartyr, and both link the name of St. Stephen to that of Maximian. This method of invoking supernatural protection and approbation was, of course, not new. Certain mosaics in Ravenna and Rome, in which a saint appears as the patron of the bishop who donated the church, convey the same concept. But Maximian imparted a peculiarly political and polemical meaning to it.

According to Agnellus, the archbishop returned to Ravenna not only with the relics of St. Stephen but with those of many other important saints. If the chronicler is to be believed, we must assume this translation of relics to have been among the most important on historical record. Besides the remains of the first martyr, it included those of John the Baptist and John the Evangelist and, even more significantly, of Peter, Paul, and Andrew.[54] We may ask whether the selection of these relics and the sanctuaries in their honor subsequently erected in Ravenna do not suggest, like the building of Santa Maria Formosa and San Vitale, an ecclesiastical strategy, directed this time not against the archbishop of Milan or of Aquileia but against the greatest of the metropolitans on Italian soil, the pope himself. The answer may be found in an anecdote which Agnellus tells in this connection.

According to the chronicler, Maximian attempted to secure the body of St. Andrew for Ravenna; but the emperor somehow got wind of the project and ordered his archbishop to bring the precious relic to Constantinople instead; for, Justinian is said to have declared, if the First Rome owned the relics of the Prince of the Apostles, it was fitting that the Second Rome (Constantinople) should house the remains of Andrew, Peter's brother. "Ambo sorores et hi ambo germani." I do not want to give St. Andrew to you, the emperor declares at the end of his alleged interview with Maximian, because only the imperial capital is the proper shrine for the remains of the apostle. Agnellus concludes the story with a narrative of how Maximian, by a ruse, was able to secure at least St. Andrew's beard. "And this is true, brethren [the chronicler exclaims], for the Roman Pontiff could never have subjugated us, if the (en-

tire) remains of St. Andrew had been buried here."[55]

The details of this story of the contest between Byzantium and Ravenna are surely an invention. But the substance deserves our consideration. The remains of St. Andrew had been in Constantinople since A.D. 357. They were rediscovered, together with those of the Apostles Luke and Timothy, during the demolition of the old Basilica of the Apostles, at the time of, or shortly before, Maximian's visit to Constantinople.[56] This explains how the bishop was able to secure some relics of St. Andrew for his see in Ravenna. But the remarks which Agnellus attributes to the emperor and which link St. Andrew to Constantinople seem too pointed to be altogether an invention. St. Andrew was not only the apostle of Asia Minor and the Balkans, allegedly the first bishop of Constantinople, and the brother of St. Peter; according to the Gospel, he was actually the first disciple to follow the calling of Christ, and it was Andrew who led even the Prince of the Apostles to his divine Master (John 1:25–31).[57] These facts must have assumed a particular significance during the great struggle between Rome and Byzantium. The rediscovery of St. Andrew's remains at this very moment may have been more than a mere coincidence. It is not even impossible that Maximian, during his visit, might have discussed with the emperor the possibility of transferring the relics of St. Andrew to Ravenna. At a moment of ecclesiastical crisis the transfer would have been a demonstration of the city's importance; it would have underscored her position as a rival of Rome itself.

Eventually, however, the emperor rejected the idea. His reasons can easily be conjectured. Ravenna was not yet sufficiently secure (in military, as well as ecclesiastical, terms) to make her the depository for so sacred a treasure. Justinian may have shrunk from antagonizing still more the other churches of Italy. Finally, and above all, from the viewpoint of his own aspirations, it was important to keep in his capital one of the great relics of Christianity. But that Maximian was allowed to take home with him some relics of St. Andrew is certain.

Whatever the merits of Agnellus' narrative, the anecdote seems to be based on evidence more reliable than his own conjectures, i.e., on the long memory of the see of Ravenna. It is hardly a coincidence that even in the ninth century the reminiscence of the ancient and bitter rivalry between Ravenna and Rome was still evoked by the relics of St. Andrew; what importance Maximian himself had attributed to these relics is shown by the fact that, upon his return from Constantinople, he redecorated the church of St. Andrew splendidly.[58]

To sum up: on the eve of setting sail for the imperial capital, Maximian had dedicated a *martyrion* to SS. Vitalis, Gervase, and Protase, thus claiming for Ravenna some of the glory of the ancient see of Milan.[59] By the acquisition of relics of Peter and Paul, of the first martyr, Stephen, and the first apostle, Andrew; by building and adorning sumptuous sanctuaries in honor of the two last-named saints, Maximian revealed a similar attitude and similar aspirations in regard to Rome itself. The erection of the archbishop's church in Pola was an attack upon Aquileia; and, immediately upon his return to Ravenna, Maximian dedicated the basilica of Sant' Apollinare, the mosaics of which, as chapter iii will show, were to convey Ravenna's claim to rank with the five great patriarchates of the Christian world. Maximian's entire architectural program would thus seem to have been executed in the service of the abiding objective of his political career.

When he was appointed to the see of Ravenna, the city had already been selected as imperial capital in the West. He owed his elevation to the rank of archbishop, with full metropolitan powers over the entire Province of Aemilia, to his stand in the struggle over the Three Chapters. In Constantinople he, alone among the Western prelates, had supported the emperor. With the three other metropolitans of Italy Justinian's bitter enemies and with two of them, Vigilius and Datius, detained in Constantinople, the emperor wished to manifest as

clearly as possible the singular powers with which the archbishop of Ravenna returned to his see. The means of this manifestation was the great architectural program which would have been impossible without Justinian's inspiration and material assistance and which marked a turning-point in the history of Ravenna. At the very moment when the churches of the West seemed ready to repudiate the emperor, the see of Ravenna was solemnly distinguished as the outpost of Byzantine theology on Western soil. The language of Maximian's churches was all the more eloquent because they rose at the very time when Rome lay deserted and in ruins.

VII

But the art of Ravenna was a demonstration in yet another direction. After a series of military setbacks, which placed the prestige and perhaps even the rule of Byzantium in Italy in jeopardy, on the eve of new and, as it proved, decisive military operations in that country, Ravenna was made a shrine of Orthodox Christianity: in the terminology of that age, such language could be understood only as meaning that Byzantium was determined not to abandon Italy to the Arian Goth.

It must be emphasized at this point that the interdependence of Justinian's struggles against the pope and against the Goth was no chronological or geographical coincidence. From the emperor's point of view, his two opponents had more in common than may appear at first sight. During the years of Gothic occupation of Italy the Roman church had drifted further and further away from Byzantium. The Latin and Gothic nations that had long lived together on the same soil were gradually drawn into a kind of symbiosis. Whatever the differences in culture, tradition, and religion, economic and social intercourse must gradually have developed ties of friendship and common interest between them. To Theodoric, Rome owed the security, liberty, and political prosperity of what appeared to some as a second golden age. If the Gothic king was a heretic, he did not threaten the established church with the intolerable claims of the Byzantine theocracy. And if the emperor should ever seek to take possession of Italy by force of arms, the pope, as ruler of the Latin population, had to fear almost as much from a military campaign on the exhausted soil as had the Goths. But these political ties between the Roman church and the Goths were strengthened by a community of interests in the religious sphere.

At the turn of the century, Byzantine Monophysitism had created the so-called "Acacian schism," which for decades separated the Roman and Greek churches (484–519). Theodoric, on the other hand, had shown singular prudence, tact, and success in his diplomatic dealings with the Holy See, while his religious policy, formulated by the great Roman, Cassiodorus, was for many years unswerving in its tolerance and unfailing in its protection of the established church.[60] Thus, during these years of dogmatic tension between East and West, the relations between Theodoric and the papacy had come to resemble more and more an outright alliance.[61] And it would not be altogether correct to assume that this situation changed radically when, after the death of the Emperor Anastasius in 518, Byzantium began to steer a political course which in regard to Rome was more conciliatory or at least more subtle. It is noteworthy that the negotiations which Pope Hormisdas initiated in order to terminate the schism had Theodoric's approval and that they were conducted by Ennodius, a relative of Boethius and later bishop of Pavia, who, as a staunch supporter of the Arian king, had hailed him in a celebrated panegyric as the wise, just, and pious protector of the Catholic church.[62]

The establishment of religious peace between Byzantium and Rome was, in the end, bound to affect the relations between the papacy and the Gothic king; it may even have been designed to drive the latter into acts of open hostility against Catholics or even the Catholic church; but the emperor was never to succeed in severing all ties between Theodoric and the papacy.

In 526 Pope John appeared in the imperial capital as Theodoric's emissary, accompanied by Bishop Ecclesius of Ravenna. Toward the end of his reign, Emperor Justinus had started his policy of persecution of the Arian church in his capital; seizure of churches and forced conversions had taken place. The pope was to deliver Theodoric's protest against these measures. That the king should have expected Catholic prelates to plead the cause of his church is less paradoxical than may appear: he had undoubtedly threatened retaliatory measures which the Catholic church of Italy had every reason to fear.[63] But such fears are poor inspiration. Pope John, a known Byzantinist who had undertaken the mission only under compulsion, conducted the negotiations so halfheartedly that the enraged king had him thrown into prison as soon as he returned. The spectacle of a Roman bishop pleading the cause of the Arian church, however, may not have left entirely unimpressed the zealot who a few months later ascended the imperial throne. And, with the election of Felix IV that same year, the papacy was, in fact, once more in the hands of a member of the Gothic party.[64]

Pope John was not the last pope to journey to Byzantium as emissary of the Gothic rulers. A second of these visits deserves our brief attention. In 535–36 Pope Agapetus sought to negotiate peace on behalf of the incapable and cruel Theodahat. The negotiations proved abortive. They were again conducted halfheartedly and under compulsion by the aged pontiff, whose attention, moreover, was arrested by issues of much graver concern to him. In Byzantium the fight between the Monophysite and the Orthodox factions had already begun. The latter hailed Agapetus as their leader; and his meeting with the Patriarch Severus of Antioch[65] evoked in the Orthodox party the memory of St. Peter's struggle with Petrus Magus. The pope acted, indeed, with great vigor. He refused to recognize the Monophysite Anthimus as patriarch of Constantinople, convicted him of heresy, and personally consecrated his successor. The Orthodox victory was complete when Severus and his friends were chased out of Constantinople. But the Monophysites and their protectress, the empress, could not fail to notice that they owed their momentary defeat to the bishop of Rome. They were one day to remind the emperor himself that Agapetus had sought also to dissuade him from reconquering Italy from its Arian masters.

It would certainly be unjust to accuse the popes of the sixth century of connivance with the Arian heresy. But it must be admitted that this may not have been equally obvious from the Monophysite point of view, with which the emperor was more and more to identify himself. Arianism had ceased to be an issue in Rome in the measure in which the danger of Monophysitism increased.[66] For a Monophysite, on the other hand, Orthodox insistence upon Christ's human nature must have had a certain affinity with the Arian denial of the Savior's divinity. From this viewpoint it seemed as if Orthodoxy as well as Arianism tended, in different degrees, to humanize the person of Christ.

In 548 the Empire faced a war in Italy on two fronts which, to Justinian's mind, were clearly interconnected. He knew that he could remain victorious only if he succeeded in crushing both opponents simultaneously. The wresting of Italy from the Goths would be futile if the Western churches were led into a schism with Byzantium. But the emperor could not even hope to conquer Italy and to hold his military gains unless the Catholic hierarchy of that country supported him. In a theocracy any threat to religious unity must also endanger the political structure of the realm. In the rebellion which Maximian had to overcome in Ravenna, moreover, there had become apparent the danger which was peculiar to the administrative organization of Justinian's empire. He had granted vast jurisdictional and legislative powers to the bishops of his realm; the age demanded that the spiritual leader of a community govern its political and social destinies as well. But this pious settlement turned into a political opponent every bishop who opposed the emperor's theological views; and it compelled the emperor to re-

gard all doctrinal controversies as political attacks upon his absolute authority.[67] It is no exaggeration to say that the unity of the Empire and the reconquest of the West depended on the outcome of the dogmatic struggle no less than on that of the military one.

These facts explain both the unique position of Ravenna under the administration of Justinian and the political function of its art. To us, the part which the cult of saints and the building of great churches in this city were designed to play in the strategy of Byzantium may reflect merely that curious blend of artistic refinement and religious fanaticism which distinguishes the political methods of Justinian and his statesmen. But the monuments of Ravenna attest, above all, the admirable logic and consistency of a statecraft capable of planning theological, as well as military, moves simultaneously, as steps leading to the same goal. Even while Ravenna was an embattled fortress surrounded by Gothic might, the architecture and, as we shall see, the mosaics of its churches were completed as monumental expositions of Byzantine theology, defying at once the Roman and the Arian points of view. The art of sixth-century Ravenna is thus a political act, and its greatness springs from this function; it had to be what it *is* in order to take up and to defy the challenge of a great historical crisis, and it prepared and preceded the twofold victory of Byzantium: in December 550, Santo Stefano, apparently the last of Maximian's churches, was completed.[68] In 551 Narses, as commander-in-chief of the imperial armies, set foot on Italian soil. In the same year Pope Vigilius was compelled to take refuge in St. Euphemia of Chalcedon. The two enemies of Justinian fell almost simultaneously.

The man who was to implement Byzantine policies in Ravenna and who epitomizes Byzantine statesmanship in its greatest phase is Maximian. Before we turn to consider the works of art which are milestones of his political career, one question remains: How much can be ascertained regarding the archbishop's actual share in the planning and execution of these monuments? Did he delegate these tasks to other men like Julianus Argentarius? Or do his artistic projects, after time has dissolved his political ones, reflect his individual genius?

On the dedicatory mosaic in San Vitale, Maximian is portrayed as he must have looked at the time. A lean, tall figure, slightly bent, the dignity of his appearance perhaps less inborn than imparted by the high office which his ecclesiastical garments indicate. The head is already bald, the face wide-eyed, lined, almost emaciated—the face of a man in his fifties who is not destined for old age. According to our concepts, Maximian's face is hardly that of a priest, it is rather that of a diplomat; and we think of a high official rather than of a statesman. The portrait, in sum, shows a man who has risen from mediocre circumstances; shrewd, indefatigable, skeptical—but not cynical. In its blend of vision and calculation, fanaticism and refinement, this countenance is supremely "Byzantine" (Pl. 2).

If we compare Maximian with other bishops who have shaped the history of the West (and, if we except the popes, who belong in a different category, there are not many) he is neither a great theologian like Athanasius nor a great noble like Hincmar of Reims, neither a great statesman like Richelieu nor a great courtier like Talleyrand. Maximian's personality seems to have been a subtle blend of the qualities of all these men.

A Byzantine bishop of an Italian see at the time of the Gothic War and the controversy of the Three Chapters, he was not a "political priest." Yet he seems to have had a singular dexterity in the use of theology and of ritual as instruments of a comprehensive political vision. The art of Ravenna reveals his ability to formulate theological and liturgical concepts poignantly and movingly; to give to the complicated, the subtle, the involved, a simple monumentality of expression which will be understood by everyone. From the little that we know about Maximian's literary activities, his genius seems to have been precisely of this kind. None of his works seems to have survived. But the titles

which Agnellus enumerates are impressive and suggest that writing must have taken up a great deal of the bishop's time. His works may be divided into two groups, the first historical, the second theological and liturgical, though in viewpoint and subject matter the two may have overlapped frequently. Whether the great chronicle "after Jerome and Orosius" is really Maximian's work is uncertain.[69] Its attribution to him shows that his fame as a historian survived him for centuries. Undoubtedly, his is the already mentioned history, perhaps in several volumes, from which Agnellus copied some passages relating to the patriarchate of Alexandria.[70] The prelate's preoccupation with history, as with art, reminds one of Richelieu; we expect it in a man for whom the cult of saints, the erection of churches, theology, and liturgy were all instruments of ecclesiastical policy. Maximian's historical writings seem to have been masterpieces of political propaganda, like those of Richelieu, which even to this day may color our estimates of the period in which he lived. Was he perhaps the author of that portrait of Theodoric which, transforming the great ruler into a monstrous enemy of the church, frightened and fascinated the Middle Ages?[71]

Among Maximian's literary works, Agnellus mentions, further, a new edition of the Septuagint, which the archbishop supervised and edited with the greatest possible care, correcting the old Latin version through collation with that of St. Jerome and using the comments of St. Augustine. He himself mentioned this fact at the end of the New Testament.[72] Such painstaking work is undertaken only by a man with genuine exegetical passion and philological, as well as theological, competence. The magnitude of the scholarly labor involved makes one marvel at the energy of the man, who in the short decade of his episcopate and in the midst of grave political decisions found time to complete such a work. Agnellus finally mentions Maximian's edition of "Misales per totum circulum anni et sanctorum omnium, cotidianis nanque et quadragesimalibus temporibus, vel quicquid ad eclesia ritum pertinet."[73] This brief reference is our only information about what must certainly have been Maximian's most important literary work. Since, unfortunately, it is lost, we cannot be certain whether it was a new edition of liturgical texts or a new composition. If the latter, it would have amounted to a veritable liturgical reform. There is good reason to believe that this may have been the case.

In the development of the liturgy the role of Ravenna may have been much more important than can now be demonstrated. Authorities like Duchesne, Baumstark, and Testi-Rasponi believe the Pseudo-Ambrosian treatise, *De sacramentis* (the historical importance of which is well known), to have originated in Ravenna.[74] Baumstark, moreover, has attempted to trace to this city the pre-Gregorian Canon of the Roman Mass; and, while his thesis appears unacceptable as a whole, evidence for Rome's liturgical indebtedness to Ravenna is not missing: the *benedictio fontis,* still in use in the church of Rome, seems to be the work of Peter Chrysologus of Ravenna.[75]

We know, on the other hand, that during the period under discussion the liturgy of Ravenna differed from that of Rome. It seems to have united certain features of the Ambrosian and Gallican rites with elements of the Byzantine liturgy. The latter can hardly have found its way into Ravenna until after the city had passed into the orbit of Byzantium. The purpose of Maximian's appointment to the see of Ravenna was to strengthen the influence of the emperor. The liturgy, no less than the cult of the saints or the theology of the fifth Ecumenical Council, was a means to this end. All this sheds light upon both the nature and the scope of Maximian's liturgical work.

A hint as to its importance may be implied in a further remark of Agnellus. He insists that certain works of Maximian were sent to Rome, and the context allows only the inference that these must have been liturgical works. Testi-Rasponi suggests that the books might have been sent to Rome at the time when Gregory the Great completed his reform of the Roman liturgy.[76] At that time relations between Rome and Ravenna were peaceful, owing in large measure to the tactful and conciliatory attitude of the popes. As we shall see later, St. Apollinaris, Ravenna's greatest and probably its only martyr, received a sanctuary in Rome early in the seventh century; and at about the same time his feast seems to have been prescribed by the Roman liturgy. The request for the liturgical works of Maximian may have been part of the same policy of reconciliation. And, since no Roman *Liber sacramentorum circuli anni* seems to have existed prior to that of Gregory the Great,[77] the work of Maximian may have served an important function in the completion of this great enterprise. If the liturgy which even today is used by the Catholic church embodies the work of Maximian, his genius could have received no greater tribute.

Our actual evidence for Maximian's place in the history of the liturgy, however, is a nonliterary source, i.e., the mosaics of Ravenna, which originated during his episcopate. Of these, only a great liturgist and theologian can have been the author. Not all of them have survived. Those which have are far more than monumental illustrations of the liturgy. They are addressed to an age in which theological doctrine and mystical experience found their expression in the holy drama of the Christian rite, an age in which this drama, in turn, molded the state as well as society. The mosaics convey this significance of the liturgy for the history of the sixth century often more clearly than do the liturgical texts of the period. In these works of art we can still comprehend the interrelation of political and religious concepts as the principle of Justinian's statecraft, which otherwise appears so cynical or so mysterious. And here, too, we may discover the minds of the three men to whom these works are due: Justinian, Julianus Argentarius, and, above all, Maximian.

CHAPTER TWO

San Vitale

I

To Agnellus the church of San Vitale seemed to surpass all others in Italy *in edificiis et in mechanicis operibus*—both as a work of architecture and as the brilliant solution of a difficult structural problem.[1] The construction of San Vitale opened, as we have seen, the great architectural program of 526. Like the *Passio beatorum martyrum Gervasii et Protasii,* the church was to proclaim the glory of Ravenna's martyrs.[2] The expenses lavished on it were such that they were mentioned even in the epitaph of Julianus Argentarius, the builder.[3] It was Justinian's will that San Vitale should surpass the sanctuaries of the Arian Goths, including Theodoric's magnificent palace chapel, now Sant' Apollinare Nuovo, which in 526 was just nearing completion. And we shall see presently that the beautiful and unusual design of the church, which antedates that of Hagia Sophia, seems to have been selected deliberately in adaptation to the liturgy of Byzantium: San Vitale was to become the stage and setting proper to the sacred drama by which the emperor meant to communicate his theological and political concepts to the West (Pls. 1, 4, 6, 7).

If San Vitale was founded in 526 and dedicated in 548, it was under construction during the very years when not only the fate of Ravenna but also the success or failure of Justinian's great political design were in the balance. In view of this coincidence, the exact dates of the mosaics, as well as of the archi-

tecture of San Vitale, acquire historical importance. After the general architectural plan had been laid down in Byzantium, its execution became the responsibility of the imperial representatives in Ravenna. The work thus must inevitably reflect not only the genius of these men but also the great political movements upon the outcome of which the realization of the artistic project depended.

Bishop Ecclesius died in 532, six years after he had founded San Vitale. The entire period between 526 and the conquest of Ravenna by the Byzantine armies in 540 must have been an extremely difficult one for the Orthodox church of Ravenna. Exposed to the material hardships of war, she was watched suspiciously by the Gothic rulers, who distrusted her loyalty and suspected her secret co-operation with the Byzantine enemy. It is not surprising, therefore, that all architectural projects of this see appear to have progressed only with great slowness during those years.[4]

With Belisarius' triumphant entry into Ravenna, the situation changed completely. From the viewpoint of Justinian's policies in the West, the event marked a turning-point; it was even more decisive for Ravenna, which the emperor selected as the imperial capital on Italian soil. In 540 begins the golden age of Byzantine art in Ravenna. What had been undertaken during the Gothic occupation of the city and continued with singular tenacity and foresight during the years of oppression was no more than preparation. From the moment of victory on, and until Justinian's death, the emperor and his archbishops lavished their resources upon an incomparably splendid artistic program.

San Vitale was not dedicated until eight years after the end of Gothic rule in Ravenna. This would indicate that a very considerable part of the architecture remained unfinished at that time, and it appears certain with regard to the mosaics. The composition in the apse shows Ecclesius and Vitalis presented to Christ by two angels. From this, the conclusion has been drawn that the work must belong in the period of Ecclesius' episcopate, i.e., the years 521–32.[5] But this chronology is meaningless unless we have concrete evidence to show that the architecture of San Vitale was sufficiently far advanced at that time to permit the execution of the mosaic. The bishop's representation as donor of the church is certainly no proof of the mosaic's execution during his lifetime. One may, in fact, ask whether the rigid theological etiquette of the age would not have demanded that a living bishop be presented to Christ by the martyr and titular saint of the sanctuary; in San Vitale, Ecclesius is juxtaposed with St. Vitalis as a person of equal dignity (Pl. 11).

One, at least, of the mosaics in San Vitale can be dated accurately. In the dedicatory mosaic there appears Maximian, together with the emperor and high dignitaries of the court. This work, then, cannot have been executed before 546 (the year of Maximian's appointment to the see of Ravenna) nor long after 548 (the dedication year of San Vitale). The character of the composition, as well as its political significance, makes it altogether impossible to assume that the figure of Maximian might have been inserted at the last moment in the place of one of his predecessors. Only one of these, Ecclesius, had any important share in the building of San Vitale; and to Ecclesius, who had accompanied Pope John to Constantinople and who seems to have enjoyed Theodoric's special confidence,[6] Byzantium would not have conceded so prominent a place in the emperor's immediate presence. The mosaic marks a definite event and reflects a unique historical situation—the assumption of the episcopal dignity by Maximian and the entry of Byzantine power into Ravenna, which this act demonstrated and confirmed.[7]

But if this composition and its counterpart, the portrait of the empress, were executed in the first years of Maximian's episcopate, there is no reason why the same should not also be true for the other mosaics in San Vitale. It is, indeed, hardly possible to assign these works to different periods; all of them, including the representation in the apse, are related parts of a comprehensive program, which the following pages will seek to elucidate. If we may anticipate our conclusions, the theological, as well as the political, aspects of this program make it appear inconceivable that it should have been executed prior to the final, spiritual conquest of Ravenna by the genius of Maximian.

The mosaics in San Vitale cover the entire sanctuary. In different symbols and images they all convey one idea: the redemption of mankind by Christ and the sacramental re-enactment of this event in the eucharistic sacrifice. The compositions must thus be understood as the setting for the rite celebrated in this room and as closely related to it. This fact we shall soon find to be of considerable importance (Pl. 4).

II

In the vault there appears the Lamb of God in the midst of a wreath, which is supported by four angels standing on globes. The image of the lamb was introduced into the Roman rite only at the end of the seventh century by Pope Sergius I, a Syrian. But in the liturgies of the East this symbol of the Christian sacrifice appears at an earlier date,[8] and we are justified in interpreting its representation in San Vitale as alluding to the eucharistic liturgy (Pl. 8).

The first arcade of the sanctuary is decorated with fifteen medallions, showing the images of Christ (restored), of the twelve apostles, and of Gervase and Protase, who, with their "father" Vitalis, were venerated in this church. In the ancient liturgy of Ravenna, all these saints are mentioned in the so-called "diptychs," the "Book of Life," listing the names of those whom the church wishes to remember at every Mass (Pls. 8 and 9).[9]

The next bay on either side shows, above the columns supporting the arcades of the galleries, two sacrificial scenes from the Old Testament. On our left, the three angels appearing to Abraham in the valley of Mambre (Genesis, chap. 18), and Isaac whom his father is about to sacrifice; on our right, Abel offering a lamb, and Melchizedek with his sacrifice of bread and wine. Above them, there appears the hand of God, the traditional symbol of the divine presence and of God's acceptance of the sacrifice (Pls. 14 and 15).

All four scenes allude to the eucharistic sacrifice. To make this significance plain, an altar is depicted between Abel and Melchizedek, on which are placed a chalice and two loaves of bread, identical in shape with that which Melchizedek offers and also with the eucharistic bread which the church used during the sixth century. The altar motif appears again in the opposite mosaic: Isaac is shown kneeling upon an altar, and even the table behind which the three angels are seated resembles the simple wooden altar of Christian antiquity. The three round cakes which Sarah has placed before the heavenly messengers are marked with the sign of the cross and recall again the eucharistic hosts of that time.[10]

In patristic exegesis and in Christian art and literature the four scenes depicted are among the most frequent symbols of the eucharistic sacrifice. Even more noteworthy is the fact that Abel, Abraham, and Melchizedek are specifically mentioned in one of the solemn prayers of the Roman canon of the Mass: "Upon which [viz., the eucharistic offerings] do thou vouchsafe to look with a propitious and serene countenance, and to accept them, as thou wert graciously pleased to accept the gifts of thy just servant Abel, and the sacrifice of our Patriarch Abraham, and that which thy high priest Melchizedek offered to thee, a holy sacrifice, a spotless victim."

This prayer is very ancient. In the fourth century it had already appeared in the eucharistic liturgy of

Milan and, in all probability, in that of Rome.[11] The representation of the three mystical antitypes of Christ's priesthood in San Vitale is striking evidence of the importance of the liturgical theme in this church—an added reason for linking the compositions with Maximian, in whose work the liturgy occupied so important a place. We shall leave undecided at this point the question of whether or not the correspondence between the biblical scenes and the liturgies of Milan and Rome suggests that Ravenna, in the pattern of her worship, belongs in the same orbit. As one studies these compositions in connection with the other mosaics in San Vitale, there emerges gradually the historical vision which prompted this monumental illustration of the eucharistic rite.[12]

Each of the two mosaics described so far is surrounded by a framing composition. The arch surrounding the Abel and Melchizedek scene (left) shows what may be called the "Mission of Moses": he appears, first, as a shepherd, guiding the flock of Jethro at the foot of Mount Horeb and, for a second time, taking off his shoes before the appearance of God in the burning bush. Two flying angels, supporting a wreath and cross, separate these scenes from the figure of Isaiah.

We meet a similar composition on the opposite wall. Here Moses is shown receiving the Decalogue, while the chiefs of the twelve tribes of Israel appear at the foot of the sacred mountain. The motif of wreath and angels leads to the figure of Jeremiah on the left side of the mosaic.

These compositions seem to abandon the sacrificial and liturgical theme. It must not be forgotten, however, that, since apostolic times, the events narrated in the Book of Exodus were looked upon as allusions to the events of redemption.

It is of special interest to note that this parallelism is expounded in the *Christian Topography* of Cosmas Indicopleustes, a work which gives an excellent idea of the prevailing religious and intellectual preoccupations of the sixth century and which, moreover, was written within the very decade in which the

[25]

mosaics in San Vitale were executed.[13] Cosmas was an Egyptian monk and undoubtedly was intimately acquainted with the symbolical and mystical Bible exegesis which had been practiced for centuries in the school of Alexandria. In the fifth book of his curious encyclopedia he demonstrates elaborately that the events narrated in the Book of Exodus are to be understood as "shadows and types" of the salvation of mankind.[14] The deliverance of the Israelites from the servitude of the Egyptians is compared with the work of redemption achieved by Christ; the divine legislation on Mount Sinai with the descent of the Hoy Ghost. Seen in this light, the Exodus scenes selected in San Vitale are indeed related to the theme of the other mosaics. Isaiah and Jeremiah, furthermore, are the prophets of the Incarnation and the Passion, respectively, and have therefore found their place in the christological cycles of medieval art.

Above these mosaics and flanking the graceful arcades of the gallery, the four evangelists are represented: Matthew and Mark on the left wall, John and Luke on the right. All four appear seated in a mountainous landscape, holding their Gospels on their knees. Their symbolic animals are seen above them; writing utensils are placed at their sides (Pls. 13 and 16).

The relation of these figures to those below is obvious: as the two tables which Moses received on Mount Sinai contained the Old Law, so the New Dispensation is contained in the Gospels. In the later Middle Ages, Christian art expressed this relation by depicting the apostles standing on the shoulders of the prophets. The mosaics in San Vitale express the same thought.

It must be noted, however, that the four evangelists are depicted not solely as the authors of the Gospels. They, too, are symbols of the sacramental life of the Christian. This function appears clearly in the ancient ceremony *in apertione aurium,* which took place on the Wednesday after the fourth Sunday of Lent and was devoted to the solemn prepara-

tion of the catechumens for their mystical rebirth in baptism.[15]

The ceremony *in apertione aurium,* "the opening of the ears," was to open the catechumen's mind to the message of salvation. As Christ himself had done in healing the physically afflicted, the bishop touched the ears of the faithful with spittle, pronouncing the word *ephpheta,* "open." There followed the instruction which initiated the catechumen into the mysteries of his faith: he learned the Lord's Prayer, the Creed, and the Gospels. These, however, were taught in a curiously abbreviated and, as it were, ritualized form; the faithful learned to identify the four evangelists with the four mystical beasts of the vision of Ezekiel; and they learned, further, that each of these animals embodied the content of one of the four holy books. The "face of the lion" of St. Mark alludes to his account of the Resurrection of Christ because the lion, according to the legendary zoölogy of late antiquity, can resuscitate his dead cub by the sound of his voice. The "face of man" recalls the genealogy of Christ in Matthew; the ox, as a sacrificial animal, refers to Christ's Passion as narrated by Luke, while the eagle, symbol of the Ascension, is the animal of St. John. The four symbols thus recalled to the Christian the four great truths upon which the mystery of Redemption rested: the Incarnation, the Passion, the Resurrection, and the Ascension of Christ.[16]

The function of the evangelists and their animals as means of visual initiation is noteworthy. They acquire the dignity of symbols which remain obscure to the unbeliever but impress the faithful with an intuitive force which no dialectical argument could equal. The same, incidentally, is true for the opening words of each of the Four Gospels. These, too, the catechumen learned by heart during the ceremony. The symbolic function of these words, their dignity as *nomina sacra,* is best shown by the wonderful calligraphy to which they inspired the illuminators of medieval gospel-books.[17]

The iconography of the evangelists must be interpreted in a similar fashion. The abstractness and the austere majesty of these figures have a profound affinity with the abbreviations of the *nomina sacra,* and both originate in the same religious experience. The symbolic animals of the evangelists had already appeared on the vault of the archepiscopal palace in Ravenna, in the fifth-century mosaics in the mausoleum of Galla Placidia, in the chapel of St. Matrona near Capua, and in Bishop Soter's baptistry in Naples. The apse mosaic in Santa Pudenziana may be the earliest monumental rendering of this theme.[18] The mosaics in San Vitale cannot rival the apocalyptic majesty of some of these earlier works. But to the symbols they add the portraits of the evangelists themselves—the earliest monumental rendering of this important subject of medieval art in existence. It is not unlikely that this innovation was inspired by the wish to render more explicit the comparison between the two Dispensations: Cosmas Indicopleustes has a similar juxtaposition of the four evangelists with the prophets and patriarchs of the Old Testament.

III

As we proceed deeper into the sanctuary, toward the main altar of San Vitale, we face the two monumental compositions which, alone among the mosaics of San Vitale, Agnellus found worthy of description and which mark, indeed, a climax not only in the art of Ravenna but in that of the sixth century in general. They are the portraits of Justinian and Theodora with their retinues. In the mosaic on our left we perceive the emperor and next to him Julianus Argentarius and Maximian, a scene we have already mentioned. The archbishop is preceded by two deacons, while the two dignitaries who follow Justinian are, in all probability, the *praefectus legibus* and the *dux armis.*[19] A group of soldiers injects a significantly martial note into the solemn processional. It has been suggested that in the figure of the *dux* we have actually a portrait of Belisarius. The presence of the conqueror of Ravenna in this composition would be eminently appropriate, and the only argument against this as-

sumption is the frequent spells of imperial disgrace which obscured the great soldier's last years (Pl. 2).

The mosaic on our right represents the Empress Theodora with her ladies and the dignitaries of her court. One cannot look at this portrait without profound emotion. The empress' eyes have retained their extraordinary beauty, but her face is mournful and already in the shadow of death (Pls. 18 and 19).

It is no exaggeration to say that no other work of art, and perhaps no other document of any kind, conveys the spirit of Byzantium with so much eloquence as do these two mosaics. If we recall that they were completed while the outcome of the Gothic War was still wholly undecided, these works appear not only as an impressive monument to Justinian's entry into Ravenna but as the proud anticipation of his victory in Italy. The significance of these mosaics can be realized fully only if we recall the official function of the imperial portrait in the Byzantine Empire.

As a political and legal institution, an emperor's portrait is proof of that unbroken tradition which linked the Christian empire with its pagan predecessor. In a very literal sense the imperial image represented the emperor and his power wherever it was displayed. The identification of reality and image, originating in the magical thought of a primitive age, had received, in the Roman Empire, a well-defined legal meaning, which we can trace back to the days of Caesar[20] and which was very much alive in the reign of Justinian. As the emperor's "representation," his image appeared in public places, on military insignia, and on coins, proclaiming his supreme authority and demanding the allegiance of everyone. Mommsen has rightly called it the "formal symbol of the monarchy."

This political function of the emperor's portrait was by no means invalidated by the establishment of Christianity. On the contrary, its significance was formalized still further, and an elaborate ceremony underscored its authoritative character. Upon the *signa* of the Christian armies, the emperor's image appeared below the labarum, representing the supreme commander and enforcing the absolute loyalty of his troops. It assumed a similar significance in the civic life of the Roman Empire. In the law courts such representations of the sovereign had a function which merged magical and legal concepts. "Remember," says Bishop Severian of Gabala in a sermon once attributed to his contemporary, John Chrysostom, "remember how many governors there are throughout the world. Since the Emperor cannot possibly be present with every one of them, his image must be placed in law courts, market places, assembly halls, and theaters."[21]

It is noteworthy that, in general, Christians do not seem to have considered idolatrous the homage which Roman citizens were required to pay before the image of the emperor. Several of the Fathers spoke out against it, and early Christian art occasionally compared those who resisted the law with the Three Children of the Book of Daniel who had refused to adore what was taken to be an image of King Nebuchadnezzar. But after the edict of Milan such opposition seems gradually to have weakened. Since the Fathers of the fourth and fifth centuries accepted the identification of the emperor's person with his image—Athanasius even uses the concept to demonstrate the unity of the Divine Persons!—one does not see how they could have objected to an act of homage before the one while tolerating homage to the other.[22] It is significant that one of the few voices of protest—that of Jerome—comes from a man living in solitude, far removed from the political life of the Empire. In the cities, the worlds of religion and of the state made peace with each other, and in the atmosphere of the imperial court we notice a general and irresistible trend toward merging the concepts and imagery of the Christian cult into what has rightly been called the *culte impérial*. In the light of this development, even Christ's "Render unto Caesar," referring explicitly to the imperial image on a coin, might well be interpreted as a permission for Christians to render homage to the emperor's portrait.

This image assumed its most important political function when an emperor had just ascended the throne or when he wished to demonstrate his authority even in the remotest parts of the Empire. Whether to legalize the imperial power or to proclaim it, the emperor's portrait was sent out in the most solemn way. When the procession carrying it approached a city, the whole population went out with candles and incense to pay homage to the new ruler. These "sacred images," as they were significantly called,[23] were subsequently erected in a public place, an act which furnished the occasion for the declaration of submission on the part of the people.

The portraits of Justinian and Theodora in San Vitale have to be seen in this light. They, too, are the *vultus sacri* of emperor-worship; and, if these images have something awe-inspiring even for the modern beholder, how much more so for an age which conceived image and reality as inseparable. Agnellus tells several stories about the miraculous life which some of the ancient mosaics in Ravenna had assumed in their time; these legends also convey the emotions with which the man of the sixth century must have looked at the portraits of his sovereigns.[24]

It is not surprising that not only Justinian's portrait but also that of Theodora should have been placed in San Vitale. We can trace the existence of official images of the empress to Roman times; and early in the fifth century the Empress Eudoxia, consort of Arcadius, effected her elevation to what amounted to the dignity and power of a co-regent by the publication of her portrait.[25] The political influence of Theodora upon Justinian's administration is well known. She was, in title and in fact, *consors imperii*. To the childless emperor it must have appeared eminently desirable to secure official recognition for the political role of his consort and to impress the public with her dignity by the solemn display of her image. Theodora's statue in Constantinople is described by Procopius. After the reconquest of Ravenna her "representation" in that city was a political gesture of equal significance. Her death within a few weeks after the consecration of San Vitale transformed this image into a funerary monument such as this great woman would have desired for herself.[26]

The selection of a sanctuary for the portraits of the *Augusti* is noteworthy. The Justinian Code has preserved a decree of the year A.D. 394 ordering the removal of pictures of a frivolous character from all public places where the images of the emperor are "consecrated."[27] The Byzantine concept of the monarch and the curiously intimate relation which it established between the emperor and Christ must have suggested, moreover, that homage be paid to the emperor in the place and at the time of religious worship. We shall presently find evidence of this thought in the Byzantine liturgy. The mosaics in San Vitale are by no means its only monumental illustration. The emperor-portraits in the Hagia Sophia of Constantinople are of much later date; but a letter of Gregory the Great attests the existence of the imperial images even in Roman churches. It relates that after the overthrow of the Emperor Mauritius (A.D. 602) the pope ordered the images of the usurper Phocas and his consort to be acclaimed by the senate and clergy of Rome; and, in order to render even more explicit the significance of this act, Gregory had the images transferred afterward to the oratory of St. Caesarius.[28]

It will be readily understood that Justinian must needs have desired a similar demonstration and confirmation of his authority in Ravenna. From this city he intended not merely to govern the political destinies of the Western Empire; from here the imperial theology, which Justinian conceived as the soul of his realm, was to be proclaimed. In announcing this program, the dedicatory mosaics in San Vitale reflect a decisive historical moment.

It is this function of the compositions which makes their execution after 540 appear certain. As long as the heirs of Theodoric retained possession of Ravenna, they would never have tolerated such a demonstration that Gothic power in the city had ended; nor would the Orthodox church have risked such language. Our reasons for ascribing the mosaics to the years of Maximian's episcopate will appear as soon as the portraits of the *Augusti* are studied in relation to the other works. Unlike the painted or carved ruler-portraits, these mosaics could not be removed after Justinian's death. It is not this physical fact, however, which welds the images of the sovereigns to the sanctuary but the liturgical act which they are seen performing.

IV

The sovereigns are shown presenting gifts and are thus marked as donors and founders of San Vitale. But the gifts that they carry are conceived as far more than symbols of that act of patronage. The emperor offers the golden paten containing the eucharistic bread, while the empress presents the *scyphus aureus* in which the wine was offered at the altar.[29] Both are thus shown participating in the eucharistic liturgy and, more specifically, in the offertory rite.

This rite is an ancient and eloquent part of the liturgy.[30] In the early church the entire congregation, men and women alike, participated in it. In their experience the oblation of the eucharistic elements appeared at once as a sacrifice of atonement and, in imitation of Christ's sacrifice, as the self-immolation of the offerer. In this dual function, the offertory procession bespoke the sacerdotal dignity, the "kingly priesthood" to which, in the words of St. Peter (I Pet. 2:9), every member of the Christian congregation belonged. In this connection the fourth canon of the Council of Mâcon, which met in A.D. 585, is of interest. Here participation in the offertory procession is strictly enjoined upon all the faithful, and all those who do not comply are threatened with the anathema. The reason for this decree is stated explicitly: by these oblations (or "immolations," as the text calls them) all may obtain remission of their sins and "may deserve to be sharers with Abel and the rest of the just offerers."[31]

We learn from this passage that the offertory was

considered a sacrifice in the strict sense of the word—a gift of atonement which represented its donor before the face of God and made him comparable to Abel and the other "just offerers."

In the Christian West the offertory procession of the laity survived well into the Middle Ages; the Roman rite has preserved traces of it to the present day.[32] In the East, however, it was abolished at an early time, probably in the second half of the fourth century.[33] The only lay person who, in the Byzantine rite, continued to participate in the liturgical oblation was the emperor.

The privileged position which the Byzantine emperor occupied in the eucharistic rite deserves our greatest attention. Its earliest trace, as far as I know, occurs in an episode related in the *Ecclesiastical History* of Theodoretus. We are told that on one occasion the Emperor Theodosius, attending Mass in Milan, did not withdraw with the rest of the laity after the oblation of gifts but remained in the sanctuary. St. Ambrose noted this and sent one of his deacons to inquire "if the Emperor wanted anything." Theodosius replied that he desired to attend the sacred mysteries. Whereupon the great bishop of Milan advised him that the place inside the *cancelli,* i.e., the sanctuary, was reserved for the clergy only and requested the emperor to leave because his place was with the rest of the laity. "The purple," Ambrose added, "makes emperors but it does not make priests." Theodosius complied graciously, remarking only that the reason for his remaining in the sanctuary was not arrogance but custom: in Byzantium the emperor at that time attended the eucharistic rite in the sanctuary.[34]

The story is interesting enough. Ambrose's decision, whether or not he could claim any precedent for it, shows that his age attributed to ecclesiastical rites a significance far beyond the context of religion and worship. The place which the emperor occupied in the church bespeaks with dramatic force the relation between *sacerdotium* and *imperium.*

If Ambrose's views in this regard have decisively affected the development of political thought in the West, they differ profoundly from those of the Christian East. This is shown very clearly by a comparison of the liturgies of the two churches. One might say that the Western rites almost forgot the emperor. He is not even mentioned in the prayers of intercession of the Gregorian Canon—significant evidence of the emancipation from imperial domination which the Roman church achieved under Gregory the Great. The Byzantine rite, on the other hand, has never failed to concede to the emperor the solemn demonstration of the sacerdotal dignity that he claimed. Even in Byzantium, it is true, the custom of the emperor's attending Mass in the sanctuary was given up after the incident at Milan.[35] But the emperor continued to present his oblation at the altar; since in his church no other layman could claim the right to exercise this priestly function, its symbolic significance must have been all the greater.

The dedicatory mosaics of San Vitale unquestionably depict the Byzantine offertory procession. As if to stress this liturgical context of the two scenes, the portrait of the emperor has been placed on the right side of the figure of Christ in the apse, i.e., the *pars virorum* of the ancient church order, while the empress appears on the left side of the sanctuary, where the female part of the congregation attended the divine service. In this connection one further detail may be not without significance. No particular background or locality is indicated in the representation of Justinian and his cortege. The implicit assumption is that we are to visualize him in the very place where his image appears, viz., the sanctuary of San Vitale. The empress, on the other hand, is shown before a doorway and next to a graceful fountain. This setting is not imaginary but reproduces, though in abbreviated form, the narthex which adjoined the apse of San Vitale.[36]

The topographical hint has something paradoxical: Theodora's portrait has been placed in the sanctuary, but at the same time the onlooker is restrained from imagining her in this sacred place. The sanctuary thus remains reserved for the emperor—at least we are to visualize him preceding his consort in the liturgical rite.

The significance of the representation of the imperial offertory becomes apparent only if we view these mosaics in connection with those adjoining them. That the figures of Abel and the other "just offerers" were understood as alluding to the liturgical oblation is attested by the canon of Mâçon which we have just quoted. Since, however, in the Byzantine rite the emperor is the only layman performing this act, the comparison took on a different meaning: Abel, Melchizedek, and Abraham were only indirectly images of every Christian attending Mass; but they appeared, above all, as images of the emperor who, as king and priest, represented his subjects in the sacred rite before God. The fact that in San Vitale the Old Testament scenes adjoin the offertory mosaics is an unmistakable indication of this significance (Pls. 10 and 12).

This is true, above all, for the image of Melchizedek. To the sixth century no figure embodied more dramatically the plenitude of power, the sacred authority, the awe-inspiring dignity of the Christian emperor than did that of Melchizedek, the King of Salem, who was at the same time "the priest of the most high God" (Gen. 14:18). The fact that St. Paul, in his letter to the Hebrews (7:1), represented the biblical priest-king as the forerunner and mystical antitype of Christ himself did not prevent the early Middle Ages from seeing in him an image of the Christian emperor whose ideal features seemed to blend imperceptibly into those of Christ.

It is noteworthy that the sixth century visualized Melchizedek as a Byzantine emperor. In the mosaic of San Vitale he wears the attire of a priest, but his headgear, cloak, and shoes are of that purple color which court ceremonial reserved for the emperor alone.[37] In the *Vienna Genesis* and also in the famous Vatican codex of the *Christian Topography* (the illuminations of which are ninth-century copies of sixth-century originals), Melchizedek is deliberately represented as a Byzantine emperor. The figure in the second work is an admirable illustration of Cos-

mas' text, in which Melchizedek is described as the king of peace and justice and, at the same time, as the high priest who resembles Christ, as the ruler who guided the education of his subjects in all works of piety and thus reconciled them with God.[38] Such language, in a theological context, sounds remarkably political. One cannot help feeling that Cosmas had before him the vision of a ruler who united in his own person the powers of *sacerdotium* and *imperium;* and this impression is singularly confirmed by the illustration. What, one may ask, prompted the artist to conceive this biblical priest as an emperor? And is even the term "an emperor" an adequate description? Kondakov seems to have been the first to be struck by the curiously vivid realism of this figure, which contrasts strangely with the style of the other illuminations; he has also called attention to the similarity between the Melchizedek miniature in the Vatican codex and the portrait of Justinian in San Vitale (Pl. 17a).[39]

That the Melchizedek image of the *Christian Topography* should have been colored by the personality of Justinian, in whose reign Cosmas and his illuminator lived, is not surprising, in view of the extraordinary political concepts of this emperor and in view of the solemn oratory in which he was wont to expound the imperial dignity as he conceived it. In the mosaics in San Vitale the comparison of Justinian with Melchizedek is inevitable.

Melchizedek was not the only embodiment of the theocratic aspirations of the Byzantine monarchy. Of equal significance is the figure of Moses. Eusebius had described Constantine the Great as another Moses and had elaborately traced the analogies between the lives of both.[40] The figure of the biblical lawgiver, who united within his person the active, as well as the contemplative, virtues, was singularly apt as the symbol of the ideal ruler; we can trace the influence of this concept even in the Renaissance. But at the Byzantine court the comparison of the emperor with Moses received the most official sanction. At solemn processions the staff of Moses was carried before the sovereign.[41]

[31]

The fact that Moses, like Melchizedek, had yet another typological significance, that he, too, was considered a mystical antitype of Christ, did not prevent such political comparisons but, on the contrary, enhanced their significance for a generation for which historical events and personalities were but shadows and symbols of an invisible reality. Already the rule of Trajan symbolized, for the Stoic, Dio Chrysostom, the divine rule of the universe.[42] For the Christian the great acts of government were images of that eternal economy from which they derived their sanction and to which they were ordered. For such speculations the figure of Moses acquired a special significance.

The *Christian Topography* gives again a fairly good idea of the theological interpretation of Moses during the age of Justinian. Cosmas[43] points out that the deeds of Moses have to be understood as "shadows and types" of those of Christ, as man's "liberation from the servitude of tyranny," the renovation of the world which will begin with the resurrection of the dead and the eternal Sabbath of mankind. The illustrations seek to make this thought more explicit. One of them depicts the First Mission of Moses: he appears as a shepherd with the flock of Jethro and again on Mount Horeb receiving a scroll from the hand of God. Another illumination represents the reception of the Decalogue with a group of leaders of the Israelites as witnesses of the event (Pl. 17b).

The similarity between these illustrations and the Moses scenes in San Vitale is most striking. The same events have been selected for representation, and the same aspects stressed. The emphasis on Moses the shepherd is perhaps most remarkable; Cosmas says explicitly that Moses appears here "adorned with the likeness of our true shepherd Christ."

But the figure of the Good Shepherd had never lost its political connotation. Originally, it had been the image of the ideal ruler of a past golden age; the Roman Empire projected this symbol into the present: in Virgil's Fourth Eclogue the world-ruler whose immediate advent is predicted appears as a shepherd. That the Roman emperors themselves encouraged and sanctioned the metaphor is shown, as Eisler has pointed out, by the clay lamps which were manufactured for the celebration of the thousandth anniversary of Rome (A.D. 248) and which bore the image of the Good Shepherd with his herd as an allusion to the Roman emperor.[44]

When Christ referred to himself as the Good Shepherd, the image took on a new meaning. It now embodied not the citizen's nostalgic dream of a golden age past or present but the hope of the faithful in the salvation of his soul from eternal death, for an eternal life in the Kingdom of God. But the image of the Good Shepherd did not entirely lose its political significance.[45] Perhaps no other symbol gives a better idea of that imperceptible transformation of a political utopia into an eschatological vision which marks the end of the classical world and the triumph of Christianity. Scholars have long noted that early Christian art renders the Good Shepherd with the features of Alexander the Great;[46] and when Constantine had the statue of the Good Shepherd placed on a fountain in Constantinople, the elaborate Moses allegories of Eusebius must have made it difficult for his contemporaries to decide whether the statue was an image of Christ or an idealized portrait of the emperor.

The ambivalence of the shepherd symbol did not remain confined to Byzantium. The comparison of the Christian bishop—and especially of the successors of St. Peter—with the shepherd originates in Christ's own words; but the wide acceptance of the comparison, of which we shall soon find an example in Ravenna itself, is evidence not only of the aspirations of the hierarchy in the West but even more of the political duties imposed upon it during the early Middle Ages.

Not only the image of the shepherd but also the two other figures of Moses in San Vitale must have been understood as alluding to Justinian. It will be recalled that both scenes depict Moses receiving the divine commands which he, as the inspired legislator of his people, is to transmit to the Israelites. In this image the emperor must have recognized himself. A preceding age had already compared the Roman and the Mosaic laws and had attempted to reconcile them;[47] Justinian conceived his own legislative work as the restitution of the Law of Moses, since Christ had not come to destroy the law but to fulfil it (Matt. 5:17).[48] And in his Code the emperor speaks with the awesome conviction of a legislator who writes under the inspiration of God.[49] More particularly, it was his dignity as *praeses doctrinae ac disciplinae ecclesiasticae*—his privilege to lay down the law in all matters theological and ecclesiastical—which convinced him of his mission. To none of his duties has Justinian ascribed greater importance; none seemed to him to express more clearly the nature and purpose of his government. And it was in presiding over the great theological assemblies of the realm, in expounding the divine doctrine to his bishops, that he appeared to his contemporaries as another Moses.[50]

To us such theological preoccupations of the ruler have something incomprehensible; yet the Byzantine monarchy was built around this concept of the emperor's prophetic mission. Of this fact we have an interesting monumental proof which, though of a later age, explains the ideas which had in Justinian their greatest exponent. Close to the imperial palace in Constantinople a small edifice was situated, the so-called "Milion" or "Golden Milestone." The structure received its symbolic significance from the fact that from it emanated the great roads into the Empire. Early in the eighth century Emperor Philippikos Bardanes adorned the Milion with a number of compositions. Since the Milion marked the heart of the Empire, these representations acquired, as has rightly been said, a specific and official significance: they must be understood as depicting the ideals, the very principles, upon which the Byzantine monarchy rested. But, instead of the great acts of the civil administration and the successes of warfare which we should expect to find commemorated in such a monument, the emperor selected representations of the five ecumenical councils, apparently personified by the emperors who had presided over them. The sovereign himself appeared, standing in the center of this cycle adorning the vault of the Milion, and with him the patriarch of Constantinople. No subject could have conveyed more eloquently the spirit of Byzantium.[51]

The series may well be compared with the mosaic in San Vitale. As the heart of Justinian's administration in the West, Ravenna's importance was surpassed only by Byzantium itself. In the place from which his decrees and his military power poured into the Empire, Philippikos Bardanes wanted to appear not as the head of his administration, the leader of his armies, but as the chief theologian of his realm, as another Moses. Justinian wanted the same message to be conveyed in the mosaics of the church that was to become the monument to his conquest of Italy. One may even ask whether these works do not preach Justinian's theological doctrines.

V

It will be recalled that the execution of the mosaics in San Vitale coincided with the dispute over the Three Chapters. The theology imposed by Justinian, while not Monophysite, made very considerable concessions to this party. Its core was the "Scythian" or theopaschite formula, *unus ex trinitate passus est carne.* The definition was not heterodox. But the popes had long opposed it on the ground that in the presence of Monophysitism the omission of any reference to Christ's humanity must almost necessarily lead to misinterpretations. In 534, John II finally complied with the emperor's wishes and declared the formula orthodox. In 553 it received the most solemn vindication by the fifth ecumenical council.[52] If we can detect any definite theology in the mosaics of San Vitale, it must be this one.

To the theopaschite point of view, all representations of the Passion, in which Christ suffered as man, must be suspicious of heterodoxy, if not of Arianism. The iconography of the Passion and the Crucifixion in the sixth century and the extreme rarity of such representations in that period have their cause undoubtedly in those theological views. It is noteworthy that the many mosaics of Ravenna depict the Passion of Christ but once: in Sant' Apollinare Nuovo; and these mosaics are almost certainly Arian in origin. In San Vitale, the emphasis on the eucharistic motif seems to render the representation of the sacrifice on Calvary inevitable. Instead, this event is no more than alluded to in the Old Testament scenes, as if all reference to the suffering of Jesus had to be omitted. And in the apse, not the Son of Man but the Second Person of the Trinity is depicted in the awe-inspiring majesty of the Second Epiphany.

But if the language of these mosaics is theological, their message transcends religious doctrine. In order to understand the vision here unfolded before us, we must look at the mosaics with the eyes of a Byzantine of the sixth century. To him these figures of Moses and of Melchizedek, in their twofold relation to the emperor and to Christ, evoked that living reality, that colorful pageant, in which his spiritual life found its realization. That reality was the liturgy of Byzantium—perhaps it would be more correct to say the two liturgies of Byzantium, since Byzantine life was encompassed by the rituals both of the church and of the imperial court. Not only do these two liturgies appear curiously entwined, but they merge into each other, embracing in one grandiose vision the two realms of human existence, the world of the citizen and that of the Christian. In our present context two examples of this union are of interest.

The feast of Pentecost commemorates traditionally not only the descent of the Holy Ghost but also the giving of the law on Mount Sinai. On the same day the liturgy of the imperial court celebrated the blessing of the imperial crown. The hymns sung on this occasion, in a significant fusion of religious and political imagery, compare the emperor to Moses.[53] Again, on the feast of Christmas, the Eastern church celebrates not only Christ's birth but also the advent of the Magi as the homage of mankind before the divine majesty of the Redeemer. The liturgy of the court blended this vision of the triumph of Christ with that of the triumph of the emperor: "The Lord," one of the hymns reads, "will exalt your power throughout the universe. He will bring all nations into your dominion; like the Magi they will offer presents to your majesties."[54]

To grasp the full significance of such language, we have to realize that the interrelation of the two rites was suggested by the identity of the place in which both were enacted and by the part which the emperor played in both of them. The great church of Hagia Sophia was, in a very literal sense, part of the Sacred Palace. Many of the great ceremonies of emperor-worship took place in this sanctuary, while the emperor vindicated the sacerdotal dignity that he claimed by the conspicuous role assigned to him in the liturgy of the Byzantine church.

Perhaps no other historical phenomenon is more difficult for modern man to grasp than the relation which Byzantine ceremonial established between church and state. We are wont to explain its earliest manifestations under Constantine the Great as a survival of pagan traditions and as evidence of this emperor's shrewd design to exploit Christianity for the enforcement of emperor-worship. But the sixth century is not the fourth. No one mistook Justinian for the Messiah or his administration for a fulfilment of the religious expectations of mankind. Nevertheless, the Fathers of the church continued to evaluate the imperial institution in a purely theological and eschatological light: it was the emperor's calling to lead his people to the eternal fruition of God. This doctrine, accepted and elaborated by Justinian, resulted in the concept of the imperial office as a sacerdotal dignity comparable to that of Moses or Melchizedek. But, to an experience which the political thought of the age tended to rationalize, popular imagination imparted a curious and fascinating life.

We know the psychological phenomenon of association. Our imagination associates or identifies not only things which evoke a similar emotional response within us but also those which logical reason connects merely through the chain of causality or by the still more distant relation of analogy. One thing may thus become the symbolic representation of another, and we may come to covet or admire the symbol without fully realizing that, in reality, we are yearning for the actuality of which it is merely the image. This mental habit must have a profound influence upon the development of political ideas and institutions. It is most noticeable in the concept of the ideal ruler. In modern democratic society the ideals of prosperity and material independence seek not only their symbol but the promise of their political realization in the homely personality of an average citizen. As candidate for the highest office, a man of such bearing will have a far better chance to be elected than any other social type, regardless of his qualifications or even of his program. Such preference on the side of the people may or may not be justified in terms of political logic. The public figure is a symbol; his acts, his tastes, his appearance, seem to embody the life which he will bring within reach of those whom he governs.

The person and dignity of the Byzantine emperor have to be seen in the same light. He is the ideal man of his age and, though he does not have to be answerable to his subjects for the acts of his administration, his appearance and his office are wholly molded by the aspirations and dreams of those whom he rules. This fact explains the extraordinary affinities between the Byzantine iconography of Christ and that of the emperor and between the rituals of the church and the court. Since the ideal Christian was Christ-like, the ruler of the *Respublica Christiana* had to be an imitator of Christ. We can trace this notion in Christian political thought down to the days of Erasmus and even of Shakespeare. But in the early centuries of the church such imitation had a specific meaning: it referred, above all, to the act of self-immolation by which Christ had redeemed mankind and of which the eucharistic liturgy was the re-enactment. Not only the life of the individual believer but the life of Christian humanity itself were conceived as an imitation of that

sacrifice. Hence the liturgy of the church took on a truly cosmic meaning; in the *City of God,* Augustine describes the goal of universal history in the grandiose vision of a liturgical offertory procession in which the citizens of the *Civitas Dei* join "all the blessed immortals . . . in sacrificing themselves to the adoration of God the Father, the Son, and the Holy Ghost."[55]

Such views explain why, in the atmosphere of Byzantium, the Christian emperor appeared as a Christ-like high priest and why the principles of his administration seemed to be symbolized in the liturgical rite. In the offertory procession he appeared like the priest-king Melchizedek, "bringing forth bread and wine" on behalf of his people, to propitiate God.

VI

Only now does the significance of the mosaics become fully apparent. And it will be realized how intimately the different works are interconnected. Moses, as well as the "just offerers," alludes to the emperor. As Moses, upon God's command, had made and adorned the Tabernacle, so Justinian had built and sumptuously furnished the church of San Vitale,[56] and, like Melchizedek, he presented the sacrificial offering at the altar. But the imperial portraits must also be related to the great central composition in the apse (Pls. 10, 12, 20).

We have described this composition but briefly. Christ enthroned upon a globe holds in his left hand the Book of Life, while his right tenders a wreath to St. Vitalis, who is presented by an angel. A second angel, on Christ's right, introduces Bishop Ecclesius. What does this scene signify?

In his hymn on the Resurrection, Ephrem the Syrian (d. 378) describes the Second Advent of Christ for the resurrection of the dead. Christ appears seated upon his "awe-inspiring throne," and with his hand he distributes the crown of glory to his saints. This is unquestionably the scene depicted in the apse of San Vitale. The four rivers of Paradise emerging from under Christ's feet and possibly also the clouds behind his head indicate the eschatological character of the scene: "For the Lord himself [writes Paul, I, Thess. 4:15] shall come down from heaven with commandment and with the voice of an archangel. . . . Then we who are alive shall be taken up together with them [the dead] in the clouds to meet Christ, into the air: and so shall we be always with the Lord."[57]

The mosaic in San Vitale illustrates this eschatological vision in the traditional way. In Ravenna itself we find the scene represented on the fifth-century sarcophagus of Rinaldo; and, in the age of Justinian, the illuminator of the *Christian Topography* illustrated the account of the Last Judgment, with which Cosmas concludes his fifth book, in a way that well deserves comparison with the mosaic: Christ appears enthroned, while the angels, the blessed souls who are already with him, and those who are rising from their graves are arranged in three strata below him (Pls. 4, 5a).[58]

The connection between the emperor-portraits and the central mosaic is obvious. As Ecclesius, the founder of the sanctuary, stands ready to receive the same award as that which is tendered Vitalis, so the sovereigns, as the primary benefactors of the church, will be rewarded for their oblation. Again it is the liturgy which gives particular significance to this thought. The Christian mystery drama, it must be borne in mind, not only commemorates the past but also anticipates the future. As the re-enactment of the deed of redemption, it makes every Christian and the entire church partakers of Christ's death and resurrection. But the resurrection of mankind will take place only with the Second Advent of Christ on the Day of Judgment; the Christian mystery drama, therefore, unfolds a vision in which the first Easter morning, the beginning of Christian history, merges into the vision of its end. This experience is very clearly expressed in the ancient liturgies, in which the moment of resurrection and the expectation of the Second Epiphany of Christ are merged.[59] The fact that no subject has been more frequently

depicted in the apses of fifth-, sixth-, and seventh-century churches than this eschatological vision is impressive evidence of its place in the ancient liturgies.

In this connection one detail in the mosaics in San Vitale is of interest. The garment of the Empress Theodora is decorated with the figures of the Magi. Biblical exegesis has interpreted the advent of the Magi as a symbol of the eucharistic sacrifice; and this thought has found expression in the liturgies themselves. At the same time, however, the scene received an eschatological interpretation: borrowing from the secular pageant and imagery of the *epiphany* of Hellenistic rulers, the church described the Magi as images of the Christian who will go out to greet the Lord on his second Epiphany as the Wise Men did on his first. This dual interpretation of the Advent scene implied no contradiction at a time when the eschatological vision found its realization in the liturgical drama (Pl. 18).[60]

The entire cycle of mosaics thus culminates in the apse of San Vitale, where the sacrifice offered by Justinian as emperor and priest is shown to be judged and accepted on the last day. The scene is the supreme vindication of Justinian's administration, all the more moving since Christ, whom he is shown confronting, appears himself as an emperor in the act—dear to the religious imagination of the age—of bestowing the wreath of glory to the victor in the *agon*. In its mixture of proud confidence and humble submission the composition recalls the solemn words pronounced at the funeral of the Byzantine emperors: "Come, O emperor, thou art called by the Emperor of emperors, by the Lord of lords."[61] The fact that the mosaics in San Vitale were completed in the midst of the Gothic War and of the controversy over the Three Chapters conveys an idea of the confidence with which Justinian faced his enemies.

There remains one final question. We have attempted to show that in the mosaics in San Vitale the Byzantine liturgy appears as a grandiose theodicy of Justinian's imperium. No theme could have been more appropriate to the historical moment for which these works were created. But could the drama be intelligible without the actor? The story of Justinian's and Theodora's actual presence at the consecration of San Vitale is evidently a myth.[62] But the myth may conceal an intention which Justinian, for reasons of state, was unable to carry out. Indeed, the emperor's visit to Ravenna on that occasion must have seemed so eminently desirable that one may assume that only grave developments—the reverses suffered by the imperial cause in 547/8 in the military as well as in the theological fields—detained Justinian in Constantinople. Whatever the reasons for his absence may have been, the images in San Vitale were designed to represent him in Ravenna in more than the political and legal sense we have discussed; they were to remind his subjects that, even while he was far away in Byzantium, even though he could not join bishop and deacons in the enactment of the sacred drama, he was, during the hour of worship, mysteriously in their midst. And the same impalpable and irresistible force which attached his people to their God was to attach them irrevocably to him.

We cannot understand this function of the mosaics unless we realize their relation to the prayers of the Byzantine liturgy. These texts and the mosaics mirror each other; the former, too, visualize the emperor as another Melchizedek, rewarded by God on the Day of Judgment for his priestly service. The mosaics, as we said earlier, must be understood as settings for the liturgical drama. Even their style, awesome and disquieting, reflects the intent of those solemn incantations to call a supernatural reality into presence.

At the time of Justinian the liturgy of Byzantium contained a solemn prayer of intercession on behalf of the emperor. Unfortunately, we have no certain knowledge of either the exact words or the place of this prayer in the eucharistic rite. The prayer of intercession in the so-called Liturgy of Chrysos-tom mentions, significantly enough, the same personages and institutions which are represented in the mosaics in San Vitale—that is, the emperor, the empress, the court, and the army; but this liturgy is of a later date. Some help is offered, however, by the liturgies of the West. The ancient rite of Milan, which reflects a time when the imperial court was residing in this city, has preserved a prayer for the protection of the pontiff, the emperor, and the kings with their consorts and descendants.[63] In the fifth century, the popes repeatedly confirmed the existence of similar invocations in the liturgy of Rome.[64]

At what moment were these prayers pronounced in the Western rites? There is every reason to believe that they followed immediately after the commendation of gifts—in other words, at the end of the offertory procession. The notion which compared those who offered to Abel and the other "just offerers" and which therefore conceived the sacrificial oblation as a sacramental remedy would naturally express itself in a prayer invoking God's blessings upon the donor. In the church of Spain such prayers for those who offer can be traced to the end of the third century; Jerome confirms their existence in his church a century later.[65] The Roman rite has such a prayer to the present day; it follows immediately upon the offertory, and in all likelihood it occupied the same position in the fifth century. In a letter to Bishop Decentius of Gubbio, Innocent I (402–17) orders that the names of those who offer be read immediately after the commendation of gifts.[66]

Is it possible to separate these prayers for those who offer from the prayers of intercession for the emperor and other persons whose names were entered in the diptychs, or Book of Life, of the church? This seems very difficult to imagine. The belief in the propitiating power of the sacrifice must attach the prayer of intercession to the oblation of gifts, regardless of whether these were offered by the person himself or in his behalf. The *Memento* of the Roman rite reminds God of those "for whom we offer or who offer up to Thee, this sacrifice."

The Egyptian rite, at the time of Justinian, also linked the intercession to the oblation;[67] this liturgy, moreover, evokes the images of Abel and Abraham in connection with the diptychs. Even more explicit is a formula for the blessing of gifts in the ancient Spanish rite in which every benefactor of the church is compared to Abel and Melchizedek. It appears probable, to say the least, that the mosaics in San Vitale refer to a similar liturgical text, though, unfortunately, the problem of the diptychs in the Byzantine rite of the sixth century remains somewhat obscure.[68]

For with the abolition of the lay offertory, the prayer of intercession must have changed not only its place but its meaning. But would this also be true for the prayer on behalf of the emperor? Would not the sacerdotal rite which he performed almost necessarily suggest some prayer on his behalf? As we said before, we have no certain knowledge of the position of the diptychs in the Byzantine liturgy at the time of Justinian. A letter of John of Constantinople regarding the prayer for the pope, dated A.D. 515, seems to indicate that even then the diptychs occurred in the same place as in the liturgy of Chrysostom, i.e., after the moment of consecration rather than after the offertory. But in this same rite, the Great Entry, which takes the place of the offertory and has preserved some of its elements, has a brief prayer of intercession: "May God remember us in his Kingdom now and for ever and until the age of ages." Can we not assume that this intercession, as long as it coincided with the imperial oblation, may have evoked, implicitly or explicitly, the image of Abel and Melchizedek before the minds of the congregation?[69]

But, beyond such considerations, we have good reason to believe that the liturgy chanted in San Vitale contained a prayer which, both by its wording and by its position immediately after the offertory, commemorated Justinian as a "just offerer." The emperor was the donor of the church. An oration on behalf of the builder of the sanctuary is pre-scribed by the Spanish Synod of Merida (A.D. 666) and the ancient liturgies preserve frequent evidence for both the existence of such prayers and their relation to the offertory.[70] If the emperor himself was the donor, as in San Vitale, this fact must have imparted special significance to the oration. One may ask whether in this case the prayer for Justinian as donor did not merge into the prayer for Justinian the emperor (i.e., the diptychs); if, in order to avoid duplication, the former prayer, which occurred immediately after the offertory, was not invested with the more solemn significance of the diptychs.

The question is of considerable interest. If the diptychs read in San Vitale referred to Justinian as donor of the church, they also suggested the comparison between him and the "just offerers" of the Old Testament which we found in the mosaics. In that case, the mosaics may be understood as illustrations of, or at least as allusions to, the diptychs, i.e., to that part of the liturgical rite which possessed actual political significance.

The place which the diptychs occupy in the theological controversies of the age is well known. The names of those who were placed on those sacred lists or were expunged from them epitomized the very object of these struggles. The victorious party demanded inevitably that the names of its great theologians be placed on the diptychs and effected the extinction of the memory of the losers with equally fanatical zeal. This practice finds its explanation if we realize that, in the sacred rite, pronunciation of the diptychs established a mystical relation between those whose names were inscribed in these lists, the congregation by whom they were remembered, and the saints in heaven. The diptychs thus became a document of allegiance of the most solemn kind.

This is, of course, equally true for the intercession on behalf of the emperor. In the diptychs of the liturgies of Basil and Chrysostom the emperor is commemorated with explicit reference to his piety and to the orthodoxy of his faith. For an age for which these were the only valid criteria of the ruler's legitimacy, such a prayer of intercession amounted to a truly awesome profession of loyalty for the sovereign, addressed not to him but to God.[71]

We may well assume the portraits of the *Augusti* in San Vitale to be a kind of visual diptychs, reminders of the sovereigns' piety—of the orthodoxy, the priestly dignity, of Justinian.[72] The idea of the sacrifice, as the sixth century conceived it, made this thought inevitable. If so, the political significance of the mosaics is considerable. They show that the liturgy, in Justinian's mind, was not merely the poetical allegory of his world view but the legal and sacramental act which committed his subjects irrevocably to his authority. In these awe-inspiring images the sovereigns, though far away in Byzantium, had actually set foot on the soil of Italy.

CHAPTER THREE

Sant' Apollinare in Classe

I

THE dedicatory mosaic in San Vitale is a testimony to Justinian's place in the Byzantine church, but it is no less a glorification of Maximian. Indeed, it provides an interesting comment on the relations between the two men. The archbishop appears by no means as the emperor's servant or functionary, but as his equal.[1] The observer is inclined to see in the two figures an illustration of the duality of powers upon which Justinian established his administration.

It is worth while to compare the position which Maximian assumed in Ravenna with that which Theodoric had held before him. In theory, the latter had also been the emperor's representative. It may be doubted whether in his metropolitan province the archbishop's power, as well as his independence, was inferior to those of the great Germanic ruler.

Although the emperor appointed his bishops, the Justinian Code conceded to them independence, immunity, and authority to an extent that must have made them sovereign lords wherever the imperial power was not immediately present.[2] In the administration of the Byzantine Empire the bishop occupied a position second to no one except the emperor himself. In the city the bishop nominated the municipal officers, maintained fortifications, aqueducts, bridges, storehouses, and public baths; supervised weights and measures; and controlled the city's finances. In the provinces it was again the bishop who recommended candidates for administrative posts and maintained a close watch on their activities, including those of the governor himself. In addition to these administrative powers, the bishop acted as judge. The emperor informed him, as well as the governor, of all newly promulgated laws. All sentences of the imperial judges could be appealed to the bishop. On certain occasions the bishop heard complaints against the administration of officials, including the governor. Diehl has rightly remarked that the governor's position must be precarious indeed as against that of a man who often spoke for the emperor and always spoke in the name of God.[3]

If all this is true for the bishops in Justinian's Empire generally, it is particularly true for the first archbishop of Ravenna. The mosaic of San Vitale is Maximian's first artistic enterprise; it marks the entry of Byzantine power into Ravenna. The image of the emperor may have had the function of presenting Maximian to the people of the city, to lend to the foreigner the visible protection of Justinian's prestige. But it also proclaims the metropolitan's authority. If, compared with Theodoric, Maximian lacked military power and popular support, this was amply compensated for by the incomparable dignity of his office. The age did not distinguish between the two sources, spiritual and political, of the bishop's power. As a bishop, Maximian was entitled to the complete allegiance of his flock in all matters; and even the political functions which the emperor might wish to bestow upon him required theological sanction. In this sense our mosaic, completed on the threshold of the Middle Ages, is one of the most eloquent documents for the antecedents and foundations of ecclesiastical feudalism.

Maximian consecrated San Vitale shortly before his embarkation for Constantinople. Immediately upon his return from that city, he consecrated the basilica of Sant' Apollinare in Classe.[4] The dedicatory mosaic in San Vitale, completed shortly after Maximian had assumed office, had introduced him to Ravenna. The great mosaic which adorns the apse of Sant' Apollinare in Classe is a monument to the task to which he returned from the imperial capital and, beyond this, an apotheosis of the episcopal office that has no equal in Christian art.

We have seen under what circumstances Maximian had undertaken his journey, what situation confronted him upon his return. If his appointment as metropolitan of Aemilia and the additions to the *patrimonium histriense* were effected during that visit to Constantinople, then these tokens of the emperor's confidence, coming at that moment, must have greatly increased the archbishop's difficulties. The churches of the West, ready to secede from Rome rather than follow Pope Vigilius into the prison of Byzantine theology, must have looked with utmost suspicion upon the man who seemed chosen to replace the bishop of Rome as primate of Italy. The military situation had not improved after the recall of Belisarius and the death of Verus. The death of Germanus in 550 deprived the emperor not only of an heir but of a figure upon whom the Empire had rightly fastened its hopes in a dark hour.[5]

Maximian remained as the one outstanding representative of Byzantium in Italy. Justinian's grants of land, dignity, and power at the expense of the other metropolitan provinces of Italy must have increased the suspicions of the hierarchy and failed to render Maximian's position more secure. In Aemilia he was threatened with defection from within the ranks of his own prelates. In Ravenna itself, the opposition which he had quelled but recently can only have gained by his absence and the events in Constantinople. The situation was tense. Wonderful and terrible signs frightened the population of the city.[6] At that moment every move of the archbishop assumed critical importance.

His first actions are characteristic. Maximian returned from Constantinople with the relics of saints and with plans and materials for churches dedicated to their memory. Had he been defeated, his name would have been expunged from the diptychs and his political downfall completed by his condemnation as a heretic. His cult of relics and his theological and liturgical writings were designed to meet this threat. His artistic projects are part of this strategy. Of these, the great mosaic in Sant' Apollinare in Classe is the most important.

According to Agnellus, the church was begun under Ursicinus. This bishop ruled less than four years (532–36), and the construction of Sant' Apollinare in Classe, like that of San Vitale, seems to have made little progress under his episcopate and even less under that of his successor, Victor: the dedicatory inscription mentions, besides Julianus Argentarius, only Ursicinus and Maximian, despite the fact that such inscriptions usually give extremely detailed credit to all who have contributed to the building.[7] Since Maximian built S. Stefano in less than a year,[8] we are entitled to attribute to him a large part of the construction of Sant' Apollinare in Classe, which was completed in the third year of his episcopate. If this is probable for the architecture of the basilica, it is certain for the mosaics which adorn its triumphal arch and the apse. We begin our description with the latter (Pls. 21, 22).

A first glance at the apse mosaic conveys the impression that the composition is divided into two spheres. The center of the upper zone is occupied by a monumental cross, studded with gems and pearls and placed in a large nimb. The vision appears against a dark-blue background, sparkling with ninety-nine stars. There are inscriptions on either end of the cross: A and Ω on the ends of the lateral extremities, ΙΧΘΥΣ above, and *Salus Mundi* below.

The cross is flanked by the figures of Moses and Elias, while the hand of God reaches down from the clouds above.

In the lower zone of the mosaic, occupying approximately three-fifths of the whole composition, we perceive a pasture planted with trees. In the foreground of this pasture and in its center there appears a figure characterized by its tunic, chasuble, and pallium as an archbishop and identified by an inscription as St. Apollinaris, the first bishop and, according to Peter Chrysologus, the only martyr of Ravenna. On either side, between herbs and white flowers, six lambs are seen proceeding toward the saint. In the background and on a higher level three more lambs appear, one on the left, two on the right, of the cross and gazing up to this vision.

The subject matter of the mosaic has been described as the Transfiguration. This interpretation is supported by the figures of Moses and Elias, both identified by inscriptions, as well as by the three lambs: they are, in early Christian art, frequent symbols of the apostles; the number of three refers here to the three disciples who were witnesses of Christ's Transfiguration. On the other hand, the figure of Christ has been replaced by that of the cross, and the whole scene has been enriched by a "proscenium" showing the heavenly pastures and the image of the martyr. Both features are unique (Pl. 23).

Few, if any, of the great creations of early Christian art have been more consistently misinterpreted, few have been treated more harshly by critics and art historians because of the latters' failure to understand the meaning and function of the work. It has been pointed out that the two parts of the composition lack all cohesion; that extraneous reasons led to the introduction of the cross, described as an alien element; that the figure of Apollinaris was a later substitution for the figure of Christ. The first objection is only apparently valid; in fact, the two segments of the composition are joined together organically and gracefully: the nimb of the cross reaches below the horizon of the pasture, while the three

lambs beside the cross are a further link between the two scenes. This aesthetic fact is significant. It leads to an understanding of the whole composition, which also invalidates the remaining criticism.

The vision of the cross appears frequently in early Christian mosaics. The splendid composition in St. Paulinus' Church in Nola is lost.[9] But the nightly vision of the cross appears in the domes of the basilica of Casaranello and of Soter's baptistry in Naples, both dating from the fifth century; even the great cross in the mosaic of Santa Pudenziana in Rome is an ancestor.[10] In Ravenna itself the representation in Sant' Apollinare in Classe has a forerunner. The shallow dome of Galla Placidia's mausoleum is adorned with eight hundred golden stars, in the midst of which there appears a cross whose foot is turned East. In the four angles of the composition there appear the symbolic animals of the evangelists.

It is noteworthy that the entire monument, architecture as well as mosaics, gives expression to the veneration of the cross. The mausoleum has the form of a Greek cross.[11] Above the entrance a mosaic represents Christ as the Good Shepherd among his sheep, holding in his hand a large cross, which seems to be at once a scepter and a shepherd's staff. The mosaic opposite depicts St. Lawrence, a martyr who enjoyed a special cult in fifth-century Ravenna.[12] This saint, too, carries on his shoulders, like a trophy or a weapon, a cross.

The empress had a special veneration for the cross. The central mosaic in the dome of the baptistry of San Giovanni in Fonte in Ravenna (the so-called "Baptistry of the Orthodox"), which dates from about the same period, depicts the baptism of Christ. St. John holds a large scepter-like cross, and this emblem appears repeatedly in the mosaics of the same building. According to Agnellus, the empress founded the church of the Holy Cross in Ravenna.[13] Her mausoleum was to be a monument to the sacred symbol which guided the destinies of her state. But the veneration of the cross continued in Ravenna long after the death of Galla Placidia.

The church of St. Zachary, built by her niece, was erected over a cruciform ground plan.[14] And in the mosaics of the sixth century the cross appears repeatedly and significantly. All these representations of the cross are surpassed by that in Sant' Apollinare in Classe.

The magnificent vision of the cross resplendent in the night sky is no invention of early Christian art. It is precisely this appearance which is described in a letter to Constantine the Great, wrongly attributed to Cyril of Jerusalem: "In the darkness of night a great cross appeared, radiating light like the sun."[15] This vision is said to have led to the miraculous invention of the Cross and is hence remembered by the liturgy of the church: "O Crux splendidior cunctis astris," she chants at vespers on the feasts of the Invention and Exaltation of the Cross (May 3 and September 14).[16] The representations in Casaranello and Naples, as well as the mosaic in the dome of Galla Placidia's mausoleum, are inspired by this vision.

So is the composition in Sant' Apollinare in Classe. The unique feature of this work, however, is that it blends what may be called the Exaltation of the Cross with the scene of the Transfiguration. It has been suggested that the cross was introduced into this composition because of the aversion of the early church to representations of Christ. Wickhoff, who was the first to advance this thesis, recalls the famous admonition of the Galatian monk, Nilus (d. 450), that the sanctuary of a church be adorned with the sign of the cross only.[17] But Wickhoff's thesis is invalidated by the fact that the introduction of the cross into our mosaic has a definite significance and purpose which are, in turn, based on a firm tradition of Christian art and liturgy: it blends the Transfiguration with another subject, i.e., the Exaltation of the Cross. An age at once as speculative and as imaginative as the sixth century cannot have done this unless it wished to express a definite theological concept.

An interpretation of the mosaic must proceed from the significance which the Gospels already attribute to the miracle of the Transfiguration. According to the Synoptics, the event alludes to the Passion and resurrection of Christ. In all three narratives the miracle takes place after a sermon in which Christ has predicted his approaching death and resurrection (Matt. 17:1-13; Mark 9:2-13; Luke 9:28-36). Patristic exegesis has, without exception, emphasized this relation between the Transfiguration and the Crucifixion.

It must be borne in mind that for early Christianity the cross was far less the instrument of Christ's suffering than the weapon and symbol of his triumph over death or, in the words of the Greek litany, the door to Paradise. The art, the liturgy, and the exegetical literature of the time provide ample evidence for this interpretation of the cross. The absence of the Crucifixion scene from early representations of the Passion, or, rather, its substitution by the labarum is not adequately explained by early Christian "aversion" to the scene. To that age, the crucifixion of Christ was, above all, the promise of his victory.

In a celebrated sermon Leo the Great describes Christ on his way to Calvary. To him the Savior at this moment appears as the most glorious conqueror of death, who carries the cross as the scepter of his power, as the trophy of his triumph. "O admirable power of the Cross!" the pope exclaims, "O ineffable glory of the Passion!"

The passage occurs in Leo's great sermon on the Passion. It is significant, however, that he evokes not the image of this event but the words of Christ related in the twelfth chapter of St. John's Gospel: "Et ego si exaltatus fuero a terra, omnia traham ad meipsum" (vs. 32). St. John adds: "This he said to signify what death he should die."[18] Patristic exegesis interpreted the word as a prediction of the glory into which Christ would enter after the Crucifixion; hence in the Roman liturgy the passage is used as the gospel for the feast of the Exaltation of the Cross.

If this view submerges the Crucifixion in the radiance of the Exaltation of the Cross, it also relates this feast to the Transfiguration. Again we quote

Leo the Great. In his sermon on the Transfiguration, the pope points out that Jesus appeared before his disciples transfigured, "in order to free their hearts from the scandal of the Cross." The humiliation of Christ's voluntary death would not disturb the faith of those to whom he had thus revealed "the excellence of his hidden dignity."[19] In predicting his Passion and resurrection, Christ had sought to convince his disciples that his suffering was but the necessary means to his resurrection. The three disciples whom he selected as witnesses of the Transfiguration were the same who later were to be present at his agony in the garden.[20] On this occasion the disciples were asleep; and so, in a sense, was early Christianity; rapt in the glory of the Transfiguration, they did not behold the Passion.

We have deliberately quoted Leo the Great. His vision embodies the theology of his age, focusing around the experience of redemption, of the participation of all mankind in the resurrection from the Easter sepulcher. This experience underlay all the great theological controversies of the fifth and sixth centuries, it lent greatness even to the Monophysite cause, and it eventually reconciled Byzantium to the theology of Rome. Justinian sought to rally the whole Empire behind this concept. In his ability to sense the religious impulses of the age and to respond to them, he was really, as Harnack says, the greatest theologian of his century.[21] Not the Crucifixion but the Transfiguration epitomizes the religious experience of the sixth century. The mosaic in Sant' Apollinare in Classe is its manifestation.

The passages we have quoted from Leo the Great are important not merely for their theological content. His language has a vigor, a blend of clarity, simplicity, and poignancy which lifts theology from subtle speculation into almost sensuous vision. Hence his influence upon the art and imagination of his age almost equals that upon theology.

Nowhere, perhaps, does the pope's genius appear more clearly than in the sermons from which we have quoted. He evokes the visions of the Exaltation of the Cross and of the Transfiguration in order to illustrate the mystery of redemption. The latter miracle assumes for Leo the Great a particular importance. It taught not only the disciples but every Christian how to see the Crucifixion. The Transfiguration is the reality of the cross.

The mosaic in Sant' Apollinare in Classe has to be studied in the light of this exegesis. The cross is not an alient shaft, driven into a context where it does not belong. The composition should be described as a union of Transfiguration and Exaltation of the Cross, and we have seen that this union is eminently meaningful. To these two motifs the artist has added the image of Christ which appears in the medallion in the center of the cross. By doing so, he has referred Exaltation and Transfiguration explicitly to the Crucifixion.

As an illustration of, or allusion to, the Crucifixion, this representation is by no means unique. On the so-called "Monza vials," which are not much later than our mosaic, the Crucifixion is represented by a cross above which there appears a medallion with Christ's image. These vials contained sacred oil with which pilgrims returned from the Holy Land. The images engraved upon them may very possibly reproduce works of monumental art.[22] If this should be true for the Crucifixion scene, the representation on our mosaic may be even closer to contemporary renderings of that event than we imagine. The difference between the Crucifixion on the vial and our mosaic lies in the fact that in the small work the medallion appears above, rather than on, the cross.[23] But this may have been rendered necessary by the small dimensions of the reproduction.

Far from being a contrivance used to avoid the representation of Christ, the cross in our mosaic thus gives magnificent expression to the theological concept which moved the age of Leo the Great no less than that of Justinian. It expounds the true meaning of the Transfiguration, and it teaches the contemplator to behold the death on Calvary as did those disciples who had witnessed the Transfiguration. By thus evoking the mystery of redemption, the composition will be for many the greatest rendering of the Crucifixion which Christian art has conceived. It is certainly the one closest to the spirit of the liturgy. In the liturgy, too, the mysteries of Passion and Resurrection appear inextricably entwined. On Good Friday the church chants the hymn in praise of the cross which evokes so vividly the vision of the mosaic in Sant' Apollinare in Classe: *Vexilla regis prodeunt fulget crucis mysterium.* The hymn was composed by Venantius Fortunatus, who was born around 530, studied in Ravenna, and almost certainly saw our mosaic.[24] The Late Middle Ages, with their exclusive emphasis on the drama of Christ's suffering, have almost blotted out the experience which inspired the mosaic as well as the hymn. It has lived on, however, in the Christian East. In a number of Byzantine ivories the scene of the Transfiguration is significantly juxtaposed with that of the Crucifixion.[25] In this parallelism there has survived the greater vision of an age which has found its monument in Sant' Apollinare in Classe.

We have already noted that the three lambs which symbolize the Apostles Peter, James, and John connect the upper part of the composition with the lower one, which centers in the figure of St. Apollinaris. The relation of this figure to the whole mosaic has so far remained unexplained. Since it does not seem to fit into the Transfiguration scene, scholars have concluded that it must be a later addition, possibly substituted for a figure of Christ or of the Lamb of God.[26]

This suggestion, while certainly erroneous, contains a grain of truth: the figure of St. Apollinaris is to bespeak that concept of the martyr's mysterious assimilation to Christ of which not only literary but also artistic vestiges have survived.[27] We notice, first of all, that he appears with uplifted hands. The term *Orans* does not explain this attitude sufficiently. In the early church this gesture had a symbolic and mystical meaning which, to judge from the innumerable references to it which have survived in patristic literature, must have been obvious to everyone. According to Tertullian, the man with out-stretched hands represents the image of the cross. In the so-called "Odes of Solomon" (42 and 47) we find expressions like "the expansion of my hands is thy sign." Egyptian papyri of the fourth century mention the *typos staurou* as an attitude of prayer; and the use of this attitude in Christian devotion is already attested by Tertullian, who demands the gesture of the outstretched hands "in remembrance of the Passion of Christ."[28] The meaning of the *Orans* gesture, then, is "representative": the believer invokes Christ's presence by impersonating him.

Not only the attitude of St. Apollinaris but also his place in the composition reveal him as an imitator of Christ. He stands immediately below the cross. As in many representations of early Christian art, this position identifies the martyr as an imitator of Christ, and it relates this concept of imitation to the miracle of the Transfiguration.[29]

The drama enacted in the sacred rites of the mystery religions (Christian as well as pagan) must be understood as the imitation of the Passion and resurrection of the Savior God; the purpose of the imitation is the union of the "imitator" with the deity he impersonates. Even in the Hellenistic mysteries such imitations frequently took on a terrible degree of reality. In the cult of Attis, for instance, representations of the god's sufferings demanded self-mutilations which often must have led to the actor's death.[30] But, unlike any of the pagan mysteries, the Christian cult was based not upon a myth but upon the death of a historical personality. And, unlike the initiates of the pagan mysteries, the Christians were subjected to bloody persecutions. As a result, the imitation of Christ's Passion was no magical fiction enacted in the dusk of the sanctuary but became stark reality: the true imitator of Christ was the martyr.

This concept of imitation originates in Christ's own words; and these are intimately related to the Transfiguration. We have already noted the connection between that event and the sermon of Christ which, according to the Gospel narrative, precedes it. The sermon contains not only a prediction but an exhortation as well. After speaking of his approaching death as the necessary way to the salvation of mankind, Christ admonishes his disciples to imitate him by taking up his cross. The content of the sermon is thus ascetical as well as theological; it is not only an explanation of the mystery of redemption but also an invitation to martyrdom. The subsequent miracle of the Transfiguration thus assumes a dual significance, which early Christian exegesis has not failed to emphasize. In the sermon on the Transfiguration from which we have already quoted, Leo the Great goes on to say that this event kindled in St. Peter the desire to participate in Christ's Passion, that it held out the certain promise not only of Christ's own resurrection but of that of his imitators as well.

The full meaning of the Transfiguration is unfolded only by the relation of that miracle to martyrdom.[31] And this relation is conveyed by the cross. In admonishing his disciples to imitate him, Christ himself had used the cross as the image for this imitation: "If any man will come after me, let him deny himself and take up his cross and follow me" (Matt. 16:24). The cross thus became the embodiment of that concept of union between the Savior and his imitators in which the Christian mystery drama itself originates (Pl. 24a).

This appears very clearly in early Christian literature, above all in the Acts of the martyrs. According to tradition, the first apostles, Peter and Andrew, were not only martyrs but died, like Christ, on the cross. In their apocryphal Acts, the cross appears as the very instrument of union between Christ and his imitator.[32] Peter, about to flee from Rome, encounters Christ and hears his words: "Romam uenio iterum crucifigi!"[33] The apostle realizes that these words predict his own martyrdom as a repetition of the Passion and also as the means of his union with his risen Master.[34] The subsequent account of Peter's martyrdom abounds in parallels with the Passion of Christ (a concept which we also encounter in early Christian art);[35] but more important is the fact that the Acts of Peter as well as those of

Andrew are far less a narrative of the sufferings of these than they are liturgical hymns to the cross as the true vehicle of the saint's transfiguration. The early church looked beyond the sufferings of martyrdom as she looked beyond those of Christ's Passion; her eyes were fixed upon the glory of man's redemption, of which the cross gave assurance to all followers of Christ (Pl. 24b).

It is significant that Origen, in his *Exhortation to Martyrdom*, interprets the gospel passage on the Exaltation of the Cross as an allusion to the martyrs and to the reward that is held out for them.[36] The same thought is frequently conveyed by early Christian art: the martyr appears either carrying the cross or standing beneath it; in either case the cross is the token of his Transfiguration.

The great cross in Sant' Apollinare in Classe is similarly related to the martyr who appears beneath it; it is significantly inscribed *Salus Mundi*. But, conversely, it now becomes clear that the figure of the saint, far from being an unnecessary addition to the iconography of the Transfiguration, renders its meaning complete. In a sense, the image of St. Apollinaris is the most significant part of the composition.

II

The Transfiguration miracle, as I have tried to show, is the promise and image of man's participation in the glory of Christ's resurrection and, as such, embodies the religious vision of the ancient church. The mosaic in Sant' Apollinare in Classe reflects both this vision and, more particularly, the great controversies of the fifth and sixth centuries in which it received its definite theological formulation. These controversies, as we have seen, affected profoundly the political actions of the emperor and his archbishop and even the entire history of the age. It is important that we try to understand this general impact of theological controversies. Gibbon was satisfied to recount, with sardonic amusement, what he took to be no more than the dogmatic squabbles of professional theologians. Not realizing

SANT' APOLLINARE IN CLASSE

that doctrine is no more—and does not aspire to be more—than an attempt to formulate rationally that which transcends reason, he never sounded the depths of religious experience which moved the age of the great councils. The inadequacies and inaccuracies of the *Decline and Fall* are largely due to the fact that Gibbon's rationalism prevented him from understanding both the nature and the power of religious experience in the sixth century. Might he not have avoided this pitfall by looking at the Transfiguration in Sant' Apollinare in Classe?

This work is certainly much more than a visual exposition of theological doctrine. The solemn magic of its language calls up before our eyes the supernatural reality which not only challenges man's mind but envelops his entire existence. This reality became present and palpable in the eucharistic rite, to which the work here under discussion—and in fact the monumental art of that period in general—is attuned. Only if these monuments are understood as stage and settings for the sacred drama of the liturgy which was enacted in their midst, does the grandeur and "incompleteness" of their style and language become intelligible. If this is realized, the Transfiguration mosaic reveals to us the spiritual experience which moved and molded the civilization of the sixth century. But it is, above all, the figure of St. Apollinaris to which the work owes its dramatic character and function.

To the Christian of that age the scene of the Transfiguration was related to the eucharistic rite in a way that is no longer apparent to us. In the language of the ancient church the term *transfiguratio* had a definite theological and liturgical meaning. Its Greek equivalent, *metamorphosis,* denotes the transformation of the eucharistic bread and wine into the body and blood of Christ. In the ancient Latin liturgy *transfiguratio* assumed the same significance.[37]

It was the imagery of the language which, to the Christian of the early centuries, evoked, at the most solemn moment of the Mass, the vision of the miracle on Mount Tabor. The scene of the Transfiguration undoubtedly owes to this fact its repre-

sentation in the sanctuary of Sant' Apollinare in Classe. It is not the only example of its kind. The same scene, though in the usual iconography, appears in the apse of the Church of the Transfiguration at the monastery of St. Catherine on Mount Sinai. This work is all the more interesting for us, since it, too, was commissioned by the Emperor Justinian and since it is one of the very few early Christian mosaics in the East which survived the tide of Islam. Monumental representations of the Transfiguration may have been more frequent than we know.[38] No scene could be more fitting for the most solemn part of the church—the place above the altar on which the liturgical drama is enacted. In the city of Ravenna, with its bilingual population and its bilingual liturgy, the Transfiguration conveyed the meaning of the eucharistic rite in a language that was universal.

The relation to the Christian cult rendered such representations of the Transfiguration in the ancient sanctuaries profoundly moving as allusions to a mystical experience of which every Christian partook. In the miracle of his Transfiguration, Christ had revealed the reality of his death and resurrection, not only in their theological meaning but in their validity for every Christian. The church has embodied in the divine office of the feast of the Transfiguration the words of St. Paul: "We all beholding the glory of the Lord with open face are transformed into the same image from glory to glory as by the spirit of the Lord": Christ's death and resurrection become present at every Mass. The language of the ancient liturgy called up the vision of the Transfiguration at the moment when the sacrificial offerings were consecrated; and, in doing so, it not only alluded to the transformation of bread and wine but also to that of the Christian who offered these. The primitive concept which identifies the sacrifice with its donor survives in the ancient prayers of consecration, which ask for the sanctification and transfiguration of both and, in fact, often name the donor in the first place.[39] No other image could have conveyed the mystery of this twofold sanctification more eloquently than did the Transfiguration; none could have evoked the experience that, in the liturgical act, every Christian shares in the resurrection of Christ.

It is important to realize that this experience assigns the martyr a place in the Christian rite quite similar to that which St. Apollinaris assumes in the Transfiguration mosaic. Christ's transfiguration anticipated the glory of his martyrs; not only his glory but theirs as well were revealed on Mount Tabor. As the sacrament of transfiguration, the Mass celebrates at once the transfiguration of Christ and that of his martyr.

The idea of the martyr's presence in the liturgical drama and of the affinity between *martyrium* and *mysterium* is very old. Perhaps its earliest expression is that tendency which we have already noted in the Acts of Peter, Andrew, and John to transform the historical narrative of the martyr's Passion into a liturgical hymn.[40] Even more significant is the use of what may be called "eucharistic imagery" in the earliest martyrological literature. Ignatius of Antioch calls himself the "wheat of God"; Polycarp, during his last ordeal, appears "like bread baked in the oven." Cyprian compares the preparation of Christians for martyrdom to the preparation of the eucharistic elements before Mass.[41]

This concept has left its traces in the liturgies themselves. The Roman rite inserts the words of Ignatius just quoted as the *Communio* in the eucharistic liturgy on his feast day. Christ's parable—"Amen, amen I say to you, unless the grain of wheat falling into the ground die, itself remaineth alone. But if it die it bringeth forth much fruit. He that loveth his life shall lose it and he that hateth his life shall win it" (John 12:24)—is taken as the gospel on the feast days of both Ignatius and Laurentius. Some of the ancient liturgies are even more explicit. On a martyr's feast day the eucharistic rite becomes here at once *repraesentatio* of Christ's death and resurrection and of the saint's martyrdom, the texts intermingling and wonderfully blending the recitals of the two Passions which in reality are one.[42] Even

more memorable is this fusion in some sacrificial prayers. We give only one example: on the feast of the Beheading of the Baptist, the so-called Gothic Missal has the following *inlatio:* "It is truly meet and just, it is right and availing unto salvation: that we should at all times give thanks to the almighty and merciful God: To the food of these sacraments we add the head of Your martyr *cum evangelica recordatione:* that it be offered on this table of propitiation like on a paten of shining metal."[43] The vision of John's head on the platter of Salome is here blended with the eucharistic prayer.

The idea of affinity between *martyrium* and *mysterium* has a twofold root. It originates, above all, in the concept of imitation, for which the martyr is the *mimos* of Christ, his martyrdom and transfiguration merging mystically into the death and resurrection of the Savior. The imitation of Christ's suffering leads to that complete union with him of which the ancient martyrological texts speak so frequently. In the Acts of the Gallic martyrs which Eusebius relates, it is Christ who suffers in the martyrdom of Blandina, while another martyr is greeted by the crowd "as Christ."[44] "Now it is I who suffer," St. Felicity said to her executioner before going to the place of her ordeal, "but there Christ will suffer in me."[45] The union of Christ and his martyr in the liturgical re-enactment of their Passion and resurrection presupposes, secondly, the peculiar time concept which all mystery religions share. Since for this experience the "myth" and its re-enactment are identical, the drama of Christ's life, death, and resurrection is not reproduced, but actually re-presented, it takes place *hic et nunc,* in the timeless presence of the mystery.[46] But this is equally true for the reiteration of Christ's Passion in his martyrs. On their feast days, the liturgy of the Mass visualizes their martyrdom as taking place here and now, and the drama of Christ's death and resurrection, which transforms each eucharistic rite into a "Little Easter," is, at the same time, the drama of the transfiguration and resurrection of the martyr.

We have not yet mentioned the factor which

rendered the unity of *mysterium* and *martyrium* most tangible to the ancient church: the cult of relics. In the first three centuries, churches and *martyria,* i.e., the burial places of martyrs, remained distinct. The custom of depositing the remains of a martyr under the altar of a church seems to begin in the fourth century. It spread rapidly in the Christian West, and by the sixth century an altar that was not the tomb of a martyr had become a rare exception.[47] St. John, according to Revelation (6:9), had perceived "under the altar the souls of them that were slain for the word of God and for the testimony which they held." In the fourth century Maximus of Turin quotes the passage and continues: "Can we imagine anything more pious and honorable than to rest below the altar on which the sacrifice is celebrated, on which sacrificial gifts are offered, and on which the Lord himself is priest? The martyrs are rightly deposited under the altar, because upon it the body of the Lord is being deposited. To bury the martyrs in the place in which we celebrate daily the death of Christ, is therefore fitting and the expression of a kind of union. Not unfairly has the sepulchre of Him who died been prepared for a kind of participation: to receive also the members of the dead Lord; those whom One Passion united with Christ, may be united to him in the sanctity of this place."[48]

This union of the martyr's tomb with the altar gave physical expression to the thought which the liturgy conveyed, and thereby rendered it more meaningful. The sacred places in which the eucharistic rite was enacted became witnesses to the idea of affinity between *mysterium* and *martyrium,* and it is not surprising if this testimony was soon evoked in the language of the liturgical texts themselves.

This is particularly noticeable in the selection of a number of Roman churches as "stations" for certain great feasts. The custom was inspired by the desire to enhance the special significance of the feast celebrated by the selection of the proper stage and setting for its enactment. But in a surprisingly large number of cases churches have been selected that were dedicated to a martyr; and it is his memory which permeates the liturgy of the day as if he were called upon to enact the sacred drama.[49] A few examples will suffice.

S. Eusebio is the stational church for the Friday after the fourth Sunday of Lent. The liturgy of this day anticipates the death and resurrection of Christ under the image of Lazarus rising from his tomb. The fact that S. Eusebio was situated close to the ancient Roman graveyard on the Esquiline must have rendered the church particularly suitable for the enactment of the day's liturgy; but it is, above all, the figure of the title saint, the martyr Eusebius, in which not only the resurrection of Lazarus but that of Christ himself seems to be embodied.

The station for the *Dominica in Albis* is San Pancrazio. The liturgy of this day, the Octave day of Easter, refers to the newly baptized who, on the day of Resurrection, had risen from the baptismal font as Christ had risen from his sepulcher. To convey this meaning of baptism as a rebirth, the liturgy speaks of the neophytes as "children." But this image must become especially meaningful in the sanctuary of St. Pancrace: he had suffered martyrdom as a child—at once the imitator of the risen Christ, whom the apostolic age compared to a newborn child (Acts of the Apostles 13:33), and the exemplar of the newly baptized.

Of special interest to us is the station for the second Friday in Lent, San Vitale in Rome. The liturgy of this day alludes again to Good Friday. This time it is Joseph, cast by his brothers into the "tomb" of the well, who serves as an antitype of the suffering Christ. But again it is the title saint of the station church, St. Vitalis, in whose martyrdom and transfiguration the mystery of the day is embodied. Does this fact explain, perhaps, the architecture of San Vitale in Ravenna? If, as a liturgical station, the Roman sanctuary of St. Vitalis conveys the idea of union between *mysterium* and *martyrium,* may not this same idea have inspired the architectural symbolism of the saint's church in Ravenna, which is at once his tomb and the Easter sepulcher of Christ, reminding the participants of every Mass that the sacrifice of the altar re-enacts the martyr's union with the transfigured Christ? The interest of this question is increased by the results of M. Grabar's recent investigations. He points out that, whereas in the East *martyrion* architecture has influenced the form and style of churches in general—the entire sanctuary becoming a kind of enlarged *martyrion*—this influence has in the West remained confined to the apse.[50] In other words, it was the close connection between the altar and the martyr's tomb which imparted to the surrounding altar-room the character of a *martyrion*.[51]

The same concept of the martyr's presence in the eucharistic mystery is illustrated in the Transfiguration mosaic in Sant' Apollinare in Classe. The work is neither the only nor the earliest rendering of that theme. In the sepulchral church of St. Agnes in Rome, the altar stood directly above the tomb of the virgin saint; and, since the sanctuary of the church was on a higher level than the nave, the congregation saw at one and the same time the tomb and the altar. As if this arrangement had not been sufficiently suggestive, St. Agnes was depicted in a beautiful relief at the entrance of the tomb. It is noteworthy that the martyr was represented, like St. Apollinaris in his basilica in Classe, with raised hands, i.e., in the *repraesentatio passionis*.[52]

The mosaic above the altar of Sant' Agnese offers another interesting comparison with the work in Ravenna. The representation alludes to a miracle said to have occurred after St. Agnes' martyrdom. Eight days after her death—again we note the number eight, a mystical symbol of the Resurrection—she appeared to her parents, splendidly dressed in those bridal garments which are also mentioned in the liturgy on St. Agnes' feast. The mosaic conveys this radiant vision. Two flames on either side of the figure, as well as a sword at her feet, recall her martyrdom and death. At the same time, however, we are not left in doubt that the image renders not the Passion but the resurrection of Agnes. On the magnificent robe of the transfigured virgin there appears the phoenix, symbol of resurrection.[53] That

the saint should thus have been depicted in the most solemn place of the church, which Christian art usually reserves for representations of Christ, is significant but not surprising. Christ's Passion and resurrection appeared in that of his martyr, and the eucharistic sacrifice offered over the martyr's tomb is also the mystery of his transfiguration (Pls. 24c, 25).[54]

The present mosaic in Sant' Agnese is of the seventh century. But an earlier work, composed under Pope Symmachus (496–514), may have shown a very similar composition;[55] such a glorification of martyrdom as the mosaic in Sant' Apollinare in Classe shows was suggested by the relation of the cult at a martyr's tomb to the eucharistic rite.

In this latter work the ancient theology of martyrdom has received its greatest monument. The Roman mosaic visualizes the martyr's transfiguration by means of her miraculous appearance after death; but the work in Ravenna conveys the same concept in a language that is at once more comprehensive and more profound. "Where there is the Cross there is also the martyr, because the Cross is also the martyr's cross," Paulinus of Nola had exclaimed in explaining the union of Christ and his martyrs in the altar tomb.[56] The cross in our mosaic is likewise an indication of St. Apollinaris' presence in the mystery of Christ's Passion and resurrection, while the scene of the Transfiguration connects the mystical experience of imitation with the liturgical experience of the eucharistic rite. I do not know whether any other work of Christian art has similarly succeeded in evoking at once the three elements of which religion is composed: the mystical experience, its theological formulation, and the solemnity of the rite in which that experience becomes present to the senses.

III

One cannot look at the mosaic in Sant' Apollinare without realizing the significance which the cult of martyrs assumed in the religious experience of that time. It modified the content of Christian worship in the direction of the particular, the concrete, and the individual. The mysteries of Christ's transfiguration belonged to the entire church; but in the figure of the martyr these mysteries were linked to the community to which he had belonged and continued to belong. Not only was the universal thus localized (to use an expression of Jakob Burckhardt), it was also brought into contact with the political *hic et nunc* of the city in which the martyr was venerated as *genius loci*. It is this fact which places our mosaic in a definite political setting and determines its historical significance.

We have seen to what position Maximian had been elevated when, upon his return from Constantinople, he dedicated the basilica of St. Apollinaris. The privileges which the emperor had bestowed upon the see of Ravenna were designed to raise the metropolitan to a rank of equality with the great patriarchs of the Christian world. Like the pope, the archbishop of Ravenna entertained henceforth an *apocrisarius,* i.e., a special envoy at the imperial court; like the bishop of Rome, he was represented in a special fashion at the councils of the Orient. And, while the metropolitan of Ravenna followed immediately behind the pope in religious ceremonies and sat at his right in ecclesiastical assemblies, he did not cede to the patriarch of Constantinople; at times, at least, he seems to have eclipsed him. According to the *Liber diurnus* (No. 9)[57] the archbishop of Ravenna is to be addressed as *reverentissimus et sanctissimus frater;* the patriarch only as *dilectissimus.*[58] Such honors could not fail to raise other questions.

One knows the argument by which the rank, the prestige, and, in fact, the jurisdictional powers of the five foremost sees of the Christian world were established. The apostles themselves had founded those sees and ruled them as their first bishops. Thus the bishops of Rome were the successors of St. Peter, those of Alexandria of St. Mark; St. James the Lesser had been the first bishop of Jerusalem; and Constantinople claimed St. Andrew as its first bish-

op, a pious legend which, as we have seen, had the most far-reaching implications in the field of ecclesiastical policies.[59]

An age which thought in such terms could not fail to inquire whether the recent dignity of the metropolitan of Ravenna could claim similar sanctions. Without these, the great aspirations of that see, the role for which it had been selected by the emperor, must have remained unrealized. The figure of St. Apollinaris and his cult, as well as the extraordinary glorification which Maximian bestowed upon him, must be seen against the background of the latter's ecclesiastical policies.

As the first bishop of Ravenna, Apollinaris seemed indeed worthy to be received into the company of the apostolic first bishops of the five patriarchates. Not only was he, like them, a martyr; but, according to the legend, he was a disciple and friend of St. Peter, appointed to the see of Ravenna by the prince of the apostles himself. The same legend asserted that Apollinaris had been a native of Antioch.[60] To the Byzantine archbishops of Ravenna this fact must have appeared to be of special significance. In writing to the patriarch of Antioch, Pope Gregory the Great liked to allude to the fact that this see had been founded by St. Peter; it seemed to explain—or to demand—the friendliest relations between Rome and Antioch, both daughters, so to speak, of the same father.[61] The Antiochene origin of the first bishop of Ravenna, on the other hand, might be interpreted in a way that was at once similar and very different indeed. At the period of rivalry with the papacy, the figure of St. Apollinaris confirmed the apostolic origin of the see of Ravenna and became, in fact, the instrument of the latter's struggle for complete equality with, and eventually for independence from, Rome.

Such radical steps were not undertaken until a century later. At the time of Justinian a break between Ravenna and Rome would indeed have jeopardized the work of ecclesiastical and theological union which Justinian had so much at heart. The Antiochene origin of St. Apollinaris, as well as his close relation to St. Peter, are asserted for the first time in the *Passio S. Apollinaris*. This work, comparable in purpose to the *Passio SS. Martyrum Gervasii et Protasii,* seems to have been written in the middle of the seventh century. In all likelihood, it originated in the chancery of Archbishop Maurus of Ravenna, who secured from the emperor the so-called *autokephalia,* which placed Ravenna on a rank of complete equality with Rome and which will occupy us later.[62] But there is some reason to assume that the legend was not altogether an invention of the time, that it may have circulated, if only orally, at least a century earlier; and that it may even have had the encouragement of Maximian himself.

Among the several pieces of evidence adduced for a comparatively late origin of the *Passio,* two deserve our special attention. The first are the sermons of Peter Chrysologus, the bishop upon whom Pope Celestine bestowed the metropolitan powers over part of Aemilia. Peter has on several occasions and with his usual vigor and eloquence defended the newly acquired rights of his see, but he has never adduced the "apostolic" argument. In a sermon on St. Apollinaris he extols the saint's virtues as bishop and martyr—but he fails to make the slightest reference to St. Apollinaris' relation to St. Peter. The same omission is notable in a set of documents as important as the sermons of Peter Chrysologus, i.e., the correspondence of Gregory the Great. In his letters to the occupants of the four patriarchal sees, the pope refers frequently to their apostolic founders. But not once, in his more than thirty letters to the metropolitan of Ravenna, does he bestow a similar compliment upon this prelate.[63]

These documents deserve to be taken seriously. Yet one may doubt whether the conclusions that have been drawn from them are entirely valid. It may be observed that Gregory's omissions are very easily explained by the facts that the pope would naturally avoid an argument which was utilized to question his own pre-eminence over the see of Ravenna; that the time of Gregory's pontificate, between the episcopates of Maximian and Maurus,

might make such restraint all the more expedient; and that, consequently, his letters by no means preclude the possibility that, even then, the legend about St. Apollinaris may have circulated in Ravenna without being accepted in Rome.

The document which lends support to this thesis is the liturgy. The feast of St. Apollinaris seems to have been introduced into the Roman liturgy in the middle of the seventh century.[64] It is at once an act of reconciliation and an attempt to maintain the primacy of Rome by means of cult and ritual. With the honor bestowed upon the *genius loci* of Ravenna, this city is brought into the orbit of Rome. This ambivalence appears clearly in the texts selected for the feast of St. Apollinaris. The gospel (Luke 22:24–30) relates the "strife amongst the disciples, which of them should seem to be the greater," in the course of which Christ exhorts the apostles to be humble: "he that is the greater among you, let him become as the younger: and he that is the leader as he that serveth."

The selection of this passage has rightly been considered an allusion to the rivalry between Ravenna and Rome. As such, however, it points to a period preceding that in which that rivalry reached its climax and rendered meaningless Rome's attempts at reconciliation.[65] It should not be overlooked that the conciliatory spirit is apparent even in the gospel selected for the feast of St. Apollinaris; while it administers a gentle rebuke to the present aspiration of the saint's see, it also bestows upon him a singular honor; if the "strife" alludes to the rivalry between Ravenna and Rome under the image of the rivalry between the apostles, the metaphor concedes to Ravenna precisely that "apostolic" dignity which it sought and upon which it based its claims.

The gospel text, moreover, should be compared with that of the lesson which precedes it. "The ancients therefore that are among you, I beseech who am myself also an ancient and a witness of the sufferings of Christ, as also a partaker of that glory which is to be revealed in time to come: Feed the flock of God which is among you, taking care of it,

not by constraints but willingly, according to God:
Not for filthy lucre's sake but voluntarily: Neither
as lording it over the clergy but being made a pattern
of the flock from the heart. And when the prince of
pastors shall appear, you shall receive a never fading
crown of glory. . . ."

These words are taken from the first Letter of St.
Peter. This fact, as well as the use of the shepherd
image, is significant. According to the Gospel of St.
John (21:15), Christ said three times to Peter: "Feed
my lambs." The words do allude to the apostolic
dignity to which Peter is thus raised. But by referring to Peter's vocation under the image of the
shepherd, the Prince of Shepherds, as Peter calls him
in the passage quoted, established a singular relation between himself and the prince of the apostles.
Christ had described himself as the Good Shepherd
who lays down his life for his flock. The application
of this image to Peter singled him out as the imitator
of Christ, not only in his martyrdom but in his
apostolic work as well.[66] This thought may be reflected in early Christian art, which occasionally
seems to have depicted Peter, Christ-like, as a
shepherd with the lost sheep on his shoulders.[67]

It is no coincidence that the lesson of Apollinaris'
feast exalts the martyr under the image of the shepherd and in the words of Peter. Dom Morin has
linked the establishment of Apollinaris' feast to the
building of a basilica in his honor in Rome. According to the *Liber pontificalis,* this church is the work of
Pope Honorius (625–38).[68] It stood in the immediate
vicinity of the church of St. Peter. This "topo-
graphic" relation seems to agree with the connection
which the liturgy established between the two
saints. It is thus permissible to attribute the composition of the texts to the same pope. In that case the
liturgy would confirm the existence of the tradition
concerning the relation between Peter and Apollinaris a generation before the *autokephalia.* But, assuming, even, that the liturgical texts for the feast of
St. Apollinaris were composed in this later period,
it seems extremely unlikely that the popes would
have used the *Petrine* symbolism in the text which

officially fixed the image of Apollinaris for the
veneration of the entire Roman church, had this
image originated only in the machinations by which
Maurus prepared the secession of his see from Rome.

It is quite possible, however, that the tradition
which linked and likened Apollinaris to St. Peter
existed, at least in Ravenna and possibly in Aemilia,
as early as the fifth century. This possibility is suggested by the sermon of Peter Chrysologus which
we mentioned before. Here St. Apollinaris is extolled above all as the martyr who is assimilated to
Christ. This assimilation is conveyed most skilfully
even by the preacher's rhetoric: "Ecce regnat et
vivit, qui pro rege suo desideravit occidi, qui vivit et
regnat cum patre . . . ," etc.; it appears, above all, in
the image under which the martyr is introduced, and
this image is that of the Good Shepherd.[69]

The sermon of the celebrated preacher could not
fail to exert an authoritative influence in his city. It
seems to have left its imprint even in the liturgy and
thus to have molded the image in which St. Apollinaris was to survive in the imagination of the faithful. In the *Kalendarium* of Ravenna the shepherd
metaphor occurs as the antiphon for both vespers
(". . . . nos autem populus tuus, et oves gregis
tui . . ."). It appears likewise in the Roman breviary: Here the fourth lesson has the narrative of
Apollinaris' accompanying Peter from Antioch to
Rome, while one antiphon hails the first bishop of
Ravenna as "Sacerdos et Pontifex, et virtutum opi-
fex, pastor bone in populo. . . ." Even more significant is the text in a Milanese missal from 1522.
Here the gospel selected is not that of the strife between the apostles but the parable of the Good
Shepherd.[70]

The Good Shepherd image does not necessarily
establish the relation between Apollinaris and Peter
of which we spoke. But the image is a rare distinction, and early Christian art and literature do not use
the same image for different persons or things, unless an affinity between them is to be conveyed. The
Passio S. Apollinaris may indeed not have originated
until the seventh century. But the ecclesiastical

aspirations for which it was to serve as basis, i.e., the apostolic rank of the see of Ravenna, could not have been expressed more effectively than under the image which hailed Apollinaris as the shepherd of his flock whom the Prince of Shepherds has rewarded in eternity, likening him at once to St. Peter and to the Good Shepherd who lays down his life for his sheep.

This magnificent language is spoken by the mosaic in Sant' Apollinare in Classe. The scene raises the first bishop of Ravenna to the dignity of the apostles. Not only does he appear in the midst of the twelve sheep, which usually symbolize the apostles; his relation to the Transfiguration relates him to the small group of the three great apostles, Peter, John, and James Major, who witnessed this miracle.

We have not yet mentioned the two features which establish what we would call the "political" significance of the work. The first is St. Apollinaris' attire: he wears the pallium. The author of the *Passio S. Apollinaris* proclaimed its hero the apostle of Aemilia, an assertion which was successful enough to find its way into the Roman breviary. The conclusion that Apollinaris also invested the bishops of that province and thus exerted metropolitan powers does not seem to have been drawn until the sixteenth century.[71] As an intimation, however, it appeared a thousand years earlier in our mosaic: the pallium on the shoulders of Apollinaris identifies him as archbishop of Ravenna and metropolitan of Aemilia.

The composition, moreover, glorifies Apollinaris at once as bishop and as imitator of Christ. This, too, was attempted later by the author of the *Passio*. But in the mosaic the fusion of the two dignities is at once so masterful and so deliberate that we must inquire into its significance and purpose.

The gesture of the raised hands and arms identifies Apollinaris, as we saw, as martyr, but it also identifies him as bishop and priest. At the beginning of the canon the priest assumes this attitude, which in the rubrics is significantly described as *repraesentatio passionis*.[72] With the canon, the mystery

proper—the drama of Christ's Passion and resurrection—opens. In this drama the priest is the *mystagogos:* the gesture of the cross identifies him as the actor, the imitator of Christ.

The bishop occupied an incomparable, a truly awe-inspiring, position in the ancient church. When Athanasius returned to Alexandria from his exile, the people went out to meet him with palm branches as Christ had been met when entering into Jerusalem.[73] The *Didascalia* says about the bishop: "He is your prince and leader; he is to be honored by you like God, since he rules in God's place; the bishop presides over you *in typum Dei,* as the image of God."[74] That the first Letter of Peter (2:25) conceives Christ as a *bishop* of souls was further confirmation of the majesty of the episcopal office.

The Christ-like dignity of the bishop originated in his dignity as a priest, i.e., as the *mystagogos* in the mystery drama. At the end of the fifth century the Syrian Narsai vividly depicted the priest as the actor of that drama.[75] Again and again he reminds his audience of the awesome majesty which this function bestowed upon the sacerdotal office. Since, during the early centuries, the bishop alone possessed the sacerdotal powers fully[76] (even today only he is empowered to administer all seven sacraments), it is not surprising that every assertion of episcopal authority would, above all, stress the bishop's office as *liturgos;* of this office the attitude of the *repraesentatio passionis* was an eloquent reminder, and Ravenna possessed at least three representations of this kind.

The sanctuary of the church of St. John the Evangelist was adorned with a mosaic depicting Peter Chrysologus celebrating Mass. The gesture of his outstretched hands marked the solemn moment of the consecration and identified the great bishop as the actor of the mystery drama.[77]

The mosaic may have had historical significance. Peter Chrysologus had consecrated the church of San Giovanni, an act which is accomplished by the celebration of Mass. In this case the rite seems to have been given special significance by the fact that it took place in the presence of the imperial family.

The dedicatory mosaic commemorated this event. In many ways the career of Peter Chrysologus parallels that of Maximian: the emperor had bestowed upon him, at least in part, the metropolitan powers which Maximian assumed a century later. The mosaic in San Giovanni Evangelista may have marked that event. If in this regard it may be likened to the dedicatory mosaic in San Vitale, the representation of Peter Chrysologus as an imitator of Christ suggests a comparison with the mosaic in Sant' Apollinare in Classe.[78]

The two works differ, however, in one important respect. Peter Chrysologus, who was not a martyr, was depicted as the *liturgical* imitator of Christ. The mosaic in Sant' Apollinare in Classe conveys the ancient *ascetical* concept of imitation, i.e., martyrdom. It glorified not only the bishop but also, and above all, the martyr. One may say that the older work alludes to the bishop's dignity only by means of the ritual in which the concept of imitation finds its symbolic expression. The miracle of the Transfiguration in Sant' Apollinare bespeaks the mystical experience and the ascetical reality, in which both the liturgical rite and the episcopal dignity originate. Hence the glorification of St. Peter Chrysologus in San Giovanni cannot compare with that of St. Apollinaris in his basilica in Classe.

The union of the dignities of martyr and bishop which this work expresses so eloquently is a concept which seemed more obvious to the early church than it does today. We have already noted that the concept of imitation provided the mystical link between martyrdom and the eucharistic mystery. That the *mystagogos* of the liturgical drama should also imitate Christ in the mystery of martyrdom seemed an almost necessary consequence during the centuries of persecution, especially when the Empire sought to destroy the church by striking at her heads, the bishops. Origen asserts that the imitation of Christ, who was at once priest and victim, imposes upon his priests the duty to immolate themselves in a similar manner.[79]

For the hierarchical organization of the church

such views had the most important consequences. If the Christian survived martyrdom, his ordeal secured for him a place in the sacerdotal hierarchy. The *Canons of Hippolytus* assert that martyrdom can rightfully take the place of the ordination to the priesthood. In many communities martyrdom was actually considered a qualification, if not for the dignity of bishop, at least for that of presbyter.[80]

Martyrdom thus replaced the sacrament of holy orders as it replaced the sacrament of baptism and, as we saw, that of the eucharist. This is not surprising. Baptism, no less than the sacrament of the altar, is a sacred imitation—the mystery drama of Christ's death and resurrection. Emerging from the baptismal font the newly baptized "acted" the resurrection of Christ. Ordination, on the other hand, prepared and initiated the priest to the dignity of *mystagogos,* which in the divine liturgy made him the image of Christ. But martyrdom, too—martyrdom, above all—was conceived as such mystical imitation of the work of redemption. Not only could it thus replace the sacramental rites, but we can imagine no more glorious vindication of the sacerdotal calling. This vision permeates the early Christian concept of the hierarchy. The dignity, as well as the authority, of the episcopal office originates in it.

This appears perhaps nowhere more clearly than in the writings of Ignatius of Antioch, who suffered martyrdom under Trajan. In the memorable letters which this bishop and martyr wrote on his way to certain execution, he has given the most solemn exposition of the hierarchical concept, but he bases his argument throughout on the theology of martyrdom.

"Permit me," Ignatius writes, "to be the imitator of the Passion of my God, that I be sacrificed while the altar is still prepared, that I may be found the pure bread of Christ."[81] The image of the eucharistic bread denotes that relation of martyrdom to the liturgy with which we are already familiar. But the bishop of Antioch is led further by this idea: "He that is within the altar is pure, but he that is without is not pure, being outside the altar means to do anything apart from the bishop."[82] Ignatius demands of the bishop that Christ-like righteousness and purity which will eventually lead him to the altar of martyrdom. For the same reason, however, the bishop may and, indeed, must exact from his flock absolute obedience: he who commands—the martyr-bishop—is "upon the altar," i.e., he is one with Christ. "Take ye heed then to have but one eucharist: for there is one flesh of our Lord, Jesus Christ, and one cup to the unity of His blood, one altar as there is one bishop."[83] As there is but one source of ecclesiastical authority, so there can be but one orthodox faith. What Ignatius has in mind is no mere analogy: "It is well to reverence both God and the bishop. The bishop is type and evidence of your immortality.[84] As therefore the Lord did nothing without the Father, so neither do ye anything without the bishop; but being come together into the same place let there be one prayer, one supplication, one mind, one hope, one love and joy undefiled. There is one Jesus Christ than whom nothing is more excellent. Do ye therefore all run together as into one temple of God, as to one altar, as to one Jesus Christ."[85] But, Ignatius enjoins, "it is fitting that ye should run together in accordance with the will of your bishop."[86]

If we attempt an interpretation of the mosaic in Sant' Apollinare, these passages deserve our careful consideration. The letters of St. Ignatius are the most impressive exposition of ecclesiastical authority in literature, as that composition is the greatest in art. Both works deduce the dignity of the bishop from the theology of martyrdom; both evoke the vision of the bishop and martyr who, as priest and victim upon the altar, appears as the transfigured image of Christ. The figure of St. Apollinaris at the head and in the very focus of his basilica in Ravenna seems to command his congregation "to run together in accordance with the will of its bishop."

It is not even impossible that the argument of the mosaic may actually be based upon the theology of Ignatius. Regardless of the date and general trustworthiness of the *Passio S. Apollinaris,* there is good reason to consider at least one fact in this narrative as authentic, i.e., the Antiochene origin of Apollinaris. The church of Ravenna seems, indeed, to have been founded by missionaries from the East;[87] if so, St. Apollinaris may either really have been a native of Antioch, or he may have considered himself a spiritual son of that great see and its greatest bishop.[88] In that case it would have been admirably fitting to extol the dignity of the bishop and martyr of Ravenna in the language of Ignatius, the bishop and martyr of Antioch.

Or, again, the mosaic in Sant' Apollinare in Classe may have been inspired indirectly by the Ignatian theology of hierarchical authority. The importance of the martyr's letters is such that they have left their imprint even upon the liturgy of the church. A passage from his letters has been embodied in the liturgical texts for his feast day. As on the feasts of martyrs and bishops, the *Commune sanctorum* gives solemn expression to his ideas.

In the Mass of a bishop and martyr, the church, otherwise so indifferent to, or even diffident of, the glory of power, hails the saint as one whom God made "the prince of the sanctuary and of his people, that to him the dignity of the priesthood should be for ever" (Eccles. 45:30). Introit and gradual compare the bishop and martyr to King David. The gospel explains this exaltation by the same argument that is used both in the Ignatian letters and in the mosaic in Sant' Apollinare in Classe: the saint has imitated Christ by taking his cross (Luke 14:26–33). This image is made even more explicit in the gospel of an alternative Mass of a bishop and martyr. Here the words of Christ are taken from the sermon which precedes his Transfiguration (Mark 16:24–27).

The eucharistic liturgy on the feast of a confessor and bishop has embodied a text which is of special significance in this connection (Heb. 7:23–27): "And the others indeed were made many priests, because by reason of death they were not suffered to continue: But this, for that he continueth for ever, hath an everlasting priesthood: Whereby he is able also to save for ever them that come to God by him:

always living to make intercession for us. For it was fitting that we should have such a high priest, holy, innocent, undefiled, separated from sinners, and made higher than the heavens: who needeth not daily (as the other priests) to offer sacrifices, first for his own sins, and then for the people's: for this he did once, in offering himself."

The passage refers, of course, to Christ's priesthood and self-immolation. In the liturgical context, however, the bishop who "has offered himself" appears as the partaker of Christ's priesthood. Here, too, the transfigured image of the saint blends into that of Christ.[89]

The affinities between the composition in Sant' Apollinare in Classe and the liturgy are noteworthy; it is not impossible that the mosaic may have inspired the selection of texts for St. Apollinaris' feast. But the interrelation is important beyond the question of sources. The liturgy is neither prayer nor hymn in the modern sense of the words. In the liturgy the City of God with its mysteries and its glory descended into the historical world of man. As the basilica seemed to widen until it merged into the Heavenly Jerusalem of which it is the image, the congregation joined the heavenly hosts of angels and archangels, prophets and apostles, martyrs and virgins, in that "great Sabbath without evening," where "we shall perfectly rest and perfectly see, that He is God."[90] And through the sacred poetry and art of the liturgy the great metaphysical concepts of Christian doctrine were conveyed with an intuitive force that made them intelligible to every believer.

This we have to bear in mind in order to understand the great homily which Maximian delivered through the mosaic in Classe. As the lone defender of Justinian's theology in the West, Maximian confronts in this work Arians as well as the defenders of the Three Chapters (whom he seems to have branded as Manichaeans) with the doctrine by which he and, indeed, the emperor meant to stand or fall.[91] This theology was not new; neither Athanasius nor Leo the Great would have disagreed with the concept of redemption as the transfiguration of human nature through participation in Christ's sacrifice. But the force and fire with which the archbishop, through the medium of art, expounded this theology were destined to tie the vision of the universal church indissolubly to the history of his career.

In the sixth century, theology had already lost itself in the opaque abysses of speculation, penetrable only to a comparatively few privileged minds. The liturgy, on the other hand (as Mr. Christopher Dawson has rightly remarked) was the one common experience which united all classes and all minds. By linking his argument to the sacred drama, Maximian translated theology into a religious reality which every believer experienced and which bestowed upon his teachings the most awesome authority.

The figure of St. Apollinaris bespeaks Ravenna's ecclesiastical aspirations, its ambition to rank with the apostolic sees. Not only is the image of the saint made to resemble that of St. Peter and thus recalls his intimate union with the Prince of the Apostles; it also proclaims the rivalry with Rome which led Ravenna to bestow upon her martyr the powers that St. Peter assumed in the life of the Roman church;[92] and in its lonely grandeur the figure seems designed to make us forget the existence of other saints and other churches of comparable dignity. A few years after Maximian's death, Justinian addressed the church of Ravenna as follows: "Sacred Mother, Church of Ravenna, truly mother and truly orthodox. While many other Churches adopted the false doctrine because of their fear and terror of princes, you preserved the true and only faith of holy Catholicism; unmoved you persevered amidst change; rocked by the storm you remained steadfast."[93] The extraordinary position to which such praise raised the see of Ravenna, its contemptuous disregard of the papacy and the other great sees of the West, are anticipated in the apotheosis of Apollinaris.

It is noteworthy, however, that the mosaic represents such convictions not as "propaganda" but as a solemn invocation, as a reality not of the future but of the present and altogether more tangible than hope. For that age sacred art was more than im-

[57]

agery. Grabar has recently stressed the *apotropaic,* or protective, function of certain murals of Christian Egypt. Here not only the sign of the cross but the images of saints have unquestionably the purpose of warding off the powers of evil and of invoking the sacred presence of the protectors of the sanctuary.[94] Such ideas should not be attributed only to the "primitivism" of Coptic art; during the sixth century they prevailed throughout the Christian world. A celebrated mosaic, once in the church of St. Demetrius at Salonika and one of the masterpieces of early Byzantine art, represents the saint between the governor and the bishop of the city. An inscription recalls that St. Demetrius, "the friend of the city," had once protected Salonika against the onslaught of the barbarians. Such protection, however, was not to be confined to the past. The saint's image invoked and, we must add, mystically realized his holy presence for the present and future.[95] It is not sufficient to explain such notions with the magical function of primitive art. They originate, above all, in the experience of the reality and omnipresence of the sacred. "The Holy Ghost," writes St. John of Damascus in the eighth century, "which dwelled in the saints while they were alive, lives, after their death, in their souls, in their entombed corpses and in their images."[96] Hence the sacred character of these images; hence, also, the belief, expressed by the same writer, that the contemplation of these images will sanctify the soul.

If we try to see the mosaic in Sant' Apollinare in Classe with the eyes of the sixth century—and we cannot fully understand it unless we do—we must realize that it evokes a sacred presence. Close to the martyr's tomb, it partook of the sanctity of his relics. Above all, the great composition must be seen in relation to the liturgical drama for which it serves as the setting and to which its imagery alludes. And in this drama the transfigured martyr was mysteriously present. Every Mass celebrated in his basilica renewed his martyrdom and transfiguration. With him, the entire congregation partook of the mystery, and by this participation the cause of Ravenna was anchored in the eternal reality from which no earthly power can dislodge man. If we recall that the mosaic was completed while Ravenna was still an embattled fortress, we realize the consolation and protection which the "sanctifying" vision was meant to offer to the defenders of the orthodox faith. It is not idle to speculate that the victorious armies of Narses may have been inspired by this composition, which conveys even to the modern beholder the full meaning of "sacred art."

The presence of Apollinaris in the liturgical drama of which the work reminds the onlooker has, finally, an ecclesiastical significance. The Christ-like dignity of the bishop and martyr was in a sense renewed in every one of his successors on the episcopal throne of Ravenna. And for the time-concept of the mystery drama, which merged present and past, the martyr whose Passion and resurrection were recalled in the Christian cult assumed imperceptibly the features of the man who, in the same pontifical robes, enacted the sacred rite. In the mosaic in Sant' Apollinare in Classe the sixth century perceived less the image of an individual, who had lived three or four hundred years before, than the saint whose dignity and authority were alive in his successor. The frail, ascetical figure in the mosaic in San Vitale portrays Maximian the man; but the martyr in Classe, transfigured under the *sceptrum potestatis,* extols his ecclesiastical career and the exalted authority that he claimed.

IV

The remaining mosaics in Sant' Apollinare deserve at least a brief description in the present essay. Though only in part the work of Maximian and his contemporaries, their subject matter and possibly the original design belong to his age. The space below the Transfiguration mosaic and between the windows of the apse is occupied by the portraits of four bishops of Ravenna, who are depicted in much the same attire as Apollinaris but hold a book in their hands instead of assuming the *repraesentatio passionis* attitude of the martyr. All four, though predecessors of Maximian (one is even older than Peter Chrysologus) wear the pallium. The obvious reason for this anachronism is that, since St. Apollinaris was depicted with this mark of his metropolitan dignity, it could obviously not be omitted from the portraits of his successors (Pl. 21).

The four almost identical figures are, according to their inscriptions, Ecclesius, St. Severus, St. Ursus, and Ursicinus. The selection of these four from among the bishops of Ravenna is significant. Two of them are commemorated as saints, two as donors. Severus, whom Agnellus hails as saint and confessor, enjoyed a special cult in Ravenna. Ursus built and consecrated (April 13, 385) the cathedral of Ravenna, called after him "Ursiana."[97] He was remembered in his city as the first of the great builders among its bishops. Ecclesius and Ursicinus have rightly received a monument in Sant' Apollinare in Classe: the first, as we saw, initiated the program of ecclesiastical architecture under Justinian; the second founded Sant' Apollinare in Classe.

The function of these four images surrounding the altar is that of the liturgical diptychs. As in these prayers of the Mass the donors are remembered "in the communion" of the saints, so the honor of visual commemoration has here been divided between the builders and donors among Ravenna's bishops, on the one hand, and the saints, on the other.

Flanking the four "visual diptychs" are two representations of considerable iconographical importance. Although they are at least a century later than the works discussed so far, they depend thematically upon works which we have linked with Maximian; and one may even ask if the mosaics of the seventh century are more than modifications of a program executed or begun during the sixth. In any event, they reflect the political program of which Maximian was the father.

The scene on the right depicts Abel, Melchizedek, and Abraham on the three sides of an altar upon which they are offering their sacrificial gifts: Abel the lamb, Melchizedek the bread, and Abraham his son Isaac. The composition is unquestionably an adaptation of the two mosaics in San Vitale. With the omission of the Visit of the Angels, however, the three antitypes of Christian priesthood have been brought together in one scene: the analogy to the *Supra quae* prayer of the Roman Canon is thus even more marked than in San Vitale (Pl. 26).

The different arrangement of the composition in Sant' Apollinare in Classe has had yet another effect. In San Vitale, it will be remembered, the sacrificial scenes, spread over two opposite walls, are each adjoined by equally monumental representations of the imperial donors. The same juxtaposition of donation and sacrifice has been attempted in the basilica in Classe. But, owing to the more modest proportions of the eucharistic mosaic, the donation scene has likewise been scaled down to far humbler dimensions. Before we inquire into the possible significance of this change, we have to consider the subject of the second composition more closely (Pl. 27).[98]

It represents nine personages, an emperor with his retinue and an archbishop of Ravenna with high members of his clergy. As in the dedication mosaic in San Vitale, of which the work is a copy, the first of these groups is placed on the left, the second on the right. The emperor is Constantine IV Pogonatus, with him (identified by inscriptions) are his sons, Heraclius and Tiberius; all three are nimbed. Some doubt prevails concerning the identity of the ecclesiastical figures. But everything leads us to assume that the archbishop in the center is Maurus, that the man on his right, who also wears the metropolitan pallium, is his successor, Reparatus. The inscription *Arcopus* ("Archiepiscopus") seems to refer to him. This prelate receives from the emperor's hand a scroll inscribed *Privilegia,* a word which allows us to identify the scene as well as the principal ecclesiastical actors.

There can be no doubt as to the "privileges" referred to. In 666 Reparatus, then deacon, but five years later archbishop of Ravenna, received in Constantinople from the Emperor Constantine IV the *autokephalia.* With this document, which granted to

Ravenna complete hierarchical independence from, and equality with, the see of Rome, the proudest aspirations of the see seemed to be fulfilled. The mosaic must allude to this event. According to Agnellus, Reparatus restored Sant' Apollinare in Classe, and the present mosaic can hardly have been completed by anyone but him. Considering the fact that he had received the *autokephalia* only as the emissary of his archbishop, the place assigned to him in the composition is somewhat surprising. Reaching rather ungraciously past Maurus, Reparatus receives the privilege from the emperor. We have, in fact, reason to believe that this arrangement does not represent the original state of the mosaic. Perhaps Maurus, who did not die until five years after the *autokephalia* had been granted, commissioned the mosaic to extol an accomplishment which he considered entirely his own. After his death, his successor Reparatus may then have caused certain changes to be made which did greater justice to his own role. We cannot even blame him for this. Ambassadors are likely to overestimate the part that they play in the political game and to belittle that of their masters. In the sixth and seventh centuries, moreover, with communications difficult and distances correspondingly vast, the ambassador's initiative must, indeed, have been far more important than modern diplomacy lets us imagine.

In this mosaic Reparatus appears as he wished to be remembered in the diptychs of his church: as the co-author of what seemed to him and his contemporaries the proudest chapter in the history of his see. The juxtaposition of the political mosaic with the eucharistic scene is again significant. It reflects the mystical and theological context in which every historical event had to be evaluated. But if the allusion to the priestly dignity of a donor (be he emperor or archbishop) invites comparison with the mosaics in San Vitale, it also underscores a remarkable contrast between the two works.

The dedicatory mosaics in San Vitale recall a comparatively modest gift (Justinian's contributions to the construction of the church) but hail the mag-nificent role for which the emperor had selected Ravenna and which, thanks to the genius of Maximian, it was, in fact, to assume. The donation referred to in the mosaic in Sant' Apollinare in Classe seemed to be immeasurably greater—but neither the emperors nor the archbishops of the seventh century were able to implement it. Soon the *autokephalia* were revoked. There is good reason to believe that the poor state of preservation of the work in Sant' Apollinare, so deplorable in contrast with the mosaics in San Vitale, may be the result of some violent changes made after the anti-Roman policies of Ravenna had met defeat. But the contrast between the two works is not entirely due to such damage but is, above all, one of quality. The two works are separated by a century. In comparing them, one cannot help reflecting upon the decline which brought the Ravenna of Maximian down to the Ravenna of Maurus. Nevertheless, the dedication mosaics in Sant' Apollinare in Classe remain valuable, in that they mark the end of the ecclesiastical policy begun by Maximian and that, in their all too obvious comparison between the emperor and Melchizedek, they confirm our interpretation of the far greater work in San Vitale.

Finally, the mosaics in the triumphal arch of Sant' Apollinare in Classe deserve description. They may be divided into five different segments. In the uppermost zone there appears the bust of Christ framed by a nimb. The Savior's right hand is raised in the Greek gesture of benediction, his left holds a book. The symbols of the evangelists appear on either side (Pl. 21).

In the zone below, six sheep are seen emerging from Jerusalem (at left), six others from Bethlehem, and ascending toward Christ. The towns are architectural symbols of the *Ecclesia ex circumcisione* and the *Ecclesia ex gentibus*.

Two fruit-bearing palm trees, symbols of eternal life, occupy the two narrow segments of the third zone, while below them, in the fourth, guarding the entrance to the sanctuary, there appear the majestic figures of the archangels Michael and Gabriel, attired like high dignitaries of the Byzantine court; the standards in their hands are inscribed with the triple *Hagios*. Finally, there are the figures of two evangelists, Matthew and Luke, added, at least in their present state, at a much later and thoroughly decadent epoch of Ravenna's art and stripped by recent restorations of almost their entire artistic and archeological significance.

Whether the various parts of this composition are part of a unified program or, at least, whether we can still restore such a program is doubtful, in view of the fact that they were obviously created at different periods.[99] On the other hand, they are all related to the liturgical drama enacted upon the stage of the sanctuary which these mosaics adorn and surround. One may ask, therefore, whether here, as in San Vitale, the subject of the liturgical drama—the eucharistic rite—does not provide the unifying motif, or even point to an original program substantially identical with the present one.

This is certainly true for the mosaics in the apse of Sant' Apollinare in Classe: not only the Transfiguration scene but the two mystical and historical mosaics and even the four bishops (through their relation to the diptychs of the Mass) are all related to the sacrament of the altar. The influence of San Vitale, noticeable in many details of the program, may also provide a clue to its significance. Thus the motif of the two cities appears already on the apsidal arch of San Vitale, though here the representation is far less elaborate. The two evangelists also have their predecessors in San Vitale. Their portraits in Sant' Apollinare, however (assuming that they figured in the original program), reflect that process of diminution which we have already noticed in regard to the dedicatory and mystical mosaics in this church: the number of the evangelists has been reduced from four to two. The selection of Matthew and Luke may be significant. As we have seen, these two symbolize Christ's Incarnation and Passion, respectively, and are thus the New Testament equivalents for Isaiah and Jeremiah. The two evangelists in Sant' Apollinare may thus not only take the place of the

four in San Vitale but also that of the two Old Testament prophets in this church. As allusions to the two mysteries which constitute the basis of the eucharistic rite, they would still be adequate.

The two archangels shown in the fourth segment are intimately related to the canon of the Mass. Michael is the angel of Revelation (1:30), "who came and stood beside the altar" and to whom, therefore, the eucharistic rite assigns a special function. His assistance is invoked in the canon as follows: "Supplices, te rogamus, omnipotens Deus: jube haec perferri per manus sancti Angeli tui in sublime altare tuum, in conspectu divinae majestatis tuae. . . ." Michael is thus the messenger of the eucharistic sacrifice, but, according to the ancient liturgy, he shared this dignity with at least one other angel. In the famous work *De sacramentis,* which possibly originated in Ravenna, we read instead of *per manus sancti Angeli* the plural *per manus angelorum tuorum.*[100] This may explain the appearance of Gabriel, along with Michael, in our mosaic.

The angels, however, allude also to the visual action of the liturgy. As the priest and especially the bishop represent Christ, so the deacons represent the angels. "Two deacons [Narsai says in describing the Christian mystery drama] he places like a rank [viz., of soldiers] on this side [viz., of the altar] and on that, that they may be guarding the dread mystery of the King of kings. . . . By their stoles they depict a sign of the heavenly beings that were clothed in beauteous garments at the temple of the tomb." In other words, the deacons represent the angels guarding the Easter sepulcher.[101] The angels in Sant' Apollinare in Classe, like the other mosaics in this church, are to make us see the things invisible, of which the visible rite is but a sign and an image.

The remaining mosaics in this church refer to the same vision. Representations of the two *Ecclesiae* in the sanctuary or at its entrance occur very frequently in early Christian and early medieval art; in the Roman churches of Santa Maria Maggiore, San Prassede, and Santa Cecilia this motif is linked to that of the twelve lambs, as it is in Sant' Apollinare in

Classe.[102] The explanation of this imagery may be found in a passage from the ancient rite for the dedication of a church: "Almighty, eternal God who through thy Son, the Keystone, hast united the two opposite walls and the two flocks of lambs under one and the same shepherd: grant to thy disciples through this office of devotion the indissoluble bond of charity, that no division of minds, no heresy may divide those whom the rule of one shepherd holds as one flock together . . ."[103] (Pl. 20).

In this magnificent passage as in the mosaic, the dual imagery of the lambs and the two churches symbolizes the vision of mankind's ultimate reconciliation under the Divine Shepherd; in both works this vision is, moreover, related to the architecture of the basilica, the opposite walls of which, united in the *lapis angularis* (keystone), are an image of the Heavenly Jerusalem. To understand this idea, we must realize that the basilica is an image of the Heavenly City of the Book of Revelation precisely by virtue of being the stage for the liturgical drama. The eucharistic rite is, at once, representation of the past work of redemption and anticipation of the future day of Christ's Second Advent. The ancient liturgies express this eschatological vision more clearly, but it is still present in the Roman liturgy; our mosaic seems to find its explanation in this liturgical vision.

The most important part of the ancient liturgies is the so-called *epiklesis*, the solemn prayer for the consecration of the eucharistic sacrifice. In the Eastern liturgies, the *epiklesis* envisages this sanctification as the descent of the Holy Ghost. In the Western *epikleseis,* on the other hand, the direction is, as it were, inverted: here the union of God with the offerer and his sacrifice is conceived as the latter's

ascent to heaven. Even the Roman rite has traces of such an *epiklesis.* We noted how one of these prayers invokes the angel of the sacrifice to carry it heavenward *in conspectu divinae majestatis;* and in the preceding prayer God is visualized as looking down *propitio ac sereno vultu* ("with a propitious and serene countenance") upon the gifts offered, "and to accept them, as thou wert graciously pleased to accept the gifts of thy just servant Abel, and the sacrifice of our patriarch Abraham, and that which thy high priest Melchizedek offered to thee." As we have seen, the one mosaic at the foot of the apsidal arch depicted precisely this threefold scene prefiguring the Christian sacrifice, while the composition opposite even originally was, in all likelihood, a representation conveying the same reference to the congregation or its "spokesman," the emperor, which we find in the prayer just quoted. The image of God looking upon the offerings would thus be particularly fitting for the place above the two sacrificial scenes.

The imagery employed in the *epikleseis* of some non-Roman liturgies comes even closer to that of the mosaic. One of them, from the so-called Mozarabic liturgy of ancient Spain, envisages God looking down upon the sacrifice *de illa aethereae arcis quadriformis machinae sede* ("from his heavenly city, seated upon his quadriform throne"; the term "quadriform" refers to the four symbolic animals); such vision is close to that of our mosaic.[104]

These few examples will suffice to show that the apocalyptic imagery employed on the arch of Sant' Apollinare in Classe is related to the liturgy; that it explains the vision which the eucharistic drama evoked during its enactment in the sanctuary of St. Apollinaris.

CHAPTER FOUR

Maximian's Throne

I

O F MAXIMIAN'S other monumental works hardly a trace remains. His great church in Pola and the sanctuaries he built in honor of St. Andrew and St. Stephen in Ravenna have vanished.[1] A little more is left of the church of St. Michael, built by Julianus Argentarius and one Bacauda, possibly an older relative of Julianus, and consecrated by Maximian.[2] Since the dedicatory inscription does not even mention the archbishop, we have no reason to assume that he took any part in this architectural project. The apse mosaic, which Frederick William IV had brought to Berlin, has suffered so much from subsequent restorations that its artistic value is questionable. It shows Christ, youthful as in San Vitale, holding in his right hand the scepter-like cross with which we are familiar and in his left an open book in which are inscribed two passages from St. John (14:9 and 10:30): "Qui vidit me vidit et patrem. Ego et pater unum sumus." The passage, in its insistence upon the unity of the persons of the Trinity, is another acknowledgment of the theopaschite theology. Christ is flanked by the archangels Michael and Gabriel. In the triumphal arch, which is possibly a later, and certainly an inferior, work, there appear SS. Cosmas and Damian and, above, Christ, bearded and seated upon a throne. He is surrounded by nine angels, two of whom carry the instruments of the Passion (lance and vinegar sponge), while the others blow trumpets. The scene refers, of course, to

Revelation 8:2. In the center of the soffit of the arch there is placed a medallion with the Lamb of God—a reminiscence of San Vitale.

Although some churches which Maximian built have perished and his share in those which still exist has remained unacknowledged, his name has survived through a celebrated work of lesser dimensions: we mean the so-called "chair of Maximian," with its splendid ivory ornaments, now in the Palace of the Archbishops in Ravenna. After some doubts concerning the meaning of a monogram on the throne, there now seems to be general agreement that it refers to Maximian (Pl. 28).[3]

Can we call the chair Maximian's work in the sense in which we have ascribed to him the mosaics? Did the archbishop commission it; did his ideas find expression in it? The answer to these questions must depend both on the chair's presumable date and on its presumable place of origin. The date does not seem to present difficulties: in the most recent monograph the chair of Maximian is assigned to the beginning of the fifth decade of the sixth century. And on the basis of stylistic evidence, this assumption appears eminently sound. As to its place of origin, the throne certainly was created in one of the great workshops of the Christian East. One iconographic peculiarity seems to point to Alexandria: in the scenes from the Joseph legend, Joseph in Egypt wears the insignia of the Egyptian god, Serapis. This fact is of equal interest from both the viewpoint of comparative religion and that of early Christian apologetics. But whether or not it provides conclusive evidence regarding the origin of the chair is doubtful, in view of the fact that, as Morath has shown, the comparison of Joseph and Serapis occurs in a number of Christian authors, the last of whom is Paulinus of Nola, a friend of St. Augustine and certainly no Egyptian. On iconographical grounds there would thus be no objection to Morath's conclusion that Maximian bought the chair in one of the ivory workshops in Byzantium.[4]

Did he buy it or did he commission it? The chair seems to have been completed just about at the time of Maximian's visits to Byzantium.[5] Is it conceivable that a work of such value, such craftsmanship, and such theological and ecclesiastical significance can have been manufactured, so to speak, in an open market and for the occasional bidder? For all we know about the economic and social position of the artist and artisan in the sixth century, this appears most unlikely.[6] What craftsman would have been able to expend the amount of skill, time, and—in view of the value of the material used—money on a work for which in the whole Christian world there were hardly more than a few score potential buyers? It could be offered for sale only to the occupants of some great episcopal sees, while the themes selected for representation seem to address themselves to communities within the orbit of Eastern theology, thus limiting still further the area of possible demand. Moreover, not even the most learned artisan but only a man of unusual theological competence could have designed the program which the original thirty-nine ivory plates reproduced. This would leave us with only two alternatives: either the work was indeed commissioned by Maximian himself, or it must have been commissioned by some other prelate to whom it was never delivered or who presented it to the archbishop of Ravenna. The second alternative appears unnecessarily complicated. It seems more appropriate to inquire whether we can discern any analogy between the ideas depicted on the chair and those reflected in the works of art that we discussed earlier.

In the ancient church the cathedra, the episcopal

throne, possessed a liturgical and symbolic significance which has rightly been stressed in connection with the throne of Maximian. Even in pre-Christian times the throne had been a symbol of authority. In the Christian church the bishop discharged his office as teacher seated upon his cathedra, and the term "cathedra" came to denote not only the throne but also the episcopal authority in all matters of exegesis and doctrine.[7] If the bishop appeared before the altar as the imitator of Christ's Passion and resurrection, he appeared upon his throne as representing Christ the teacher and the authoritative character of the divine teachings. This was particularly true during the baptismal rite. In the course of the solemn *scrutinia,* which preceded the baptism of the catechumens, the bishop received the catechumen's profession of faith, seated upon this throne.[8]

The throne's function in the rite of baptism explains the five large representations of the Baptist and the four evangelists which adorn its front. As in San Vitale and elsewhere, the latter are abbreviations for the mysteries contained in the Gospels into which the catechumen is initiated before baptism. The other plaques, still existent, which represent the life of Joseph in ten scenes and the life of Christ in twelve (originally twenty-four), may also find their explanation in the light of such catechetical instruction. Joseph is one of the Old Testament antitypes of Christ. The Fathers frequently explain the life of the patriarch, his miracles, his immersion into, and deliverance from the well, as analogies to the life, Passion, and resurrection of Christ. We have in this parallelism an example of that exegesis of which Origen was the author and which was to dominate the interpretation of the Bible for a thousand years. Selection of the Joseph cycle for the exegetical homily delivered from the cathedra must be all the more impressive for the catechumens, since Joseph's "tomb" in the well evoked the image of the baptismal font from which the newly baptized rose in the great ceremony of Easter night, as Christ had risen from the Holy Sepulcher (Pl. 29).

The scenes from the life of Christ may be divided

into two groups: scenes from his childhood and scenes from his adult life as miracle worker and teacher. It will be noted that here, as in the mosaics of Ravenna, the Passion is excluded or, rather, that here again it appears only symbolically, in a figure from the Old Testament. One can hardly avoid the conclusion that this sudden change from the narrative of Christ's childhood and miracles to a mere allusion to his Passion and resurrection reflects the same theopaschite theology which we have discerned elsewhere.

The theological influence of Byzantium, however, is particularly noticeable in the scenes from Christ's childhood. Here we find a surprisingly large space conceded to the Virgin Mary: she appears in a number of episodes which have their source not in the Gospels but in the apocryphal literature. The purpose of their introduction in early Christian art seems fairly clear; these representations were to focus attention upon the dignity of Mary as virgin and mother of God. This argument had been greatly furthered by, if, indeed, it did not have its origin in, the Nestorian controversies. In the sixth century it seems to have assumed renewed importance. Two theological questions, we are told, commanded the attention and kindled the emotions of Justinian's Byzantium. The first of these was Christ's relation to the Trinity; the second was "whether the virgin Mary can properly and truly be called the mother of our Lord Jesus Christ."[9] On the chair of Maximian the Byzantine answer to the first of these questions appears in the omission of any direct representation of Christ's Passion and death. The answer to the second question is made explicit in the place granted to Mary in the infancy cycle.

Ingeniously, then, the cathedra has been used to expound Byzantine theology; and the liturgical function of the throne has made it possible to deliver this doctrine with the full weight of episcopal authority, since the four evangelists represent the authoritative source of Christian theology. The majestic figure of the Baptist is a magnificent embodiment of the plenitude of episcopal dignity.

Christ himself had called him the greatest of them "that are born of women" (Matt. 11:11), thus raising him even above the apostles. On his feast day the liturgy of the Roman church, which has bestowed extraordinary honors upon this saint, seeks to explain his pre-eminence: The words of Isaiah (49:1 ff.) are here referred to St. John: "The Lord hath called me from the womb: from the bowels of my mother he hath been mindful of my name. And he hath made my mouth like a sharp sword. In the shadow of his hand he hath protected me and hath made me as a chosen arrow. In his quiver he hath hidden me. And he said to me: thou art my servant Israel, for in thee will I glory. . . ." The liturgy also chants the Gospel words (Luke 1:76): "Thou, child, shalt be called the prophet of the Highest; for thou shalt go before the face of the Lord to prepare his ways."

St. John appears great here as a preacher and as the prophet of redemption. It is significant that on the chair he is depicted holding a lamb. The Baptist had referred to Jesus as the "Lamb of God" (John 1:36); in this prophetical exposition of the mystery of redemption his apostolic calling appeared most eloquently.

But St. John embodies not merely the bishop's authority as a teacher but also his dignity as dispenser of the sacraments. The image of the Baptist upon the throne where the bishop received the catechumen's profession of faith, fittingly recalls the greatness of the sacrament to which Christ himself had submitted. In its dignity, as in that of the Eucharist, there originates the dignity of the bishop who bestows it. It is this idea which is solemnly conveyed on the cathedra of Maximian.

Baptism and eucharist are comparable, inasmuch as both are re-enactments of the Passion and the Resurrection. But in baptism it is the catechumen who is the imitator of the dying and rising Savior, whereas in the eucharistic rite this role is primarily assumed by the bishop and the priest. But in the liturgy of baptism, too, the bishop appeared as an image of the Savior, representing not the drama of redemption but those miracles by which Christ bestowed health or life to the afflicted as tokens of the eternal life to which he had come to restore mankind.

Because these miracles were intimately related to the renewal of human nature in the work of redemption, they were specifically evoked and, in fact, enacted during the rite of baptism. The so-called *illuminatio* of the catechumen, which took place during the solemn *scrutinia* recalled the healing of the blind. According to St. Augustine, the blind man whose sight is restored by Christ is an image of the catechumen's illumination; hence the Gospel narrative of this miracle was read during the ceremony mentioned.[10] The exorcism of "every unclean spirit" during the baptismal rite recalled Christ's exorcism of demons. In subsequently touching the catechumen's ear with saliva and pronouncing the word *ephpheta,* the bishop repeated the gesture and word with which Christ had healed the deaf and dumb (Mark 7:34); two other moments from the life of Christ as a teacher are especially recalled in the liturgy of baptism: the *Benedictio fontis,* the blessing of the baptismal font, still in use in the Roman church and attributed to Peter Chrysologus of Ravenna, recalls the miracle of Cana.[11] Christ's conversation with the Samaritan woman has been embodied in the liturgy of the fourth Friday in Lent, which initiated the catechumens into the symbolism of the baptismal water. Like the water Moses struck from the rock, as related in the lesson of the day (and already adduced by St. Paul [1 Cor. 10:4] as a symbol of baptism), the water for which the Samaritan woman asks, "that I may not thirst," is understood as an allusion to the sacrament of baptism. The scene is depicted in the oldest baptistry known, that of Dura-Europos, which dates from the first half of the third century.[12]

The majority of the christological scenes on the cathedra of Maximian still extant refer to baptism: the "Healing of the Blind and the Halt,"[13] the "Baptism of Christ," the "Miracle of Cana," and Christ's "Conversation with the Samaritan Woman." The

"Multiplication of the Loaves" refers to the sacrament of the altar and is recalled in its liturgy. The gesture of Christ who, "looking up to heaven, blessed and brake and gave the loaves to his disciples" (Matt. 14:19) is repeated by the bishop or priest at the moment of consecration.[14] We note that here again the miracle represented is not merely a symbol of the sacrament but the reality which the bishop enacts in the liturgical rite.

This is particularly obvious in regard to "Christ's Entry into Jerusalem," the last of the existing christological plaques on the cathedra. As an anticipation of the *resurrectio vitae,* this scene, too, belongs liturgically to the Easter cycle and hence to the sacrament of rebirth.[15] But in the thought of the church, Christ's entry becomes also an image of the sacerdotal dignity of the bishop. According to Gregory Nazianzen, Athanasius' solemn entry into Alexandria was deliberately patterned after the biblical event.[16] In the liturgy the representation of the entry enacted on Palm Sunday becomes an act of homage to the Christ-like majesty of the bishop.

We can trace this solemn pageant to the fourth century. The pilgrim Etheria has described the procession which descended from the Mount of Olives to the church of the Anastasis in Jerusalem. Old and young, carrying palm and olive branches, accompanied the bishop as the "type" of the triumphant Christ.[17] It would not be correct to say that the bishop impersonated Christ in the sense of the modern drama. To that age, a mystical tie connected image and invisible reality; and in that ceremony the bishop was perceived as Christ himself. The magnificent hymn with which he is greeted in the procession of the Roman rite—Theodulf of Orleans' *Gloria, laus et honor tibi sit, Rex Christe Redemptor*—dates only from the ninth century. But the emotions that it conveys are no different from those of the fourth. In the hymn Christ is greeted as the king of heaven, the son of David, who is now welcomed into the church as the Hebrews once welcomed the "merciful King Christ." The song is chanted by singers who have remained inside the church, while the procession on its return halts outside, before closed doors. To the present day it is a breathtaking moment when, after such suspense, the great doors open, and the bishop or priest is seen entering with his procession.

II

It is noteworthy that every one of the christological scenes of the cathedra, while depicting the life-giving powers bestowed upon the faithful by the two sacraments of resurrection, exalts the bishop as a type and image of Christ. Morath has already suggested that these events from the life of Jesus "point to Christ as the fountainhead of episcopal power."[18] What is more important, however, is the fact that the scenes convey the idea that the sacraments are actually *repraesentationes* of Christ's miracles and that the bishop who administers them bestows new life and health in a far more than allegorical sense.

For modern man it has become difficult to relive a religious experience which encompassed man's entire existence, body as well as soul. There cannot, however, be the slightest doubt that this was the religious experience of the Gospels and the ancient church. Christ had referred to himself as a physician (Luke 5:13); and the act of faith that he asked of the afflicted or found in them also restored their physical health. The rebirth in Christ was experienced as a recovery of body as well as of soul. The etymology of the Germanic languages still attests to that unity of what today is called "psychosomatic experience" for which *holy* and *hale, heil* and *heilig*, were one.[19]

This is the light in which the nature of the sacraments must be understood. It is significant that the Fathers refer not only to eucharist and baptism but to the sacrament of penance as a "medicine."[20] It is equally significant that the ancient church looked upon the bishop who administered the sacraments as a physician. The *Apostolic Constitutions* (*ca.* 400) contain a lengthy instruction to the bishop for the treatment of penitents in the form of a detailed comparison with the medical treatment of the afflicted.[21] But the concept of the bishop as physician was more than a metaphor.

Epiphanius' treatise *Against Heresies* contains a curious anecdote. He relates that the Jewish patriarch Ellel (*ca.* 300) desired to become a Christian but refrained from doing so for fear of the Jews. Only on his deathbed did he take courage and send for a bishop who was also a well-known physician. When the bishop arrived, Ellel informed him secretly of his desire to receive baptism. Whereupon, the bishop, pretending that he needed water for some medication or cure, sent the servant out to fetch some. And under the guise of medical treatment he administered the baptismal rite to the dying man.[22]

The story is not, as Harnack thought, evidence of fraudulent practices in the early church but attests to a religious experience which attributed life-giving power to the sacrament. That baptism was here administered as a medicine and that the bishop was also a physician are significant. The legend of Sylvester and Constantine is, in all likelihood, a reflection of the same experience: the emperor is healed of leprosy by the baptism that he receives from the pope; as the Roman breviary defines the dual effect of the sacrament, St. Sylvester cleansed the emperor, through baptism, of the leprosy of unbelief.[23]

One last work has to be mentioned in this connection: the *Passio S. Apollinaris*. This legend, as we have seen, was in all probability compiled in the seventh century as a means of buttressing the political aspirations of the see of Ravenna. It enumerates a number of alleged miracles of the saint, which, as was first noted by Lanzoni, resemble in the most striking manner the miracles of Christ. Even the wording of the narrative follows closely that of the Gospels. This fact is, of course, only further proof of the spurious character of the work. But it seems to be no coincidence that the miracles selected are healings of the afflicted, that is to say, those works of Christ which lived on as sacraments of the church administered by the bishop as the physician of his flock. To depict the first bishop of Ravenna as such an imitator of Christ is a thought which from the viewpoint of the ancient church contained a profound truth. More important, however, is the fact that the attribution of the "sacramental" miracles to Apollinaris appears in a work written for the purpose of establishing the authority and dignity of the archbishops of Ravenna. It is this consideration which leads us back to the iconography of Maximian's cathedra.

The argument conveyed by its ivories—the Christ-like dignity of the bishop—would have been appropriate in any of the great sees of the sixth century, certainly in those within the orbit of Byzantine theology. But the peculiar emphasis with which it is delivered here would seem to have been nowhere so purposeful as in the Ravenna of Maximian. There exists, moreover, a certain affinity between the rhetoric of the cathedra and that of the great mosaic in Sant' Apollinare in Classe which seems to point not only to the same political situation but also to the same author. Do not both works resemble each other in eloquence, in vividness of imagination, in profoundness of thought? In order to exalt the bishop of Ravenna, the mosaic exhausts the theology of martyrdom; the chair, that of the sacraments. In both works the political argument emerges from the depth of mystical vision. It is difficult to imagine that twice within the same generation the great historical movements of the age should have evoked the same oratory, that two different personalities in the same station and office should have possessed such identical gifts and genius. That a century later the *Passio S. Apollinaris* advanced the same argument for political purposes is additional reason for assigning the program for the cathedra to the bishop with whom that political vision originated.

We may sum up as follows: It is certain that the cathedra was purchased by Maximian and belonged to him. The artistic quality of the chair is as high as that of all other works of art that Maximian commissioned or inspired. The subject matter cannot, of course, be proved to have been created by the same personality that designed the program for the mosaics. But the thematic affinities are certainly very close. The ideas expounded on the cathedra seem more fitting for Ravenna than for any other of the great sees of that age; in its tendency to argue political principles in theological and liturgical terms the cathedra belongs to a whole family of documents, literary and artistic, which originated under Maximian. Since, moreover, stylistic evidence permits us to assign the chair to the period in which he was archbishop of Ravenna, we may assume that he commissioned this work, hardly prior to his Constantinopolitan journey in 548 but definitely in connection with the vast artistic program which was to initiate and to proclaim the ecclesiastical role for which Ravenna had been selected by Justinian. This work, like the others which we have studied, reveals its beauty only if one recalls the program of ecclesiastical policy of which Maximian was the artist.

CHAPTER FIVE

Sant' Apollinare Nuovo

I

MAXIMIAN died suddenly and prematurely in 556, at the age of fifty-eight.[1] His death closed an episcopate of only ten years, which had been singularly rich in critical events and important accomplishments. Justinian outlived his great servant for another nine years. As he grew older, his religious fanaticism became more intense. His savage persecution of all minorities not within the fold of the state religion reminds one of Diocletian. The repercussions of this fanaticism were also felt in Ravenna. Under Maximian's successor the entire property of the Arian church, the existence of which must have been precarious indeed since the defeat of the Goths, was finally confiscated and turned over to her Catholic rival. It was on this occasion that the emperor bestowed upon the see of Ravenna the title of "Orthodox," with the fierce and bitter implication that the other churches of the West, including that of Rome, had made common cause with the Arian enemy by resisting the emperor in the controversy of the Three Chapters.[2] It is significant that an imperial declaration couched in such language accompanied the suppression of the Arian church: it implied a warning of what might befall all dissenters—as if Justinian's treatment of Pope Vigilius and his intimidation of the fifth Ecumenical Council had not already taught this lesson adequately. But the works of art which Justinian's last and largest donation to the see of Ravenna called forth

bespeak not the terrible spirit of intolerance but that of generosity, of toleration. We have here to consider the man who, as Maximian's successor, determined the ecclesiastical policies of Ravenna from 556 to and beyond the emperor's death and whose statesmanship those works of art reflect.

Agnellus, namesake of the chronicler, was a personality altogether different from Maximian. A man of noble birth and great wealth, he had originally embraced a military career. The death of his wife made him resign the world.[3] Consecrated a deacon by Bishop Ecclesius and more than ten years older than Maximian, Agnellus must have witnessed at close range the tempestuous career of this extraordinary man. Whether he admired or disapproved of the younger prelate's policies we do not know. The latter's temperament, education, and origin differed profoundly from his own. Such contrasts do not always lead to understanding or sympathy. And even where a man continues the traditional policy of his predecessor, a different outlook and a different personality must profoundly affect the course of events. When Maximian died, Agnellus was nearly seventy. Even in his old age he was a man of vigorous and even splendid appearance. In his portraits, with which he decorated several churches, his complexion seemed rosy, his figure somewhat stout.[4] A career in the world and the comfortable circumstances of his early life may have disposed him toward tolerance. A man of his age and his experience is not easily inclined toward unnecessary zeal. Justinian would not have appointed him, had he not been convinced of his loyalty; but we do not know what Agnellus' early attitude in the controversy over the Three Chapters had been; and if he disapproved of the opposition to the appointment of Maximian, history has not recorded the fact. Unlike the humble deacon from Pola, Agnellus was a native of Ravenna. He knew the emperor little and owed him far less than did his predecessor. Whatever his aspirations for the prestige of his see, he could not have conceived it as merely an instrument of Byzantine policy. When he ascended the cathedra of Maximian, the great war against the Goths and the great war against the Three Chapters were won and over. Now it was necessary to undertake the work of pacification.

The position which the see of Ravenna had gained by means of force and opposition could be maintained only by peaceful and conciliatory means. Of such a policy Agnellus seems to have been a master.[5] In his metropolitan province he was at one time threatened by a serious defection; during the schism of Aquileia the bishops of northern Tuscany sided with the opposition, and the hierarchy of Aemilia seemed inclined to follow their example. But Agnellus persuaded them to desist.[6] He was no less successful in Ravenna itself. Upon Maximian's death the "Manichaean" opposition appeared once more. But it seems to have been easily quelled by peaceful means, and I do not find that it re-emerged during Agnellus' episcopate.

There remained the suppression of the Arian church. Agnellus could only have welcomed a measure which, in addition to restoring unity of faith in Ravenna, added vast possessions to his see. But if he approved of the militant document by which the transfer of ecclesiastical property was effected, neither his work as a statesman nor the artistic works that he commissioned show any mark of such intransigence in the broad strategy of his ecclesiastical policies. Agnellus cannot have overlooked the emperor's age; he may have foreseen the inner weakness of Byzantium which must come to the fore upon Justinian's death and must then demand a revision of Ravenna's entire position.

Agnellus was not a builder. Here, too, he differs profoundly from Maximian. In the fourteen years of his episcopate he seems to have commissioned but one work of ecclesiastical architecture, a monastery which he dedicated to St. George, the military saint to whom he may have felt a special attachment since the years of his military career.[7] Yet the more modest proportions of Agnellus' artistic patronage may not be due altogether to personal indifference or inability.[8] The great projects of Maximian owe their quality to a peculiarly militant character, such as the historical moment required. They were acts of defiance, hurled at once against the Goth laying siege to Ravenna and against the anti-Byzantine hierarchy of Italy. But when Agnellus assumed office, all the objectives had been secured which those works of art had demanded or defended. Cities, as well as individuals or nations, have their *kairos,* the irretrievable moment when history seems to surrender itself to their initiative and fortune. For Ravenna that moment had come with Maximian and had passed away with his death. What remained for Agnellus was not to build and to add but to maintain the unsurpassed prestige which Maximian had gained for his see. Agnellus was the ideal man for this task; but he was neither a fighter nor a builder. His artistic sense delighted in the perfection of comparatively small works of liturgical furniture, in the splendid and appropriate adornment of already existing monuments. To this day the fine pulpit in the cathedral bears his name.

The sequestration of the Gothic church of Ravenna made certain artistic projects necessary. The orthodox archbishop had to rededicate the Arian sanctuaries which now passed into his possession. The chronicler mentions the churches of St. Sergius in Classe, of St. Zeno in Caesarea, and in Ravenna itself St. Eusebius, St. George, St. Theodore with its baptistry, S. Maria in Cosmedin, and, above all, the palace chapel, St. Martin and the adjoining baptistry.[9] All the names given are those which the sanctuaries received after their "reconciliation." With one exception, the original names of the Gothic churches are unknown, and with two exceptions the buildings themselves have vanished. The exceptions are: S. Maria in Cosmedin, the Arian Baptistry, and St. Martin, which, originally dedicated to Christ, changed its name once more in the ninth or tenth century and became Sant' Apollinare Nuovo.

This church had been built, or at least begun, by Theodoric as his palace chapel and also as the Arian cathedral; it was dedicated to Christ the Savior and seems to have been the greatest of the king's architectural projects. With the splendor of its mosaics intact, the basilica ranks, with San Vitale and Sant' Apollinare in Classe, among the greatest monuments which the greatest century of Byzantine art has left us (Pls. 38, 39).

The rededication of this church to the Orthodox cult demanded certain artistic revisions. The architecture was left intact, but Agnellus sought to adapt the mosaic decoration to the liturgy of his church as well as to the veneration of the saint in whose honor the sanctuary was now dedicated. This artistic "reconciliation" was hardly less difficult than the ecclesiastical one. Today we can judge the success of Agnellus' artistic undertakings only in the case of Sant' Apollinare Nuovo, where the problem must have presented the greatest difficulties because of the excellence of the works which required modification. But in this one instance, at least, Agnellus was as masterful a "conciliator" as he seems to have been in his statesmanship.

Unfortunately, the basilica is no longer intact. Under Archbishop John V (724–ca. 750) an earthquake destroyed the apse or at least a part of it.[10] Thus, when the chronicler Agnellus wrote his *Liber pontificalis,* the original mosaics in this part of the church had vanished either partly or entirely. But he did see an inscription above the windows which named Theodoric as the founder of the sanctuary and which Archbishop Agnellus had not found it necessary to destroy.[11] The same spirit of tolerance is noticeable in his treatment of the magnificent mosaics of the nave.

II

These mosaics may be divided into three zones. The upper one, above the clerestory, in thirteen scenes on each side depicts the miracles and the Passion of Christ. These scenes are not even mentioned in the *Liber pontificalis,* a fact that seems all the more remarkable, since, of all churches of Ravenna either still intact or described by the younger Agnellus, this one alone contained representations of the life and Passion of Christ. The omission is justified, however, if we assume that these mosaics were not executed by Agnellus and that the chronicler described only those works of art of which the archbishop was the author. Hence it has been concluded that the mosaics showing the life of Christ belong to an earlier time and that they were executed when the basilica was still the palace church of the Arian kings. This assumption is borne out by other evidence. The mosaics in San Vitale and Sant' Apollinare in Classe, as well as the later compositions in Sant' Apollinare Nuovo itself, are Byzantine in inspiration; but the christological cycles in this last church depend, both stylistically and iconographically, upon the art of Rome, especially that of the catacombs[12] (Pls. 32, *a*, *b*, and 33).

This fact is of considerable importance. We must conclude that the Roman orientation of the mosaics reflects the taste and interests of Theodoric himself. The Gothic king looked upon Rome and its monumental remains with profound admiration; he sought to preserve and to revive the great cultural tradition to which he had fallen heir; and he urged that the works of the ancients be studied, that they be imitated wherever possible. While commanding that ancient monuments be preserved and restored with the utmost care, he instructed his architects to execute new buildings after the model of the ancient ones; time and again he demands a style emulating the glory of the classical model without uncritically copying its defects.[13]

Whatever such classical formulations of the Renaissance viewpoint may owe to Theodoric's prime minister, Cassiodorus, they undoubtedly reflect the king's own views. His mausoleum, blending Roman and Germanic elements, is itself magnificent testimony to a taste for which ancient art was not a dead model but a living source of inspiration. One may ask whether his ecclesiastical buildings did not, perhaps, reflect a similar spirit. The mosaics in Sant' Apollinare Nuovo suggest that the king's admiration was not confined to Rome's classical art but extended to its Christian antiquities as well. If so, Theodoric's taste and the art he commissioned were eloquent expressions of his political convictions.

We have stressed the community of interests which united Goths and Latins, Theodoric and the popes. But on the king's part such attitude was not dictated entirely by expediency. Catholicism, as Pfeilschifter remarks, was for Theodoric an integral part of Roman culture, the pope as the Lord of Rome was the legitimate representative of a tradition which the king revered.[14] For him, as for his contemporaries generally, no chasm separated the classical and the Christian heritage of the Eternal City: the first, as Leo the Great had put it a century earlier, had prepared the way for the second, and in the church the Roman Empire had found its continuation and fulfilment.

Upon the Catholic religion itself the Arian ruler seems to have looked with favor and respect. His own mother, Erelieva, professed this faith, and some of the most distinguished members of his court were Catholics. When Theodoric had reached Rome on his famous first journey of A.D. 500, the basilica of St. Peter was, as a Catholic chronicler notes with astonishment, the object of his first visit "as if he had been a Catholic himself."[15] This attitude may have resulted in part from Theodoric's admiration for the Roman tradition and partly from his inborn tolerance and respect for all religious convictions. But to this disposition the general course of political developments imparted special significance.

As relations between the Gothic king and Byzantium became strained, the emperor made the Arian religion the target of ever increasing attacks. Under such conditions, it was not political considerations alone which made Theodoric draw closer to the church of Rome, whose leaders (not only an Ennodius of Pavia but great popes like Gelasius and Hormisdas), suppressing all doctrinal disagreements, warmly reciprocated his tolerance and respect.[16] The king must have found it more and more difficult to recognize in the orientalized New Rome the Roman tradition which he admired; and, violently rebuked in his religious convictions, he turned to what must have appeared to him as the purer sources of the apostolic tradition. That Boethius composed his theological treatises against monophysitism at Theodoric's court may reflect on the latter's part an attitude more positive than toleration or indifference. Gothic theological writings of that epoch point to a spirit of rapprochement between the Arian and the Catholic doctrines.[17] The savage measures against Catholics to which Theodoric resorted eventually, and the exploitation of these measures by his enemies have unduly affected the estimate of the king's religious policies. May not even such savagery reflect an affection that finds itself betrayed?

If Theodoric had always been aware of an unbridgeable chasm dividing Arians and Catholics, such awareness is not evident in his palace chapel. Here, in the artistic vision of the early Roman community itself, are depicted the great events from the Gospel upon which the Catholic church had built its doctrine. Was the onlooker to be convinced that the church of the catacombs, the epoch in which the Christian faith had found its first martyrs and theologians, had been preserved in—or restored to—their original purity in the Ravenna of Theodoric? The claim to cherish the purer doctrine is common to all movements of religious protest. If presented in the palace chapel of the ruler, such claim must acquire official significance as a statement of Gothic policy in regard both to Rome and to Byzantium. It is strange to reflect that Roman doctrine is expounded in this Gothic Arian basilica with that same exclusiveness that distinguishes the visual expositions of Byzantine theology elsewhere in Ravenna.

Were the two artistic programs conceived as rivals? (Pl. 32.)

Sant' Apollinare Nuovo was, in all probability, not constructed until the very last years of Theodoric's life. Even the mosaics of Arian origin may have been completed only after the king's death, possibly under his daughter and successor, Amalasuntha.[18] They seem to reflect not only the political and cultural legacy of the great ruler but also Gothic reaction to Justinian's ecclesiastical policy in regard to Ravenna. The general program for these compositions is of singular magnificence; the political circumstances under which the program was conceived render its significance all the greater. The two monumental cycles of the life and Passion of Christ, if they are not the first ever created, are certainly the oldest in existence.[19] To their simple, dignified, and moving insistence upon the humanity of Christ, the awesome and majestic rendering of the Second Person of the Trinity in San Vitale may have been a deliberate answer and certainly offers a strange contrast. The visitor to both sanctuaries feels that two theological worlds, each self-containing and comprehensive, confront each other in these compositions.

The scenes from Christ's life and Passion had already been depicted by early Christian funerary art; to the mosaicists in Sant' Apollinare Nuovo these works even served as models. And during the fifth and sixth centuries, Christian art both in Italy and in the East occasionally recorded Christ's Passion and death. The cycle in Sant' Apollinare Nuovo surpasses all these representations by its monumentality and by the number of scenes selected. In Ravenna, moreover, this representation is the only one of its kind. In none of the great churches built and sumptuously adorned by Maximian do we encounter any scene from Christ's suffering and death. This omission, originating, as we have suggested, in the Theopaschite, if not Monophysite, leanings of the Orthodox see, must have rendered the christological cycles in Sant' Apollinare Nuovo all the more conspicuous. The selection of this theme is itself a conclusive argument in favor of a pre-Byzantine origin of the mosaics; it amounts to the statement of a theological position. And this position was underscored by an iconographical feature: whereas in the miracle scenes of the basilica Christ appears youthful and beardless, he is shown bearded in the Passion cycle on the opposite wall. This distinction must have made the most profound impression upon the Christian of the sixth century.[20]

The great christological controversies of the fifth century had found an illustration and, as it were, a test case in the interpretation of the Passion. For the school of Antioch no unity of persons existed between Christ the God and Christ the man. The Syrian theologians conceived not only two natures but two persons in him.[21] Hence, it was a mere man who had been born, who had trembled in agony, who had suffered and died upon the cross.

This doctrine had not been altogether destroyed, even though its leader, Nestorius, had been condemned by the Council of Ephesus. The opposition to Nestorius had driven the great Eastern sees— above all, that of Alexandria—into the arms of monophysitism, which, in turn, forced the popes, who had been equally instrumental in the refutation of Nestorius, to adopt a doctrine that appeared Nestorian to the East. In his letter to Flavian, Leo the Great defended, against the Monophysites, the union of the two natures in the person of Christ. The human nature, he asserted,[22] has not been absorbed by the divine nature; on the contrary; the Word and the flesh, while acting in communion, operate according to what is proper to their distinct natures. Hence the events of the Gospels are divided between the two natures of him in whom they are united. The miracles are performed by the divine nature—Leo mentions specifically the multiplication of loaves and the Samaritan woman—the Passion is suffered by the human nature: "aliud tamen est, unde in utroque communis est contumelia, aliud unde communis est gloria."

The pope goes on to show that this personal unity also united the two natures, so much so that it is no paradox to say that the Son of Man descended from heaven, that the *opera* of the two natures can, and, in fact, must, be exchanged. Nevertheless, the two natures continue to reside in Christ individually. Even though Christ be both Word and flesh, it must be understood that these two are not the same.

At that time religious speculation did not always separate the pure abstractions of theology from the vivid imagery of sensuous experience. Interest in theological questions was general. The doctrine which Leo the Great had formulated could hardly fail to lead to speculations about the life and Passion of Christ which seemed to disregard or even to undo the works of the councils.

At the colloquy that Justinian convoked in 533 he sought to reconcile the Orthodox and the Monophysite points of view. In the speech which he himself delivered in the last session of the assembly, he solemnly declared that one and the same person had wrought the miracles of Christ and suffered the Passion; that he who had suffered in the flesh is God and one of the Trinity.[23]

The statement was to have been equally acceptable to the Monophysite and to the Roman points of view. Its explicit juxtaposition of Christ's miracles and his Passion is nevertheless significant. The emperor's insistence that not two persons but one had acted in both cycles of events sounds not only like a rejection of the Nestorian viewpoint but like an answer to the distinction between the two natures which Leo the Great had made. It is obvious that any simultaneous treatment of miracles and Passion in an artistic program raised a theological problem of cardinal importance.

It is worth while in this connection to compare the mosaics in Sant' Apollinare Nuovo, the earliest monumental representation of the two cycles extant, with the contemporary *Codex Rossanensis*, the earliest known illustration of the two themes in a manuscript. This work, which originated in the East, is so scrupulous in avoiding any mistake as to the identity of Christ's person in the two cycles that even the Good Samaritan, as the typological image

of the Savior, is rendered with Christ's physiognomy and even with his halo.[24] The opposite is true in Sant' Apollinare Nuovo. Christ's youthful appearance in the miracle scenes and the bearded type in the Passion cycle can hardly have failed to raise the doubt which Justinian's remark sought to quell. The Christ of the miracles represents the same idealized type of the Divine Savior which we met in the Theopaschite art of Maximian. The bearded sufferer of the Passion cycle, on the other hand, is of the Syrian type. The very contrast is like an illustration of the distinctness of the two natures which Leo the Great had stressed. To Byzantine eyes such a distinction must have been indistinguishable from Nestorianism (Pl. 32).

In their theology, then, no less than in their style and iconography, the mosaics in Sant' Apollinare Nuovo are Roman in inspiration. The selection and arrangement of the scenes, however, seem to point in yet another direction. The Passion cycle ends at the entrance of the basilica, seemingly following an inverse order; no chronological order at all is discernible in the arrangement of the miracle scenes. One possible explanation of this curious arrangement has been offered by Baumstark. He has pointed to the striking analogy between the subjects of the christological mosaics in Sant' Apollinare Nuovo, on the one hand, and the liturgy of the Syrian Jacobites, on the other.[25] The miracle scenes represented in the Arian sanctuary are identical with the gospel readings for the Sundays of Lent in the Syrian office; the Passion scenes with those of Passion week, from Maundy Thursday to Easter Sunday. Baumstark concludes that the liturgy of Ravenna at the time of Theodoric must have been, in important aspects, Syrian; that "Jerusalem, Edessa, and Antioch, in their commemoration of Christ's Passion and resurrection, were sisters of Ravenna."

This interpretation presents difficulties, in view of the fact that, as Baumstark himself admits, the mosaics were executed at a time when Sant' Apollinare Nuovo was still dedicated to the Arian cult. It seems, at first, difficult to believe that the Gothic church of Ravenna, in the king's own chapel, should have expounded the liturgy of those great centers of Orthodox theology in which the opposition to Arianism had once originated. It would seem, on the other hand, that the Arian liturgy differed little, if at all, from that of the Catholic church and that Arian bishops attempted consistently to efface rather than to emphasize differences of worship between their churches and the Orthodox ones.[26] In Ravenna itself, political considerations may have suggested a liturgical rapprochement between the church of Theodoric and other Christian communities, as the mosaics suggest the more difficult theological rapprochement with Orthodox Rome.

The strength of Syrian influence in Ravenna is beyond question. The chronicler Agnellus asserts that from Apollinaris to Peter Chrysologus every bishop of the city was a Syrian.[27] This fact is not surprising, in view of the close relations between the Adriatic port and the East, and the unrivaled prestige of Syria as a center of Christian piety and wisdom. In the sixth century this prestige increased even further in the West as a result of the role that Syrian theologians played in the struggle against Byzantine theology.

In 512, Severus, the leader of monophysitism, ascended the see of Antioch. But while still in Constantinople, he had encountered the adamant opposition of two Italian theologians. One of these, he says, was a Roman; the other was Renatus, the pupil and emendator of Boethius and a native of Ravenna.[28] Once installed upon the see of Antioch, Severus hurled his anathema against the Council of Chalcedon and the tome of Leo the Great. The opposition was mercilessly silenced or deposed. It was natural that the victims of this persecution sought and found refuge not only in Rome but in Ravenna as well, where, as the example of Renatus and later the opposition encountered by Maximian show, the Syrian enemies of monophysitism had many supporters among the Catholic clergy. This sympathy may account for the influence of these theological refugees in Orthodox Ravenna; I see no reason for

making light of Sidonius Apollinaris' reference to the "Syrians in Ravenna chanting the psalter";[29] the liturgy may have been considered by themselves and their friends as their proper domain.

This prestige may not have remained confined to the Orthodox community of Ravenna. At a time when Theodoric or his successors realized that the clash with Byzantium was inevitable, such homage to the spiritual hegemony of Syria, like the homage to the theological hegemony of Rome, would have been, from the Gothic and Arian viewpoint, excellent strategy. It would at once deny the Byzantine claim that its anti-Gothic policy was a crusade in defense of orthodoxy; would secure a more friendly attitude among the Catholic population of Italy; and, by stressing those principles of theology and worship which the Arian church shared with the anti-Byzantine opposition everywhere, would cement the alliance against the common enemy. From the Gothic viewpoint such religious policy would have been wise even at the cost of dogmatic compromise.

But we have to assume such compromise only if we accept Baumstark's thesis. It seems entirely possible to follow his valuable suggestion regarding the liturgical significance of the mosaics in Sant' Apollinare Nuovo without going as far as he did in linking them to the liturgy of Syria. The thesis that we should like to advance is as follows: the christological cycles in Sant' Apollinare Nuovo convey a cult experience which can be traced to the origins of the church and which, as a comparison of the liturgies of the different sects shows, all Christians in the sixth century shared, their theological disagreements notwithstanding. The allusions to the liturgy of Syria, like the allusions to the theology of Rome, are significant and quite possibly intentional. But the essence of these mosaics is what may be called their "ecumenical spirit": they draw their inspiration from the earliest and deepest sources of the Christian faith; they explain the meaning of these sources for Christian wisdom and worship, and they make the onlooker feel that the pristine experience of his faith is present even today and that the vision of the oldest centers of Christianity is universally valid. Does not this spirit reflect the tolerance of Theodoric himself? We are likely to confuse this word with indifference; but the tolerance of the Gothic ruler stemmed from a respect for tradition which enabled him to revere the Rome of the popes and the primitive church no less than that of the Caesars. This spirit is reflected in the mosaics in Sant' Apollinare Nuovo; it explains the selection and arrangement of the subjects no less than their iconography and style.

III

The subjects of the Passion scenes, in their order from the entrance to the nave, is as follows: The Incredulity of Thomas; The Road to Emmaus; The Two Marys at the Sepulcher; The Carrying of the Cross; Christ before Pilate; Judas' Repentance; Peter's Denial; The Prophecy of Peter's Denial; Christ before Caiaphas; Christ taken Prisoner; The Betrayal; Gethsemane; The Last Supper.

On the opposite wall and in the same order: The Healing of the Paralytic at Bethesda; The Gadarene Swine; The Healing of the Paralytic at Capernaum; The Last Judgment; The Widow's Mite; The Pharisee and the Publican; The Raising of Lazarus; Christ and the Samaritan Woman; The Healing of the Woman Having an Issue of Blood;[30] The Healing of the Two Blind Men; The Calling of Peter and Andrew; The Miracle of the Loaves and Fishes; The Miracle of Cana.

Of these twenty-six scenes, the last two on either side could not fittingly have appeared in any place other than the one they occupy at the end of the nave near the sanctuary.[31] The Last Supper, with which the Passion cycle begins, obviously belongs in the vicinity of the altar, where the Last Supper is celebrated and commemorated. The adjoining scene, The Agony in the Garden, would seem equally appropriate for the next place, even apart from the chronological sequence. In the Gethsemane scene Christ prayed "if it be possible, let this chalice

pass from me" (Matt. 26:39). The Roman canon mentions the *Calix Praeclarus*, the chalice of Christ's blood, in the words of Institution.[32] One cannot help feeling that this vision of the chalice is also inspired by the event which, in the Gospel narrative, follows the Last Supper, that the chalice used in the eucharistic rite is to remind us of Christ's anguish in its meaning for the mystery of redemption (Pls. 30, 33).

It has been suggested that, since the narrative of Christ's Passion begins near the altar, the same order had to be observed in the miracle cycle; hence the Miracle of Cana had to appear opposite the Last Supper, since, according to the Gospel, it was the first of Christ's miracles. In point of fact, however, the first two scenes of the miracle cycle are as appropriate in their place as are those of the Passion. The Miracle of Cana alludes not only to baptism but also to the transubstantiation of the eucharistic wine into the blood of Christ. The Multiplication of the Loaves, too, is, as we have already noted, an illustration of the eucharistic rite. The early church, moreover, conceived the Miracle of Cana and the Multiplication of the Loaves as closely related. Peter Chrysologus of Ravenna himself mentions them in one breath,[33] and in early Christian art they are paired innumerable times, just as in Sant' Apollinare Nuovo.[34] Are the selection and arrangement of the other christological mosaics in Sant' Apollinare Nuovo as appropriate as those of the four mosaics discussed so far? (Pl. 34.)

At the opposite end of the nave and on our right as we enter, three mosaics represent events from the Easter cycle: The Women at the Sepulcher, The Road to Emmaus, The Incredulity of Thomas. It seems, at first, surprising that we are thus led to contemplate the Easter events before the Passion. But this seeming "inversion" finds its explanation if we recall that, just as the end of the nave, adjoining the sanctuary proper, relates to the sacrament of the altar, so the church entrance is dedicated to the sacrament of baptism.[35]

Baptism, the rite of Christian initiation, may indeed be described as a sacrament of entry. It takes place at the church door, and the admission to the sanctuary symbolizes the catechumen's admission to the communion of saints, to the Heavenly City of which the basilica is the image. Leading the catechumen into the church and to the baptismal font, the priest speaks as follows: "Enter into the temple of God, that thou mayest have part with Christ, unto life everlasting."

The representation of the three Easter scenes near the entrance to Sant' Apollinare Nuovo is explained not only by the general relation of the sacrament of baptism to the Easter mysteries but also by the fact that Easter was the day of baptism in the ancient church. The three mosaics stand in a more specific relation to this sacrament.

The Emmaus and Incredulity of Thomas scenes record two appearances of Christ which opened the eyes of those who, blinded by lack of faith, were not yet partakers of the Easter mysteries. These disciples the catechumen impersonates. As he enters the basilica, he is as yet unillumined by faith. At the very beginning of the baptismal rite the following dialogue takes place: *Priest:* "What dost thou ask of the Church of God?" *Catechumen:* "Faith." *Priest:* "What does faith bestow upon thee?" *Catechumen:* "Life everlasting." The catechumen who entered the basilica in order to receive faith bestowed by baptism could not have found a more beautiful confirmation of his hopes, a more moving reflection of his suspense and expectation, than the two scenes in which Christ appeared to the "foolish and slow of heart" at Emmaus and to the doubting Thomas. As early as the fourth century these events were commemorated in the liturgy of Easter week, which may truly be called a liturgy of the newly baptized.[36]

The third scene, that of the Easter sepulcher, is, of course, even more obviously related to baptism, since the baptismal font is an image of Christ's sepulcher, with the newly baptized, emerging from the sacred water, representing the rising Christ. It is not inconceivable that the mosaic in Sant' Apollinare Nuovo may be placed just above the site where the baptismal font once stood.

Our interpretation of the three compositions is confirmed by the corresponding scenes on the opposite wall. The first of these, showing the healed paralytic of Bethesda carrying his bed, appears already in the baptistry of Dura. In the Roman liturgy (Ember Friday of Lent) this miracle appears also as an image of baptism. The casting-out of devils in the country of the Gadarenes (Mark 5:8) recalls Christ's exorcism of the possessed which the priest repeats in exorcising the catechumen. The miracle of Capernaum, finally, is as dramatically related to the baptismal rite as is the sepulcher scene on the opposite wall: the catechumen, immersed in the font, appeared as an image of the paralytic man who was lowered down from the roof (Mark 2:12)[37] (Pl. 35).

The Easter mysteries, however, do not refer to the newly baptized only. The feast, as St. Augustine points out, is not a remembrance of an event past, as even Christmas is in some respects. The Easter events are ever present and are not only witnessed by every faithful but "operate" in him.[38] In other words, Christ dies and rises from the tomb in every Christian; every believer is a *Christus*, experiencing and enacting the Easter drama. "Though our outward man is corrupted (writes St. Paul, II Cor. 4:16), yet the inward man is renewed day by day." The passage originates in the experience of the Christian mystery; it also bespeaks the very essence of liturgical life.

It is noteworthy that the church retained what may be called the "baptismal symbolism" in its liturgy even after Easter had ceased to be the day of baptism. Since the resurrection of Christ takes place every year, every believer becomes in a profound sense a catechumen during the preceding season of Lent, yearning for his redemption and preparing himself for the rebirth on Easter morning. The occurrence of all the miracle scenes represented in Sant' Apollinare in the Syrian liturgy of Lent and of four of them in the Roman rite confirms the ever renewed presence of these events in the liturgical year and in the mystical life of the faithful. The same is true, of course, for the Passion and Easter cycle: since every Mass is a "little Easter," representing the Christian's death and resurrection in Christ, the mosaics in Sant' Apollinare allude to this mystery, as well as to the historical Easter events.

The liturgical significance of some christological scenes in Sant' Apollinare Nuovo is not so obvious as is that of the ten compositions discussed so far. In the early centuries of the church an untiring exegetical speculation discovered in the great events of Christ's life a wealth of meaning which we can no longer hope adequately to retrace. Certain general features do stand out. In the eight Passion scenes not yet discussed we notice a striking emphasis on the virtue of faith and its active manifestation in confession and martyrdom. This appears, positively, in Christ who is represented before Caiaphas and again before Pilate as "giving testimony to the truth" (John 18:37). This concept of Christ as the ideal martyr and confessor appears also in the ancient liturgies.[39] The four other scenes, on the other hand, depict the reverse of this virtue: two mosaics are devoted to the traitor Judas and two to Peter's denial of his Master. These alternating contrasts are all the more impressive, since, as we enter the basilica, the first Passion scene that we perceive is the *Via Crucis,* Christ carrying the Cross; the scene, which resembles a triumphant procession rather than a journey of agony, is a dramatic exhortation to imitate Christ's martyrdom (Pl. 32, *e, f*).

The Passion in Sant' Apollinare Nuovo is conceived both as the mystery of redemption and as a manifestation and triumph of faith, this term here understood in its ancient, austere sense, which implies assent as well as devotion and surrender. The same idea of faith is apparent in the opposite sequence. Every one of the miracles depicted imparted, or was the result of, faith. The Calling of Peter and Andrew is represented as following the miraculous draft of fish, which inspired such faith in Christ's disciples that they left everything to follow him (Luke, chap. 5). The two blind men are cured after they cry out: "O Lord, thou son of David, have

mercy on us" (Matt. 20:30 ff.). The woman with the issue of blood knows she will be healed by touching Christ's garment. Christ says to her: "Thy faith hath made thee whole" (Luke 8:48). The Samaritan woman believes in Jesus and asks Christ for the water of life (John, chap. 4). Lazarus is revived after Jesus says to Martha: "Did not I say to thee that if thou believest, thou shalt see the glory of God?" (John 11:40.)

Since we noted a certain correspondence between the baptismal scenes on either side of the entrance to the nave and between the eucharistic mosaics at its end, the juxtaposition of other scenes on the two opposite walls may also be deliberate. How eloquent, for instance, is the contrast between the denials of Peter and the faith of Martha and the Samaritan woman on the opposite wall; between the repentance of Judas and that of the publican; between Peter and Andrew, who leave their nets to follow Christ, and Judas, who betrays him; between the Way of the Cross and the Parting of the Goats and the Sheep (Matt., chap. 25) in the Judgment parable, with its promise to Christ's imitators and its threats to those who refuse to follow him; between Pilate's washing of hands and the mite of the widow, who "cast in all she had, even her whole living" (Mark 12:44)[40] (Pl. 42).

In other instances the correspondence is not caused by contrast but by affinity. Thus the testimony of the blind man to the divinity of Christ is juxtaposed to Christ's being led away captive to his martyrdom, in which he is to "give testimony to the truth" (John 18:37). This comparison is even more striking in the adjoining scenes: the woman of the issue of blood, and Christ before Caiaphas. The Fourth Gospel interprets this last scene as a twofold testimony to the work of redemption. Not only is Christ here a confessor, but so is even his enemy, Caiaphas, "who had given the counsel to the Jews: That it was expedient that one man should die for the people" (18:14). According to patristic exegesis, these words find their explanation in the priestly dignity of Caiaphas, which revealed to him Christ's mission even though

Caiaphas, the man, himself remained unaware of it (Pl. 32, *c, e, f*).

Our study of the christological mosaics in Sant' Apollinare Nuovo suggests two conclusions. (1) The scenes depicted must be understood not as narratives of Christ's life but as representations of the liturgical drama. To the Christian the content of the Gospels is neither an epic nor a myth: the Savior's life, death, and resurrection did not happen once in the dim past (as had the stories Homer tells about his gods and heroes) but take place mystically within the faithful themselves as they are enacted in the liturgy. Hence (2) the figures of Christ and his disciples in the mosaics are images of the priest and the congregation as *actors* in the mystery drama.

In this connection attention may be called to one significant difference in the two cycles. In the miracle and sermon scenes the believer identifies himself not with Christ but with those to whom health is restored or salvation promised. This is also true for the two appearances of the risen Christ on the opposite side. But in the Passion scenes, it is obviously not only Peter and Judas but, above all, Christ with whom the believer is to identify himself: in the Passion and resurrection of Christ the Christian is to perceive the mystery of his own redemption. It would not be altogether untrue to say that the Passion cycle refers to the sacrament of the eucharist, as the miracles refer to baptism; that one cycle represents man's life before, the other his life after, his redemption. Before his rebirth man resembles the sick whom Christ healed; in the sacraments he is reborn in the image of Christ.

IV

The reader will notice that the way in which these religious ideas are mentioned presupposes a concept of the nature of artistic imagery and its imitative function which is related to the experience of the ancient church and requires a few words of comment. The Transfiguration mosaic in Sant' Apollinare in Classe revealed the mystical and ascetical aspects of the concept of imitation: the Christian, like the initiate of the other mystery religions of late antiquity, becomes, through baptism, the imitator of his Savior God, re-enacting—either in the sacred play of the mystery drama or in the reality of martyrdom—the "myth" of the god who died and rose again from death; by enacting these events, the "imitator" partakes of the divine victory over death and is, indeed, transformed into the god himself. It is difficult for modern man to appropriate the experiential meaning of this religious concept of imitation; its reflections in art and poetry may be even more incomprehensible to us.

If we speak of works of art and poetry as imitations, we understand the term to mean no more than an image which copies the appearance of a thing and is thus its imitation in a purely fictitious sense. Our aesthetic experience and, in fact, reason itself refuse to see between the work of art and the thing it depicts a relation which is much closer and much more mysterious than that between "reality" and "appearance," a relation in virtue of which the work of art partakes of the reality that it "imitates." Such a concept of art appears to us not only as "primitive" but as excluded by the definitions of art which modern aesthetics has evolved. It is this concept of artistic imitation, however, which explains the nature and the function of the sacred art of the ancient church. Contemplators of the mosaics of Ravenna, if we believe the chronicler Agnellus, did not experience aesthetic enjoyment but were overcome by awe and fear as if in the presence of sacred reality.[41] Christian art would not have come into existence without that more "primitive"—we might say "magical"—concept of imitation.

The first to direct attention to the experiential significance of early Christian art seems to have been Edmond Le Blant, who noted a striking parallelism between the subjects most frequently depicted in early Christian funerary art, on the one hand, and, on the other, those which occur in a number of liturgical prayers for the dying or dead. These prayers, some of which are contemporary with, or even later than, the mosaics in Sant' Apollinare Nuovo, mention certain miracles of Christ—above all, the healing of the afflicted or the raising of Lazarus. The reason for commemorating these miracles in the context of the prayers is fairly clear. The sick, the dying, or even the dead, are here identified with the biblical person to whom health or life has been restored. For that age, language had not yet lost its magical power to create the reality it invoked. The "imitation" of Christ's miracles in those prayers transferred the events mentioned from the past into the present and its effect from the biblical person who had experienced it to the ailing or dying Christian for whom the prayer was said.[42]

The visual representation of the same scenes in early Christian funerary art has, in all probability, the same function. The miracle scenes so frequently depicted in the catacombs or on sarcophagi have not unjustly been described as "visual prayers."[43] To the "representations" or imitations of biblical scenes in works of art, the experience of Christian worship imparted a special significance. The liturgy, as we have seen, regarded the events of the Savior's life not as past but as universally present. In looking at representations of Christ's miracles and, a fortiori, of his Passion and resurrection, the Christian perceived a reality not past, but mysteriously present and related to his own life and death, his own sufferings and hopes. Not only must this fact have determined the effect of this art; it is also reflected in the awesome grandeur of its style.

Unfortunately, students of early Christian art have, almost without exception, failed to consider its relation to the religious experience in which it originated. Not even scholars like Le Blant or Wulff have followed up their original observations. More recently, a school of interpretation has gained some popularity by asserting the function of early Christian art to have been purely narrative. The negative value of this claim lies in its refutation of older interpretations that were based too injudiciously on patristic exegesis. Since the Fathers used the authority of the Bible for the solution of every theological

argument, they were likely to be extremely imaginative in their exegesis and to vary their interpretation of a biblical event according to the context with which they were concerned at the moment. Hence scholars, following them in their interpretations of early Christian art, were often led astray and saw allegories of doctrine in works of art which are certainly not allegorical in essence. To give but one example that has often been quoted: "Daniel in the den of Lions may represent the resurrection, the eucharist, the prayer for the dead, the Passion of Christ, or an example of steadfastness in martyrdom." In patristic exegesis these different interpretations, as we have said, result from the difference of context in which they occur. But can we conclude, from such seeming inconsistencies, that the representation of this and similar scenes in early Christian art has no purpose except a narrative one? Such an assertion, if refreshingly sober, is also disconcertingly unhistorical. How are we to assume that the images from the Old and the New Testament are depicted for the purpose of narrative only, if we know that the Bible was not read as a narrative and that its events were all thought to relate to the mystery of redemption of which every Christian is the actor? With reference to this liturgical experience, the different exegetical interpretations of one and the same event are neither so contradictory nor even so distinct as we may be inclined to believe at first.[44]

In the example just mentioned, Daniel must obviously be understood as an image of both Passion and resurrection, since, as we have seen, these events were inseparable in early Christian worship; but, by the same token, Daniel is also an image of eucharist and martyrdom, because both are conceived as mystical enactments of Passion and resurrection. Since, finally, the Christian is conceived as an imitator of Christ, the Old Testament image of the Resurrection was not only fittingly invoked for the dying man but also represented him. In other words, every one of the apparently contradictory interpretations of Daniel in the lion's den refers to one and the same experience.

These observations, we believe, are relevant not only for the interpretation of early Christian funerary art but also for that of the christological mosaics in Sant' Apollinare Nuovo. The miracle scenes do not refer here to the death or health of the individual Christian as they do in the catacombs and in the prayers for the dying. The fact that the mosaics use the same subjects and often even copy the composition of the sepulchral scenes is nevertheless significant. If Christ's miracles and his Passion and death were conceived as present both in the physical recovery of the faithful and in the sacramental life of the church, we have here again proof for that wholeness of religious experience of which I have already spoken in connection with the cathedra of Maximian. The style of the mosaics resembles that of the catacombs as that of the liturgy resembles the ancient prayers for the dead; in both cases the greater generality of imagery and application and the increased austerity of form indicate the transition from religious experience as an individual concern to religious experience as a universal truth of the entire church. Religious worship must always undergo the development from the individual and spontaneous to the universal and authoritative which the sacred art of the sixth century reflects no less than does the sacred hymnody that received its final form at the same time. But, like the liturgy, the mosaics in Sant' Apollinare Nuovo still use the "medical" language of the apostolic age in order to appeal to man's entire being. In this appeal lies the message of the mosaics which we have studied and the secret of their greatness.

V

A second group of mosaics in Sant' Apollinare Nuovo deserves a brief comment, since it raises some of the same problems as those posed by the works which we have discussed so far and may contribute to their solution. The fields between the christological compositions are decorated with uniform motifs, combining shells (usually symbolizing immortality or resurrection) with a cross, a crown, and doves (which represent the apostles). These objects, like most of the ornaments in the mosaics of Ravenna, have probably symbolic significance, but it is doubtful whether they are related to the figures which appear in the lower zone and between the clerestory windows of the basilica. The figures represent thirty-two (originally thirty-four) men in white robes, holding books or scrolls in their hands, but with no other attribute which might permit their identification; nor are there any inscriptions. It has been suggested that these figures may represent the patriarchs, prophets, apostles, and evangelists mentioned in the ancient Greek litanies of the Orthodox church of Ravenna.[45] This theory again encounters difficulties if we assume that the mosaics were executed under Arian occupancy of the basilica, as may be inferred from the silence of Agnellus. The four patriarchs, the four major and twelve minor prophets, the twelve apostles, and the two evangelists not enumerated among the apostles are, however, mentioned in several ancient litanies[46] (originally all these categories of saints seem to have been commemorated during the eucharistic rite[47]); and the mosaics in the Arian church of St. Agatha in Rome, commissioned by Ricimer, another great Germanic ruler, showed figures of the apostles that were comparable to those in Sant' Apollinare, if the drawing in the Vatican Codex 5407 is to be believed.[48] The images in Ravenna present little evidence of their chronological place, especially if we assume their execution during the last years of Gothic reign of the city. They present an ancient type which can be traced back to the synagogue of Dura and beyond that to classical antiquity (Pls. 33, 40).

VI

The mosaics that we have considered so far would have made Sant' Apollinare Nuovo justly famous. Below these, however, and directly above the arcades, there appear two processions of virgins and martyrs, which are among the greatest works of mosaic art extant and rank with the masterpieces of all times and of any artistic medium. These mosaics alone are described as the work of Archbishop Agnellus in the *Liber pontificalis*.

The chronicler is not quite exact; even these works do not wholly belong to Agnellus. They are, at least in part, creations of an earlier age. The two processions of saints on either wall of the nave are seen emerging from two representations of architecture. The one on the right, inscribed "Palatium," shows Theodoric's palace as an abbreviation for the city of Ravenna;[49] the opposite mosaic depicts the port of Classe (Pls. 35, 36, 37).

These representations undoubtedly date from the time of the Goths. In the portico of the Palatium and in front of the columns there can still be seen the shadowy remnants of figures which have been effaced. This destruction must have taken place under Archbishop Agnellus, obviously as part of the work of "reconciliation" to which the chronicler refers. We cannot say precisely what composition occupied this place originally—certainly, a procession, probably that of Theodoric and his cortege and, possibly, an offertory procession not unlike that in San Vitale. It has even been suggested that this later work received its inspiration from the mosaic in the Arian basilica. This must, however, remain conjecture, since we have good reason to believe that the Gothic mosaic was never completed. Testi-Rasponi has pointed to the remark of the *Anonymus Valesianus*: "palatium usque ad perfectum fecit, quem non dedicavit," i.e., Theodoric completed the palace but died before he could occupy it.[50] Since the mosaic in Sant' Apollinare Nuovo depicts this palace of Theodoric, it must have been executed after the king's death. We have no means of knowing whether Amalasuntha and her successors, during the stormy last years of Gothic rule of Ravenna, were able to bring the great mosaic program to conclusion. Modern scholarship is inclined to attribute not only the architectural mosaics but also those at the other end of the nave, depicting Christ, the Virgin, and their attendant angels,[51] to Theodoric—a suggestion which appears possible on the basis of stylistic evidence but

dubious in view of the fact that these works are attributed to Archbishop Agnellus by his namesake, the chronicler, whose authority is accepted for the dating of the mosaics elsewhere.

What is, above all, noteworthy is the moderation with which the archbishop carried out only such destructions as were absolutely necessary and the admirable ingenuity with which he blended the elements that he himself had to add with the older works that he had been able to preserve. The fact that he left intact the christological mosaics, although they reflect a theology conflicting with that of Byzantium, is remarkable enough. In this moderation on the part of Agnellus we may detect evidence of a new attitude toward Rome, which will occupy us later. The elimination of the portraits of the Arian king and his retinue was unavoidable. A zealot would have destroyed the architectural mosaics as well, for these represented the great buildings which Theodoric had commissioned: behind his palace there appear the Arian baptistry and what is apparently a representation of Sant' Apollinare Nuovo itself. Kibel's restorations have greatly affected the representation of Classe, but here, too, the ancient mosaic may have depicted Gothic buildings only. In this regard not only are the two mosaics a tribute to Theodoric as a patron of the arts, but the twin cities of Ravenna and Classe are here identified with him to such an extent as to suggest that they owed to him their very existence. Archbishop Agnellus did not find it necessary to destroy this impression; but, by his additions to these mosaics, Agnellus transformed the largely political imagery into an exposition of the liturgy comparable only to the great mosaic in Sant' Apollinare in Classe. We forget today that the mosaics in Sant' Apollinare Nuovo are not the work of one man. They have been welded into a unified program and appear as the work of one mind.

On our right, a procession of twenty-five martyrs is led by St. Martin, the ancient titular saint of the basilica, into the presence of Christ. That the sanctuary, having been wrested from the Arian church, was dedicated to St. Martin is noteworthy. The bishop of Tours was one of the great enemies of the Arian heresy which the Christian West had produced; on his feast day the ancient liturgies solemnly commemorated this fact.[52] Though not a martyr in the strict sense of the word, he is singularly honored in the mosaic in Sant' Apollinare Nuovo. Garbed in a red tunic, he leads the procession of martyrs. With the exception of him and of St. Lawrence, who wears a golden tunic, all saints are garbed in white robes. We are reminded that in the language of the ancient church the terms *togatus* and *candidatus* designated the martyr and the saint, the garment thus marking the citizen of the Heavenly City as it had once marked the Roman citizen.[53] The transformation of this symbolism has its source in the Book of Revelation (7:13 ff.): "These that are clothed in white robes, who are they? And I said to Him: My Lord thou knowest! And He said to me: These are they who are come out of the great tribulation and who have washed their robes and who have made them white in the blood of the lamb. Therefore they are before the throne of God. And they serve him day and night in the temple. And he that sitteth on the throne shall dwell over them. They shall no more hunger nor thirst; neither shall the sun fall on them nor any heat. For the lamb which is in the midst of the throne shall rule and shall lead them to the fountains of the waters of life: and God shall wipe all tears from their eyes" (Pl. 38).[54]

Whoever has entered Sant' Apollinare Nuovo on a hot, glaring summer day will have experienced in the solemn shadows of the basilica the wonderful sensation which the Apocalypse evokes: the vision of eternal bliss under the image of the *refrigerium*. The liturgy, which grew in the Mediterranean world, has kept alive this vision. The passage we have just quoted is chosen as a lesson for the Mass of several martyrs. It has also, as Schermann pointed out, influenced the ritual of the Mass proper: the church conceives the host of white-robed martyrs as present at every eucharistic rite, "serving God day and night in his temple"; she evokes for the com-munion of the eucharistic elements the vision of the martyrs being led to the fountains of eternal life. We have here the first evidence of the relation of the procession mosaics to the Christian mystery drama.

The mosaic on our left shows a procession of twenty-two female saints, to whom Agnellus refers only as "virgins" but who are also martyrs. They are led by the Three Magi before the Virgin Mary and the infant Christ, who are attended by four angels. Above their white tunics the virgins wear magnificent dalmatics of gold, in addition to a *lorum*.[55] Diadems and other jewelry complete the exquisite splendor of their attire (Pls. 39, 42, 43).

The liturgy of the Roman church hails her virgin martyrs as brides of Christ in the heavenly splendor of their nuptial attire; it likens them to the ten virgins who went out to meet the bridegroom (Matt. 25:1 ff.) and again praises their beauty which, in the words of the Psalmist (Ps. 44), "the heavenly king greatly desires." Whereas on the anniversary of a martyr the eucharistic feast is conceived as the heavenly repast by the fountain of life, the same mystery appears as a heavenly wedding on the feast of a virgin. The two visions do not remain entirely distinct, however, but merge in a third, i.e., that of the parable of the marriage feast (Matt., chap. 22). Here, again, the liturgy reflects the apocalyptic vision of St. John, who perceived the blessed as those "that are called to the marriage supper of the Lamb" (John 19:9). The church conceived the eucharistic sacrifice under the image of that heavenly feast to which only those are admitted who wear a wedding garment, as do the martyrs, who have washed their robes white in the blood of the Lamb, and the virgins, who have gone out in their bridal beauty to meet the Spouse.

It will be recalled that on the left wall of Sant' Apollinare Nuovo, above the procession of virgins, the Miracle of Cana refers to the Eucharist under the image of a wedding meal; that on the opposite wall, above the martyrs, the same mystery is represented as the Last Supper, celebrated in memory of Christ's death. These two images are united, as it were, by the altar that stands between the two walls and on which the drama is enacted that is both sacrifice and heavenly feast. So are the two processions of virgins and martyrs, which are so beautifully attuned to the older mosaics above them. The canon of the Mass visualized both these groups of saints surrounding the altar whenever the Eucharist is celebrated (Pls. 33, 34).

The martyrs and virgins depicted in Sant' Apollinare Nuovo are all identified by inscriptions. Most of them are the same that are mentioned in the diptychs of the canon of the present Roman Mass and

in those of the still older canon of the liturgy of Milan. The remaining saints are invoked in the ancient litanies of Ravenna. Because of the close relation which usually prevails between the lists of saints mentioned in the diptychs of a church and those invoked in its litanies, we are entitled to conclude that the processions of virgins and martyrs in Sant' Apollinare Nuovo illustrate the diptychs of sixth-century Ravenna. A comparative list follows of the "literary processions" which appear in the canons of Rome and Milan, of the litanies of Ravenna, and, as is presumed here, of the "visual" diptychs represented in the mosaics here under discussion.

RAVENNA		MILAN	ROME
Litanies	Sant' Apollinare Nuovo	Canon of the Mass	Canon of the Mass
S. Stephanus	S. Martinus	Xystus	Linus
S. Apollinaris III	S. Clemens	Laurentius	Cletus
S. Vitalis	S. Xystus	Hippolytus	Clemens
S. Ursicinus	S. Laurentius	Vincentius	Xystus
S. Gervasius	S. Hippolytus	Cornelius	Cornelius
S. Protasius	S. Cornelius	Cyprianus	Cyprianus
S. Laurentius	S. Cyprianus	Clemens	Laurentius
S. Vincentius	S. Cassianus	Chrysogonus	Chrysogonus
S. Johannes	S. Johannes	Johannes	Johannes
S. Paulus	S. Paulus	Paulus	Paulus
S. Nicander	S. Vitalis	Cosmas	Cosmas
S. Marcianus	S. Gervasius	Damianus	Damianus
	S. Protasius	Apollinaris	Johannes
	S. Ursicinus	Vitalis	Stephanus
	S. Namor (sic)	Nazarius	Matthias
	S. Felix	Celsus	Barnabas
	S. Apollinaris	Protasius	Ignatius
	S. Sebastianus	Gervasius	Alexander
	S. Demetrius	Victor	Marcellinus
	S. Polycarpus	Nabor	Petrus
	S. Vincentius	Felix	
	S. Pancratius	Calimerius	
	S. Chrysogonus	Johannes	
	S. Protus	Johannes	
	S. Hyazinthus	Stephanus	
	S. Sabinus	Andreas	
		Petrus	
		Marcellinus	
S. Agatha	S. Euphemia	Agnes	Felicitas
S. Agnes	S. Pelagia	Caecilia	Perpetua
S. Caecilia	S. Agatha	Felicitas	Agatha

RAVENNA—*continued*		MILAN—*continued*	ROME—*continued*
Litanies	Sant' Apollinare Nuovo	Canon of the Mass	Canon of the Mass
S. Lucia	S. Agnes	Perpetua	Lucia
S. Christina	S. Eulalia	Anastasia	Agnes
S. Valeria	S. Caecilia	Agatha	Caecilia
S. Eulalia	S. Lucia	Euphemia	Anastasia
S. Justina	S. Crispina	Lucia	
S. Marina	S. Valeria	Justina	
	S. Vincentina	Sabina	
	S. Perpetua	Thecla	
	S. Felicitas	Pelagia	
	S. Justina		
	S. Anastasia		
	S. Daria		
	S. Emerentiana		
	S. Paulina		
	S. Victoria		
	S. Anatolia		
	S. Christina		
	S. Sabina		
	S. Eugenia		

It is worth while to examine these lists more closely. Out of twenty-six martyrs represented in Sant' Apollinare Nuovo, fifteen appear in either the Roman or the Ambrosian Canon or in both. Another, Ursicinus, is mentioned in the litany of Ravenna. Martinus, who, as titular saint of the church, leads the procession, is mentioned in the canon of Milan. Among twenty-two virgins on the opposite wall, eleven are mentioned in the diptychs of Milan and Rome, three more in the litany of Ravenna.

From the historical viewpoint the list is striking enough. We have already noted the importance of the diptychs as a compass of ecclesiastical policies. The saints included in the great prayers of intercession indicate the political and theological orientation of the see in which they are thus honored. If we study our mosaics with this question in mind, the result is surprising. Already Delehaye has noted the extraordinarily weak representation of Eastern saints in this Christian Pantheon of a "Byzantine" city.[56] Among the martyrs, only two—Demetrius and Polycarp of Smyrna—are Eastern saints. Likewise, among the virgins only two—Euphemia and Pelagia—seem to belong to the East. On the other

hand, the two processions of saints are magnificent homage to Ravenna's great sister churches on Italian soil, Rome and Milan.

Likewise revealing is the order in which the virgins and martyrs are depicted. In the Roman Canon the martyrs are enumerated in strictly hierarchical order: first the popes; next the bishop of the sister-church of Carthage, Cyprian; after him the deacon Lawrence; finally, five laymen. The Ambrosian Canon is less strict in its observation of the hierarchical order but very respectful of the churches of Rome and Ravenna. Here the procession of the diptychs opens with three Romans, followed by Vincentius, the illustrious martyr of Spain, who also enjoyed a special cult in Rome;[57] that he should interrupt the group of Roman bishops and precede Cornelius is nevertheless striking. Apparently he was to be honored in a special way. Since Cyprian always appears together with Cornelius,[58] the only way to give Vincentius precedence over all non-Romans listed in the Ambrosian Canon was to give him precedence also over Cornelius.

After the saints of the Roman Canon the Milan diptychs mention the great martyr of Ravenna:

[85]

Apollinaris; only then follow the saints claimed by Milan: Vitalis, Nazarius, Celsus, Protasius, Gervasius, Nabor, and Felix. The mosaics in Sant' Apollinare Nuovo show a different order. Here St. Martin is followed by a group of five Romans and these, in turn, by Cyprian. Next comes Cassian, who apparently precedes SS. John and Paul for historical and political reasons: Cassian is a saint of Imola, one of the cities of Aemilia over which the archbishop of Ravenna exercised metropolitan powers. The ties between the two cities must have been close; Peter Chrysologus died on St. Cassian's feast day while saying Mass in the saint's sanctuary at Imola.[59] Whether the bishop's visit on this occasion had been a token of Ravenna's special veneration for St. Cassian or whether such veneration originated in the circumstances of Peter's death, the historical occurrence seems to explain the place of honor conceded to the saint of Imola in Sant' Apollinare Nuovo.

After the Roman martyrs, John and Paul, there follows a group of four local martyrs of Ravenna: Vitalis, Gervasius, Protasius, and Ursicinus. We have seen that the *Passio SS. Martyrum Gervasii et Protasii* declared the first three of these to be members of one family and located the martyrdom of Vitalis and Ursicinus in Ravenna. The appearance of Ursicinus in the group, as well as that of Valeria among the female martyrs on the opposite wall, is in all probability also inspired by the *Passio*. Only then do two martyrs of Milan, Nabor and Felix, make their appearance. The next figure, that of Apollinaris, has led to some conjectures. That this great saint of Ravenna should appear in such a comparatively humble place is certainly significant. Lanzoni has suggested that here, as in the diptychs of Milan, the "strangers" among the martyrs have graciously been given precedence over their "hosts," the local martyrs of the city.[60] This assumption is convincing if we assume that Vitalis, Gervasius, Protasius, and Ursicinus are represented as martyrs of Milan. According to what has been said earlier in these pages, however, regarding the political significance of the *Passio* and its reflection in the art of Ravenna, this

appears unlikely. To cede these four martyrs to Milan would have despoiled Ravenna of that number of titles to her ecclesiastical aspirations, titles which this see had deliberately claimed by means of the sumptuous sanctuary erected in honor of Vitalis and his alleged sons. The place assigned to St. Apollinaris, on the other hand, may well mark an act of deference to Milan. If the liturgy of the age speaks the language of diplomacy, it speaks it with a charming simplicity to which we have become altogether unaccustomed. There follows Demetrius of Salonika, who seems to have enjoyed an ancient cult in Ravenna, and Polycarp, the illustrious martyr of Smyrna and a friend of Ignatius of Antioch.[61] Baumstark has already suggested that his presence in the mosaic may be an act of homage to the theology which Ignatius represented. This would be significant in view of Ravenna's claim that her "apostle" Apollinaris was a native of Antioch. Polycarp is followed by the Spaniard Vincentius, by the Romans Pancratius and Chrysogonus, Protus and Hyacinthus. Sabinus, the last, is a martyr of Spoleto.

Even more significant is the order observed in the opposite mosaic. The procession of virgins is led by Euphemia, the celebrated martyr of Chalcedon. In the sixth century, her appearance must have amounted to a theological manifesto. The Council of Chalcedon had assembled in St. Euphemia's sanctuary. Her name remained associated with the doctrines proclaimed on that occasion in solemn and dramatic fashion. When Pope Vigilius, at the height of the controversy over the Three Chapters, escaped from Constantinople, he took refuge in St. Euphemia of Chalcedon. From here he waged the fight in defense of the Chalcedonian settlement. Duchesne[62] has already observed that the pope's base of operations was singularly well chosen: "the memory of St. Euphemia and that of the Council had somewhat merged. Above the theological quarrels, the mysterious doctrines, the terrible verdicts, hovered the image of the young martyr." Her image appeared now in the great sanctuary of Ravenna.

Nowhere, except in Byzantium itself, does this

tribute paid to St. Euphemia appear more surprising. The churches erected in her name throughout the Christian world expressed the most solemn assent to the theology of Chalcedon. In the West, where the condemnation of the Three Chapters was considered as an attack upon the Council, the veneration paid to St. Euphemia must, during the years of the theological struggle, have amounted to an act of defiance of Byzantine ecclesiastical policies.

This struggle was over when Agnellus rededicated Sant' Apollinare Nuovo. He placed the image of St. Euphemia at the head of the procession of virgin martyrs, opposite the figures of the title saint of their basilica, or possibly of St. Stephen. No other image could have expressed more movingly and more gracefully the metropolitan's convictions. Officially, Byzantium had never approved of the position taken by Monophysite extremists, such as Severus of Antioch. The emperor had declared repeatedly that the condemnation of the Three Chapters did not in any sense constitute an attack upon, or even a criticism of, the Council of Chalcedon or its spiritual leader, Leo the Great. Now in Ravenna, the western capital of the Byzantine Empire and the only metropolitan see of the Occident that was regarded as an exponent of Byzantine theology, the image of St. Euphemia paid the most solemn homage to the genius of Chalcedon.

It is significant that this gesture was not altogether an innovation on the part of Archbishop Agnellus. His predecessor, Maximian, at the very moment when the struggle over the Three Chapters had reached its climax, thought it necessary to act in a similar manner. Among the relics which he deposited in St. Stephen—he almost certainly acquired them while in Constantinople—were those of St. Euphemia. Maximian went even further. An ancient baptistry in Ravenna, annexed to the church of St. Probus, had long been identified with the place where Apollinaris himself was said to have administered baptism for the first time. This baptistry was dedicated to St. Euphemia. We do not know at what time pious legend had first linked in this fash-

ion Ravenna's greatest saint with the holy patroness of Chalcedon. But we know that Maximian renovated the church of St. Probus, and considerations entirely different from our own have led Testi-Rasponi to suggest that the archbishop on this occasion enlarged the modest baptistry of St. Euphemia into a church.[63]

Whereas Maximian's part in the tribute paid to St. Euphemia remains partly conjecture, the mosaic in Sant' Apollinare Nuovo leaves no doubt about Agnellus' position. Through the medium of these images he speaks a language that is at once forceful and conciliatory. By means of the procession of martyrs the see of Ravenna declared his sympathy and respect for the great sees of Italy. The saint of Chalcedon is followed by Pelagia, who enjoyed a special cult in Antioch and whose image, therefore, like that of St. Polycarp, may be a testimony to the theological and ecclesiastical ties between the two cities.[64] Four Roman virgins—Agatha, Agnes, Caecilia, and Lucia—surround Eulalia, the martyr of Spain. Crispina is an African martyr; Valeria, the wife of Vitalis, belongs to Ravenna. Vincentina (like Paulina) cannot be identified. Perpetua, Felicitas, Anastasia, Daria, Emerentiana, and Eugenia are again Roman saints. Justina is the saint of Padua. Victoria and Anatolia are saints of ancient Sabina and share the same feast (July 10) in Jerome's martyrology.[65] Christina is a martyr of Tyre, whom an ancient tradition, however, linked to Bolsena;[66] Sabina is a Roman saint.[67]

It is illuminating to compare Sant' Apollinare Nuovo with San Vitale and Sant' Apollinare in Classe. In these two churches the local martyrs of Ravenna are extolled in such a way as to make the onlooker forget that the church universal extends beyond the confines of Ravenna. The mosaics in Sant' Apollinare Nuovo, on the other hand, transform this basilica into a veritable pantheon of Christianity. In the solemn harmony of these processions there appear some great saints of the Eastern church (Polycarp, Euphemia, Pelagia) in whom a theological tradition with which Ravenna wished to associate herself found its embodiment. Homage is also paid to the churches of Africa and Spain. Above all, however, the mosaics convey the unmistakable impression of unity among the three great metropolitan sees of Italy: Rome, Ravenna, and Milan. If one recalls the spirit of fierce rivalry which Maximian's mosaics bespeak, the conciliatory message of these works of his successor is most remarkable, particularly in regard to the relations between Ravenna and Rome. This will become fully apparent if we realize that the processions point, if not to an adaptation of the Roman rite by Ravenna, certainly to a significant liturgical *rapprochement* between the two great sees.

VII

In the canons of Rome and Milan the "processions" of martyrs and virgins whom we have enumerated are divided into two groups. The first of these is mentioned at the very beginning of the canon; it occurs in a group of prayers the function of which has been described as linking the offertory prayers, which precede them, to the subsequent act of consecration. Following are the first prayers of the canon:

"Wherefore, O most merciful Father, we humbly pray and beseech thee, through Jesus Christ, thy Son, our Lord, that thou wouldst vouchsafe to receive and bless these gifts, these offerings, this holy and unblemished sacrifice, which in the first place we offer thee for thy holy catholic Church, that it may please thee to grant her peace: as also to protect, unite, and govern her throughout the world, together with thy servant N., our Pope, N., our bishop, as also all orthodox believers who keep the catholic faith. Be mindful, O Lord, of thy servants and handmaids, N. and N., and of all here present, whose faith and devotion are known unto thee; for whom we offer, or who offer up to thee, this sacrifice of praise for themselves and theirs, for the redeeming of their souls, for the hope of their safety and salvation, and who pay their vows to thee, the eternal, living, and true God: communicating, and

reverencing the memory first of the glorious Mary, ever a virgin, Mother of our God and Lord Jesus Christ; likewise of thy blessed apostles and martyrs [there follow the names of the twelve apostles and of the first twelve martyrs mentioned in our list] and of all thy saints; by whose merits and prayers grant that in all things we may be guarded by thy protecting help. . . . Through the same Christ our Lord. Amen.

"We therefore beseech thee, O Lord, to be appeased, and to receive this offering of our bounden duty, as also of thy whole household; order our days in thy peace; grant that we be rescued from eternal damnation and counted within the fold of thine elect. Through Christ our Lord. Amen."

The first prayer invokes the divine blessing over the sacrificial gifts offered; the second is a prayer of intercession for the faithful, "for whom we offer, or who offer up to thee, this sacrifice." The parallelism of these two prayers originates in that mystical concept of identity between the oblation and its donor with which we are already acquainted. In the subsequent prayer there appears the first "procession" of martyrs; its relation to the preceding prayer is remarkable.

It will be noted that the enumeration of the twelve apostles and the twelve martyrs does not form a separate sentence but is linked grammatically to the prayer for the sanctification of those who have offered the sacrifice. At the end of the *communicantes* the hope is expressed that the "merits and prayers" of the saints may secure divine help and protection for the faithful. But this is an afterthought. The preceding passage speaks of the presence and the communion of the martyrs,[68] and the last of the preconsecratory prayers returns to this thought: "Grant that we be . . . counted within the fold of thine elect." Explicitly and emphatically the Gregorian Canon thus establishes a relation between the faithful who offer their oblation and the martyrs. The significance of this thought is re-created in the mosaics in Sant' Apollinare Nuovo.

The procession of virgin martyrs is preceded by

the Three Magi, who are shown offering their gifts to the infant Christ. It is the scene which the Roman church has raised to extraordinary dignity: her liturgy commemorates the advent of the Magi as the great feast of the Epiphany, the manifestation of Christ. Hence the representation of the Epiphany scene in Sant' Apollinare Nuovo should not surprise us. But, in order to understand its relation to the processions of martyrs, we have to interrupt our consideration of these works and to inquire into the meaning of the advent of the Magi for the religious imagination of the ancient church (Pl. 34).

The first clue is provided by patristic exegesis. The Fathers are almost unanimous in one regard, i.e., the symbolic significance of the gifts offered by the Three Magi. The gold offered by the first of them is interpreted by Irenaeus and Origen as an act of homage to Christ's kingship; the frankincense as an allusion to Christ's godhead; the myrrh as a prophetic symbol of his Passion.[69] This interpretation deserves our attention, all the more since even the chronicler Agnellus, in his description of the mosaics in Sant' Apollinare Nuovo, repeats it at length, in the apparent notion that the scene of the Three Magi has a theological intention which the beholder is not to overlook.[70]

Leo the Great devoted eight important sermons to the feast of the Epiphany.[71] He, too, dwells on the symbolic meaning of the Magi's presents: the gold is an acknowledgment of Christ's kingship, the myrrh is offered by the Christian who believes that the Son of God has united to himself the true nature of man; and we honor him with frankincense if we confess him to be in no sense different from the majesty of the Father. In this interpretation allegorical exegesis takes on a new meaning. In the shadow of the great theological controversies of the age the simple presents of the Magi become symbols of the doctrine that triumphed at Chalcedon. Different in kind and distinct in nature, the gifts of the Magi honor and acknowledge the union of the two natures in Christ as Leo himself had conceived and expounded it. It is significant that the pope, in the

same sermons, makes the polemical meaning of the Epiphany symbol emphatically clear. The Christ Child, he says, whom the Magi saw and adored, was small and frail and in no way different from other children of man. As the resplendent star had announced to the Magi the divine majesty dwelling invisibly in Christ, so the humble manger attested to the incarnation of the word by which the eternal essence of the Son of God had taken on the true nature of man. Henceforth the mystery of faith can no longer be disturbed by the diversity between the wonderful miracles wrought and the ordeal of the Passion suffered by Christ. That diversity finds its only explanation in the conviction that our Lord Jesus Christ was at once true God and true man.

The Magi thus embody every Christian who believes in the mystery of redemption as the Council of Chalcedon had formulated it; to him the star and the manger will always be evidence and token of the two distinct natures which have been reconciled in the person of Christ. At this point Leo the Great launches into an attack upon the "Manichaeans": those who assert that Christ had not really taken on human nature, since it would have been unworthy of the Godhead to be born of the womb of a woman. Leo does not perceive in the humility of the Incarnation any insult, any pollution to the majesty of God, but only the glory of his mercy. Light is not dimmed by the darkness which it illuminates. In order to redeem what it has created in its own image, the Eternal Light has united itself to man. It has suffered no damage from this union.[72]

Patristic homiletics has produced little that is comparable to these Epiphany sermons of Leo the Great and perhaps nothing surpassing them. To the clarity of his theology, to the irresistible sweep of his eloquence, he adds here the power of dramatic vision. The gifts of the Magi acknowledge the twofold nature of Christ and are, as such, symbols of theological doctrine which everyone will remember. But to the pope the entire story of the Magi is a symbol. Man's pursuit of ultimate wisdom, the Christian's assent to a revealed truth which surpasses all understanding—these can find no more moving image than the long journey of the three Wise Men and their final homage before the simple and ineffable scene in the manger.

It is not the specific theological significance—one might almost say the "polemical slant"—of this exegesis that is most remarkable, but its way of linking theological doctrine with the living pageant of the liturgical drama. The feast of the Epiphany had been introduced into the West in the second half of the fourth century; and Ambrose as well as Augustine already knew its identification with the advent of the Magi.[73] But Leo is the first to relate this feast to the innermost core of the Christian faith, in which liturgy as well as doctrine originate. For him worship and doctrine were as one. Theology was one way to experience the mysteries of the faith, the liturgy another; but the abstractions of the first retained all the vividness of poetical vision, while the sensuous pageant of the second conveyed even to the illiterate the profoundest concepts of Christian speculation. One wonders whether Leo the Great's almost equal influence upon the theology, the liturgy, and the arts of his and succeeding ages was due more to his singular genius or to the close affinity which at his time united those three. We can trace the Epiphany liturgy of the Roman church to the time of Gregory the Great, i.e., *ca.* A.D. 600. But the entire rite is so sublime an illustration of the views expressed by Leo the Great in his Epiphany sermons that one is tempted to attribute it to him also.

The catechetical purpose of the feast appears quite clearly in some of the liturgical texts: "Grant us, we beseech thee, O Lord our God, that what we celebrate with solemn office we may attain by the understanding of a purified mind." Or again: "Enlighten, we beseech thee, O Lord, thy people, and kindle their hearts always with the splendor of thy glory, that they may forever both acknowledge and truly perceive their Savior." The illumination of the mind is here clearly conceived as one of the fruits of the mystery. It takes place intuitively during the solemn enactment of the Epiphany drama.

It may be said that on this feast the entire eucharistic rite is transformed into the pageant of the Three Magi. As the gospel passage is read: "And entering into the house, they found the child with Mary his mother and falling down they adored him," the whole congregation kneels down, imitating the homage of the Magi. The offertory is taken from Psalm 71: "The kings of Tharsis and the Isles shall offer gifts: the kings of the Arabians and of Saba shall bring presents: and all kings of the earth shall adore him; all nations shall serve him."[74] The offertory hymn was chanted while the faithful carried their gifts to the altar; this procession is here again interpreted as an image of the Epiphany. Even more significant, however, is the following prayer: "Graciously regard, O Lord, we beseech thee, the gifts of thy Church, in which are offered now no longer gold, frankincense, and myrrh, but he whom those mystic offerings signified is immolated and received, even Jesus Christ thy Son our Lord. . . ."

This prayer, the ancient *oratio super oblata* or *Secreta*, is the oration specifically devoted to the oblation of the faithful. In the Gregorian sacramentary every one of the *secreta* texts seeks to elucidate the mystical significance of this act. The text for Epiphany is of unusual significance, however: in the offertory hymn the oblation of the faithful was described as an act of homage to the divine majesty of Christ; the prayer *super oblata* perceives them as an image of the Passion. The two texts repeat the dual exegesis of the Magi's presents with which we are already familiar from patristic literature. In the Epiphany liturgy, however, not only the gifts but the entire advent of the Magi ceases to be an allegory of doctrine and embodies, as it were, the ritual act in which the mystery of redemption was realized by the Roman church. Is not this the reason why she elevated this biblical event to the rank of a great feast and why Leo the Great, in his sermons, focused his theological vision upon that solemn pageant?

The Epiphany texts that we have quoted distinguish the two motifs of Christ's Passion and man's homage before the divine King. These are the very elements which compose the Christian mystery drama, the eucharistic rite itself. Some scholars have even sought to identify these two elements with two distinct sources of Christian worship: a memorial repast with the *epiphany* of the God, after the model, or in analogy, of the Hellenistic mysteries, and an oblation of the eucharistic elements originating in the Jewish sacrifice. The two acts are said to have merged under predominantly Jewish influence: the mystery of Christ's Epiphany thus being transformed into that of his mystical oblation, accomplished by the priest. By this transformation, we are told, the ancient offertory act, the oblation of gifts by the faithful, lost its mystical significance until it was finally abolished.[75]

If this thesis is dubious from a historical viewpoint, it makes even less sense as a description of the eucharistic rite. The *epiphany* and sacrifice motifs appear indissolubly united in the liturgy, the sacrificial oblation being at once an act of homage to the *epiphany* of the divine Redeemer and the enactment of Christ's death and resurrection.

Neither the words nor the action of the liturgical drama makes this meaning entirely clear. Accustomed as we are to the "imitation" of modern drama, we should expect the Christian rite, as the drama of Christ's death and resurrection, to reproduce the events on Calvary in their material reality. Instead, the liturgical drama presents the Easter mysteries as a sacrifice experienced and enacted by the faithful; and—as the solemn confirmation of the reality of this representation and the faithful's participation in its life-giving power—the commemoration of the words of Institution spoken by Christ at the Last Supper. It is important to realize that for religious experience it is precisely the double imagery of repast and sacrifice which conveys the idea of participation in the divine work of redemption.

The mystical significance of the meal is very explicitly stated in the New Testament: Only if a man incorporates Christ's body and blood as "meat" and "drink" (John 6:56) will he become truly united with him and share in the transfiguration of human nature which Christ accomplished in his resurrection. "He that eateth my flesh and drinketh my blood abideth in me: and I in him" (*ibid.*, vs. 57). St. Paul, who writes "if we be dead with Christ, we believe that we shall live also together with Christ" (Rom., chap. 6), linked this belief to the sacred repast: "The bread which we break, is it not the partaking of the body of the Lord? For we, being many, are one bread, one body: all that partake of one bread!" (I. Cor. 10:16 f.).

Not the sacramental meal by itself, however, is the realization of the mystery of redemption. The sacrifice is its essence. The crude and pristine ritual of the Dionysian mysteries may explain the meaning of this oblation. Here the initiate offered a young goat, which he himself slaughtered and devoured. By an ambivalence typical of the Hellenistic mystery cults, the victim represented at once the initiate and the god and thus became the means of magical union between them: the victim's slaughter denoted the initiate's own death, while the particularly fierce form of its dismemberment represented the death of Dionysos Zagreus. In the subsequent repast the initiate literally incorporated the sacrificed god and thus partook of the divine nature which overcame death. In other words, in this rite the sacrificial oblation was at once the representation of the god's death and resurrection and the means of the initiate's mystical union with him. We may ask whether the oblation of the Christian rite does not have a similar significance.[76]

The church inherited the offertory from Judaism. In speaking of the spirit in which the Christian is to present his "gift" at the altar, Christ himself had sanctioned the continuation of this act in Christian worship (Matt. 5:23). Irenaeus has referred these words of Christ to the liturgical oblation and has thus linked the rite of the church to that of the Temple.[77] The Lord's words are also echoed by St. Paul: "I appeal to you by God's mercy," he writes (Rom. 12:1), "to offer up your bodies as a living sacrifice, holy, pleasing unto God, your reasonable service." This moral and ascetical exhortation, like so many others of the apostle, must be seen in relation to the Christian mystery rite from which its imagery is borrowed. And in this rite the oblation was conceived as a sacrifice—a sacrifice in imitation of that on Calvary and in which the believer was to assimilate himself to the Divine Lamb, the only "living sacrifice" that Christianity knew. If such notions reflect the influence of the Hellenistic mysteries, they have also had a profound effect upon the pattern of Christian worship. The influence of St. Paul's sacramental doctrine upon the shape of the liturgy is beyond question. His words regarding the believer's spiritual self-immolation in imitation of Christ's Passion called for mystical realization in the action of the sacramental rite.

Recent theology is inclined to locate the enactment of Christ's death and resurrection in but one part of the eucharistic rite, i.e., the consecration of bread and wine upon the altar. But the ancient liturgies fail to support this interpretation. They identify the representation of Christ's death with the offertory act. "When we remember," we read in the mother of liturgies, that of Hippolytus (*ca.* A.D. 200) "his death and resurrection in this way, we bring to thee the bread and the cup." The liturgy of Serapion states this symbolic function of the oblation of bread and wine even more explicitly: "we have offered the bread as a representation of Christ's death."[78] The same thought appears also in the Roman liturgy: ". . . calling to mind the blessed Passion of the same Christ thy Son our God, and also his rising up from hell, and his glorious ascension to heaven, [we] do offer unto thy most excellent majesty, of thine own gifts bestowed upon us . . . the holy Bread of eternal life and the Chalice of everlasting salvation." The prayer occurs in the canon. It is all the more remarkable that it, too, conceives the offering of the sacramental gifts as the image of Christ's death and resurrection.

It is inconceivable that this image should have been confined to the language of the liturgy. The eucharistic rite is, above all, action—*actio*, as the ancient language of the church calls it significantly.[79]

The acts and gestures of the liturgy, sparse, simple, and solemn, are designed to effect the sacred reality which the accompanying prayers invoke. The imagery of language (*oblatio* in Latin, *prosphora* in Greek) visualized the Christian sacrifice as a "bringing-forward" of gifts and hence as a solemn procession toward the altar in analogy to the Jewish oblation. St. Paul (Rom., chap. 12) had interpreted this act as an imitation of Christ's self-immolation. These facts could not fail to bestow upon the Christian offertory procession the most solemn significance.

The first authoritative description of this rite occurs in the *Ordo Romanus*, which, in substance at least, goes back to Gregory the Great.[80] But this solemn procession, in which every member of the congregation, men and women alike, carried the eucharistic species of bread and wine to the altar, is certainly much older. It is already depicted in the floor mosaic of the ancient basilica of Aquileia, which seems to date from the second decade of the fourth century; and, from what has been said above, it is hard to conceive that the offertory procession should not be as old as the liturgy itself (Pl. 45, *a*).[81]

Our interpretation of the significance of the offertory rite can also be traced to the patristic age. Both St. Ambrose and St. Augustine assert that this rite is inseparable from Communion and in dignity hardly inferior to this sacrament.[82] To explain this notion, it should be recalled that, according to patristic theology, the eucharist is a twofold sacrifice, consisting in the sanctification of the faithful as well as in the sanctification of bread and wine. In other words, the mystery of Christ's death and resurrection is incomplete unless the Christian "imitates" these events by immolating himself.[83] It must be stressed that this sanctification of the faithful can in no way be conceived as separate from the sanctification of the eucharistic species. It nevertheless precedes the latter act in the liturgy in order to lend special emphasis to the twofold nature of the sacrifice. If, in our discussion of the Transfiguration, we have described the consecratory act as a *repraesentatio passionis,* this term may likewise be applied to the offertory procession as the self-immolation of the faithful.

In the ancient liturgies this meaning of the offertory is stated explicitly, often in the very words of Romans, chapter 12: "O pure and spotless lamb," we read in the liturgy of the Syrian Jacobites, "who offered to his father an acceptable offering for the expiation and redemption of the whole world: vouchsafe us, to offer ourselves to thee a living sacrifice . . . and like unto thy sacrifice which was for us, O Christ our Lord, forever. Amen."[84]

The same thought occurs in the Roman liturgy. On Monday in Whitsun week the Gregorian sacramentary has the following prayer *super oblata:* "Hallow, we beseech thee, O Lord, by the invocation of thy holy name the victim of this sacrifice and through its means make us too an eternal offering to thee. . . ." It is this idea of the believer's mystical share in the sacrifice which he offers that prompted, as late as A.D. 813, a synod at Mainz to enjoin participation in the rite upon every believer as a "great remedy of the soul."[85]

The advent of the Magi is a *mysterium,* or, in the language of Leo the Great, a *sacramentum*—a feast actualized not only on the day especially devoted to its commemoration, but, as the Fathers point out repeatedly, at every Mass.[86] The presents of the Magi prefigure Christ's sacrifice; they also are symbols, however, of the other element of the eucharistic rite, which is not commemorative but eschatological.

The Christian mystery drama not only remembers the Easter events; entwined with this representation of the beginning of the Christian church is the anticipation of its end. As if the ages had become like one moment before the eyes of God, the liturgy unfolds the entire panorama of Christian history, and the vision of Christ's resurrection from the Easter sepulcher blends into that of the resurrection of mankind on the Day of Judgment. It is significant that, of all the canonical books, none has inspired the Roman liturgy more than has the Revelation of St. John. Hence the sacred repast commemorates the

Last Supper and also evokes the vision of the marriage feast of the Lamb; hence the sacrificial oblation represents the self-immolation of the Savior but also the adoration of "every creature which is in heaven and on the earth and under the earth," who render to the Lamb "benediction and honour and glory and power, for ever and ever."

This eschatological element of the liturgy preserves the most ancient Christian experience. After his resurrection, Christ had appeared among his disciples and had again broken bread with them. His promise that he would be present wherever two or three of his faithful were assembled in his name must have imparted a feeling of awe, of suspense, of expectation, to the celebrants of the ancient *agape*. But this rite was overshadowed by yet another promise of Christ. During the Last Supper he had promised the apostles that he would drink with them again "of this fruit of the vine . . . in the kingdom of my Father" (Matt. 26:29). Inevitably, the vision which these words unfolded must have been present whenever the sacred meal was enacted by the early church. That age expected the *parousia,* the Second Advent of the Lord, in the very near future. As Christ's appearance, his "descent" upon the sacred species of the sacrifice was invoked, there appeared before the eyes of the ancient Christians the vision of the heavenly repast which would unite them with the Lord in his Kingdom.[87]

This eschatological vision remained part of the liturgy even after the belief in the imminence of the *parousia* had waned. And this vision, too, is conveyed by the advent of the Magi. Christian imagination likened that first manifestation of Christ to the Three Wise Men to his manifestation to all mankind on the day of resurrection. The Magi represent the awe and devotion with which all humanity will then acknowledge the majesty of Christ. In his Epiphany sermons Leo the Great dwells emphatically on this eschatological motif. The Kingdom of God, he says, will not come to those who sleep but to those who wake, who labor to fulfil his commandments. For him, the image of the Magi embodies the Christian who abandons all other concerns and makes haste to arrive in the company of the blessed before the throne of God.[88]

To us the eschatological significance of the advent of the Magi must be less clear than it was to the Christians of the first centuries. To them, the simple Gospel narrative of the event evoked a pageant less religious than political, in which the emotions of homage, surrender, and devotion received their most solemn expression, for their thoughts quite naturally turned to the *epiphany* ceremonial of the Hellenistic and Roman monarchies. The meaning which the term "epiphany" had assumed in the ruler-worship of the age is significant. It denoted the manifestation of divine powers in the king or emperor—an Ephesian inscription describes Caesar as ἐπιφανὴς θεός—and hence set the pattern for his worship.[89]

Christian imagination conceived Christ's Epiphany before the Magi in analogy to the *epiphany* motif in contemporary ruler-worship because it saw in the biblical event the manifestation of Christ's kingship and its acknowledgment by the Three Wise Men. On the triumphal monuments of imperial Rome there often appear representations of Orientals presenting gifts, especially golden crowns. These crowns have been identified as the *aurum coronarium* which the defeated enemy solemnly offered to the victorious emperor. The ceremony denoted, of course, the surrender of sovereignty by the vanquished and his acknowledgment that this sovereignty had passed to the conqueror. As Cumont has shown, this triumphal imagery was adopted by early Christian art in representations of the Three Magi: they are dressed as the barbarians are on Roman monuments; they approach Christ in the attitude in which the representatives of vanquished nations are shown to approach the emperor; and the first of the Magi often presents a crown.[90] This last feature is no more than an accurate translation of patristic exegesis into visual imagery. The Fathers, as we have seen, interpreted the gold offered by the first of the Magi as an acknowledgment of Christ's kingship; undoubtedly, they had in mind the golden

crowns presented in Roman *epiphany* ceremonial, a thought which the early Christian artist conveyed by depicting the gold as the *aurum coronarium*[91] (Pl. 45, *b, d*).

All these features made the advent of the Magi the appropriate image to evoke the vision of Christ's Second Epiphany in the liturgical rite. Their journey and adoration embody what may be called the "eschatological," as distinct from the sacrificial, meaning of the offertory procession. The presentation of gifts is an eloquent expression of the sentiments of submission and devotion. "Praise and beauty are before him: holiness and majesty in his sanctuary. Bring up sacrifices, and come into his courts: adore ye the Lord in his holy court." In the Roman liturgy these words from the Ninety-fifth Psalm bespeak the devotional spirit of the eucharistic rite. It is characteristic that the vision of the Second Advent is evoked especially in the hymns chanted during the offertory: as the congregation proceeded toward the altar, it resembled the Epiphany procession of the Magi:

"Rejoice greatly, O daughter of Sion, shout for joy, O daughter of Jerusalem: behold, thy King cometh to thee, holy and the Savior" (Zach., chap. 9 [Ember Saturday of Advent]).

"Lift up your gates, O ye princes, and be ye lifted up, O eternal gates: and the King of glory shall enter in" (Ps. 23 [Christmas Eve]).

"The kings of Tharsis and the Isles shall offer gifts: the kings of the Arabians and of Saba shall bring presents: and all the kings of the earth shall adore him, all nations shall serve him" (Ps. 71 [Epiphany]).

"Sing joyfully to God, all the earth, serve ye the Lord with gladness: come in before his presence with exceeding great joy, for the Lord is God" (Ps. 99 [Sunday, within the Octave of Epiphany]).

Not the hymns of the liturgy, alone, however, evoked the vision of an *epiphany* procession. The eucharistic bread which the congregation brought to the altar had the shape of a crown and was actually called *corona*.[92] The analogy with the *aurum co-*

[94]

ronarium underscored the dual significance of the oblation as sacrifice and *epiphany* offering.

There is neither discordance nor contradiction in this twofold meaning of the oblation. Sacrifices of atonement or propitiation have always been conceived as the expression of man's surrender before the deity; Christianity conceives the sacrifice of man's self as the only offering worthy of God. The mystery of redemption has elicited an oblation through which the believer is united to Christ by imitating the sacrifice of him who was at once victim and priest. The Roman liturgy conveys this ambivalence of the Christian offertory in a way that is especially noteworthy in our present context. On the Sunday within the Octave of the Epiphany the lesson is taken from the letter to the Romans: "Brethren, I beseech you by the mercy of God, that you present your bodies a living sacrifice. . . ." Liturgically, the feast of the Epiphany and the following Sunday are intimately related. The vision of the advent of the Magi illuminates both days. Hence the self-immolation to which St. Paul exhorts the faithful merges here into the image of the Magi offering their gifts; these prefigure the Passion as the Christian oblation represents it. Both are acts of homage to the manifestation of the Lord.

We may sum up as follows: the advent of the Magi, visualized as a procession of the faithful offering gifts in honor of Christ's epiphany, has become, at least since Leo the Great and probably as a result of his exegesis, the image of the Christian's approach to the mystery of redemption. As such it embodied at once the "approach" of the mind in theological perception and that of the entire person in the physical action and mystical reality of the liturgical oblation. Is not this the reason why the advent of the Magi became for the Roman church the mystery of Christ's manifestation to mankind?

VIII

The martyrs have no less a part in the Epiphany vision than did the Magi. In Leo the Great's sermons this idea is expressed very clearly, at first in an intellectual and polemical context. As we have seen, the pope interpreted the feast in the light of the great theological controversies which occupied his mind. Christ's Epiphany appeared to him as the manifestation of the Incarnation, the unfolding of God's union with human nature, a mystery which man cannot perceive without being himself transformed by it. Leo the Great interprets the gifts of the Magi as allegories of this *illuminatio* (the Latin equivalent of the Greek *epiphany*), which the feast renews in every Christian. And he exhorts his flock to be "enlightened" like the Magi, to surrender, to assimilate themselves to the truth which the Epiphany reveals to them. It is in this context that the idea of martyrdom receives a new interpretation.[93]

Leo the Great recalls the "little martyrs," the Innocents slaughtered as martyrs of Christ's birth. He goes on to quote the celebrated passage from the Letter to the Romans (8:35 ff.): "Who then shall separate us from the love of Christ? Shall tribulation? Or distress? Or famine? Or nakedness? Or danger? Or the sword? As it is written: For thy sake we are put to death all the day long. We are accounted as sheep for the slaughter."

The passage has always been understood as an exhortation to physical martyrdom. In the Roman liturgy it is read on the feast of Ignatius of Antioch, as if this martyr himself were pronouncing it. But in the fifth century the danger of persecution had passed. The theological controversies of the time might occasionally involve physical dangers for the leaders of a losing faction; the average Christian felt not his life but the integrity of his faith threatened by denials or distortions of what he held to be orthodox doctrine. This is the peril that Leo the Great had in mind when he declared the steadfast acknowledgment and courageous profession of Christ's nature, as the ecumenical councils had formulated it, to be comparable to martyrdom.

This concept of martyrdom, if characteristic of the age of theological struggles which followed the age of persecution, appears to us pale and diluted in comparison with the vision of the catacombs. And we may be inclined to deny the connection between the heroic fortitude of the martyrs and the obstinate insistence on abstract doctrine. Yet both originated in the same vision, and the theology of the fifth century was an attempt to realize that vision no less fervent, often no less heroic, than was the martyrdom of the third. To the early church the martyr's death and transfiguration confirmed the promise of man's share in the glory of redemption. It was the same religious experience which the great theologians of the following epoch strove to retain in their definition of the union of the divine and human natures in Christ. The ancient Christians saw in martyrdom not only the act of physical courage but, above all, the realization of their faith in man's entire nature. The theologians of the fifth and sixth centuries saw in the attainment of theological truth not only the solution of a philosophical problem but, above all, the illumination of the mind by the divine light which again confirmed the union of God and man on which their hope in the resurrection rested. Both ages conceived the lives of the soul, the mind, and the body as one—hence martyrdom as the realization of truth and truth as the illumination of man's entire existence, since it proved the Incarnation of the Divine Word in human nature.

This experience explains why, as has often been observed, the language of the ancient church hardly distinguishes between the terms "martyr" and "confessor."[94] It also explains why the Three Magi—embodiments of the virtue of confession, as Peter Chrysologus calls them in his Epiphany sermon—are so often likened to the martyrs. Both in the catacombs and on early Christian sarcophagi the Magi appear juxtaposed with the three children in the fiery furnace as if to invite comparison between the first three confessors of the Incarnation and the three martyrs of the Old Testament.[95]

Nevertheless, the mystery of Christ's Epiphany appears fully only in his martyrs. The liturgy conveys this thought time and again, most clearly, per-

haps, on the feast of the protomartyr, Stephen. That it occurs on the day after Christmas is already noteworthy: the martyr's *natalitia*, the anniversary of his birthday (as the church calls his martyrdom), is thus linked to the birthday of Christ. In Stephen's martyrdom the Incarnation bore its first fruit, it became manifest in man. The liturgy chants the words with which the protomartyr gave up his spirit: "I see the heavens opened and Jesus standing at the right hand of the power of God." It is significant that Stephen beholds this vision at the moment of his death. His mind perceives Christ's glory as his body suffers Christ's Passion; and, as the first imitator of Christ, the martyr is also the first to behold the manifestation of Christ's heavenly majesty. The liturgy could not have conveyed the relation of martyrdom and Epiphany more clearly than by placing the feast of the protomartyr between Christmas and Epiphany; in his martyrdom, he seems to embody the mysteries of both days. Once more we invoke the testimony of Leo the Great; in his fifth Epiphany sermon he calls upon the faithful to celebrate this feast by joining those in whom it had become manifest: "Join the society of patriarchs, prophets, apostles and martyrs. Enjoy what they enjoy. . . . For we shall share their dignity whose devotion we have shared. While you still have to execute the commandments of God, glorify God in your bodies [I Cor. 6:2], and shine, beloved, as lights in the world" (Phil. 2:15).[96]

As we have pointed out earlier, however, the mysteries of the church are present not only in the feasts devoted to them but in every eucharistic rite. This explains the presence of the martyrs in the solemn oblation of the sacrifice. Again it is the liturgy on the feast day of St. Stephen which expresses this thought most clearly. Its prayer *super oblata* reads as follows: "Receive O Lord our offerings in commemoration of thy saints: that, as their sufferings rendered them glorious, so our devotion may render us innocent." In other words, the Christian's devotion, of which his oblation is the sacramental token, is here compared to the Passion of the martyr. The clue to this comparison between the liturgical offering and martyrdom is provided by the word "devotion."

In the language of the early church this term had a meaning that it has lost entirely today. Livy calls the death vow of Decius Mus *devotio,* and in speaking of Christian devotion Thomas Aquinas reminds his readers of this ancient meaning of the term.[97] Lactantius uses the word to denote the loyalty, the devotion unto death, which the Christian, like a good soldier, owes to his leader, Christ. By the time of Tertullian, however, *devotio* had already acquired ritual significance as well. Leo the Great calls the eucharistic rite *devotio,* and the ancient liturgical books use the term in this sense. But even in this context it had not lost its original meaning, i.e., the consecration of a sacrificial offering, a gift or a person, to God. The comparison between St. Stephen's *passio* and the *devotio* of the faithful in the text quoted was possible because the donor and his sacrifice were mystically conceived as one.[98]

The commemoration of the martyrs at the moment of the offertory—the vision of the faithful offering his gift in "communion" with the martyrs—finds its explanation in this concept of Christian devotion. The martyrs embody St. Paul's exhortation that the Christian offer up his body as a living host.

Martyrdom and sacrificial oblation, however, were similar not only as acts of devotion but, above all, as representations of the same mystery. We have seen how the early liturgies apply St. Paul's exhortation that the Christian offer his body as a living sacrifice to the ritual oblation. But the martyrs were living embodiments of that exhortation. The Fathers often interpret the dual significance of St. Paul's words in order to convey that relation between *mysterium* and *martyrium* of which we spoke in an earlier chapter.

Of particular interest in this connection are two sermons which Peter Chrysologus of Ravenna delivered on the passage in Romans, chapter 12. He reminds his flock that they are partakers of the regal priesthood of Christ and must therefore imitate his sacrifice. As Christ was at once victim and high priest, so his faithful must also immolate themselves. The bishop of Ravenna is referring to the eucharistic oblation, but he illustrates its sacramental meaning by reminding his audience of the passion of the martyrs.[99]

According to this vision, the offertory procession became a mystical procession of martyrs. In this connection we recall the magnificent *Inlatio* from the Feast of the Baptist's Beheading in the *Missale Gothicum,* quoted in an earlier chapter, in which the believers are envisaged as offering the sacred head of St. John on the altar. It is also significant that the faithful, in the prayer of self-immolation of the Roman rite, impersonate the Three Children in the fiery furnace by repeating their words.[100]

"What the table of the mighty is, we know," writes St. Augustine, "it is the table where the body and blood of Christ are being offered. He who approaches this table must offer the same. And what does it mean to offer the same? As Christ gave his life for us, so we must give our lives for our brethren." "That is what the blessed martyrs did in burning love. And if we do not want to celebrate their memory in vain, if we do not want to come in vain to the meal at which they satisfied themselves, we have to follow their example and prepare something similar; that is why we celebrate the memory of the martyrs on this table. . . ." Because Christ offered his suffering as a repast, only those who imitate his passion are truly partakers of his body and blood: "Coenam suam dedit, passionem suam dedit; ille satuaratur, qui imitatur."[101] These words explain why the martyrs are commemorated at every Mass: the oblation of the faithful becomes a true sacrifice only if he is "in the communion" of the true imitators of Christ.

But the martyrs recall not only the sacrificial nature of the oblation but also its eschatological significance. In his hymn to the eighteen martyrs of Zaragossa, the Spanish poet, Prudentius, paints a grandiose vision of the Last Judgment. In that hour, he says, every Christian city will send out its martyrs to meet the Divine King. Each will carry the instruments of his martyrdom as a sacred gift of propitiation.[102]

This vision of the Christian poet, it will be realized, was not entirely one of things to come. It became mystically present at every Mass. The eucharistic drama, as we saw, re-enacts at once the Passion and the resurrection of Christ and the death and triumph of his martyrs. At the same time, however, it is inspired by the Book of Revelation and its vision of the last things. As the liturgy is celebrated, the basilica becomes the Heavenly Jerusalem, and the living congregation joins the heavenly hosts in adoration of the Lamb. The early Christian experienced this communion with the apostles and martyrs in the hour of worship as an almost tangible reality.[103] As he commemorated their triumph during Mass, he beheld the sublime vision of their entry into the Heavenly Jerusalem and into the presence of the Divine King.

The ancient writers evoke this vision time and again. In the ancient Gallican rite of the dedication of a church the translation of relics into the sanctuary is accompanied by the hymn "Ambulatis sancti Dei, ingredimini in civitatem."[104] The entry of the relics into the basilica is here visualized as the entry of the saints into the Heavenly City. In a sermon delivered prior to the deposition of relics in his church, St. Victricius of Rouen (*saec.* IV) has elaborated this vision. He beholds the majestic procession of martyrs, resplendent in robes and jewelry, which symbolize their virtues, taking possession of the sanctuary as if the Gospel passage had come to life: "Sancti mei fulgebunt sicut sol, in regno Patris."[105] In the liturgy the entry of the apostles and martyrs into the Heavenly Jerusalem and their arrival before the throne of God are not confined to the moment when their relics are deposited in the newly dedicated church. Victricius reminds his listeners that the martyrs have ascended the throne of the Redeemer by the sacrifice of their bodies, by the offering of their passion; that by this imitation of Christ they have really become his body. Hence every re-enactment of Christ's immolation in the eucharistic mys-

tery is also the renewal of the death and transfiguration of his martyrs, and we behold in the liturgical oblation their entry into the Eternal City. The martyrs, as the author of the treatise *De aleatoribus* puts it, are present whenever the oblation is deposited upon the altar.[106]

This is the significance of the commemoration of the apostles and martyrs at the beginning of the canon, and we now understand the relation of this prayer to the offertory cycle. Like the advent of the Magi the mystical procession of saints evokes the twofold meaning of the offertory rite as representation of the Passion and as anticipation of the eternal adoration of the Lamb. The liturgical texts themselves, so restrained, so austere in their language, do not reveal this grandiose meaning of the *Communicantes* entirely. Fortunately, we have the mosaics in Sant' Apollinare which were designed to illuminate the liturgy. We must return to them.

IX

The mosaics in Sant' Apollinare Nuovo are stage decorations, not fully intelligible unless we know the drama for which they were designed. The Christian of the sixth century, who saw them as the backdrop of the offertory rite in which he himself took active part, knew the meaning of these compositions instantly. Even to him, however, these mosaics must have unfolded a vision of unexpected grandeur.

The processions in Sant' Apollinare Nuovo represent the offertory of the congregation. Beginning at the entrance of the nave and solemnly following its rhythm, the martyrs and virgins reach their goal at the end of the nave, i.e., just above the place in front of the altar where the faithful surrendered their oblation during the eucharistic rite.[107] The relation of the mosaics to the congregation is further indicated by a remark of the chronicler Agnellus.[108] He points out that the martyrs are represented *parte virorum*, on the side of the nave assigned to the male congregation, while the virgins appear to address themselves to the women assembled on the opposite side. In its moral and ascetical appeal, early Christian art may not infrequently have taken into consideration the division of sexes which the ancient church order prescribed. The scenes from the Old Testament in Nola, which we know from the description of Paulinus, were selected and distributed according to the same principle.[109] In Sant' Apollinare Nuovo, however, the identification between onlooker and image was designed to be not moral but mystical. The congregation assembled in the basilica knew these saints to be with them in the hour of the mystery.

We have not yet mentioned the feature which must have rendered this identification most moving. The martyrs and virgins are shown offering crowns; the eucharistic bread offered at the altar by the men and women of the congregation was also shaped like a crown and, as we have seen, actually called *corona*. It was this symbol in all its simplicity which revealed the twofold meaning of the offertory which we have described. A few words must be said here about the symbolism of the crown (Pl. 15).

For Christians and Jews, as well as for the rest of the Hellenistic world, the crown was a symbol of immortality and divine glory; hence its function in the initiation rites of nearly all the mysteries.[110] The crown of the Christian martyr has a more specific meaning: it singles him out as the victor in the *agon*, "who has fought a good fight" (II Tim. 4:7). It is noteworthy, however, that in our mosaics the martyrs appear neither wearing their crowns on their heads nor receiving them from Christ but carrying them in their hands. This gesture deserves a word of comment, since, among early patristic writers, both Minutius Felix and Tertullian attest to its significance. The latter's explanation is of special interest for us.[111]

In his treatise *De corona*, Tertullian tells of an occurrence that happened during the distribution of the imperial bounty in a Roman army camp. As was customary on such occasions, the soldiers had appeared with their heads crowned with a laurel wreath. There was one exception. One of the soldiers carried the crown not on his head but in his hand, and, by this gesture alone, Tertullian asserts, he

made it known to everyone that he was a Christian. The consequence of his courage was inevitable. The soldier died at the hand of the executioner and thus earned "the white crown of martyrdom." Tertullian continues as follows:

"Blush, ye fellow soldiers of his, henceforth not to be condemned even by him but by some soldier of Mithras who, at his initiation in the gloomy cavern . . . when, at the sword's point a crown is presented to him, as though in mimicry of martyrdom, and thereupon is put upon his head, is admonished to resist and cast it off, and, if you like, transfer it to his shoulder, saying that Mithras is his crown. And thenceforth he is never crowned; and he had that for a mark to show who he is, if anywhere he be subjected to trial in respect to his religion and he is at once believed to be a soldier of Mithras if he throws the crown away—if he says that in his God he has his crown."

What is remarkable about this curious passage is not only the spirit of rivalry between Christianity and Mithraism which it suggests. It shows that the ritual and imagery which the mystery religions shared often were derived from the political ceremonial of the ancient world. The gesture by which Tertullian's martyr acknowledges his allegiance to Christ recalls the presentation of the *aurum coronarium* to the Roman emperor. The oblations of the martyrs and virgins in Sant' Apollinare Nuovo are likewise inspired by the secular pageant. In fact, it is not only the individual figure but also the processions, in their entirety, which here reflect the *epiphany* ceremonial of Hellenistic ruler-worship. We have only to compare the mosaics with descriptions of the pageant which greeted the advent of the earthly monarch to perceive the similarity: the population of the city went out to greet the sovereign, dressed in white robes and carrying golden crowns or, occasionally, certain sacred objects. The order of these processions indicated the social order of the population, precedence being conceded either to the great political dignitaries of the city or to the priesthood.[112]

Now we have seen that the processions of virgins and martyrs in Sant' Apollinare Nuovo, like the "literary" processions of the liturgical canons, also observed the hierarchical order of the saints represented. The same is true of the order in which the members of the Christian congregation in the basilica carried their gifts to the altar. They were reminded by the images of the white-robed martyrs and virgins above them that the liturgical procession, too, had an eschatological meaning.

Early Christian vision of the Second Advent was profoundly affected by the Hellenistic *epiphany* rite. St. Paul's description of the Lord's appearance on the Day of Judgment and of the living, the dead, and the risen going out to meet him borrows its imagery from that secular ceremonial,[113] and so does early Christian art in illustrating the prophecy of the apostle and enlarging upon it. As renderings of the eschatological motif, the processions in Sant' Apollinare Nuovo are not without parallel. Apostles carrying crowns appear in the fifth-century Baptistry of the Orthodox in Ravenna and in the sixth-century basilica of Parenzo; the composition in SS. Cosmas e Damiano in Rome is the most magnificent among many similar compositions which attest to the importance of the vision of the *parousia* in the ancient liturgies.[114] A slight variation of the theme was presented by the mosaics with which Sixtus III (432–40) adorned the basilica of Santa Maria Maggiore in Rome.[115] Here, as in the vision of Prudentius, the martyrs appeared with the instruments of their passion; as the inscription would indicate, however, the martyrs were seen approaching the Virgin, a theme especially fitting in this church, which was to be a monument to Mary's dignity as Mother of God, which the Council of Ephesus had just proclaimed. In representing the Virgin as receiving the homage of martyrs, the mosaics in Santa Maria Maggiore seem to have been an interesting antecedent to those in Sant' Apollinare Nuovo, although these are unique both in their explicit relation to the liturgy and in their linking of the *epiphany* processions of the martyrs to the Advent of the Magi. It is this feature which

conveys the mystical and liturgical significance of the oblation as the *aurum coronarium* offered to the Divine King. The advent scene has been heavily restored. But the analogy of early Christian iconography suggests that here, too, the first of the Magi may have been depicted offering a crown. This object would have made the relation between the Magi and the martyrs even more explicit.

The mosaic on the opposite wall conveys the relation of martyrdom to the liturgical sacrifice. Facing the advent of the Magi is Christ enthroned—an image of unforgettable grandeur—surrounded by four angels.[116] The scene is like an illustration of the Introit for the Sunday within the Octave of the Epiphany: "Upon a high throne I saw a Man sitting, whom a multitude of Angels adored singing together: 'Behold him the name of whose empire is to eternity' " (Pls. 30, 41).

Into Christ's presence St. Martin introduces the host of martyrs. The pre-eminence given to this saint is justifiable, in view of the fact that Archbishop Agnellus dedicated the basilica to him. It is not impossible, however, that here, too, as in the Advent mosaic, restorations have not left the original composition intact. A Franciscan chronicler of the late sixteenth century, entirely reliable otherwise, mentions explicitly that the procession of martyrs was headed not by St. Martin but by St. Stephen and that the title saint occupied the second place. This assertion appears all the more likely, since the present mosaic seems to leave a slight gap between the figures of Christ and St. Martin[117] (Pl. 44).

The image of the protomartyr in this place would have been eminently appropriate. He enjoyed a special cult in Ravenna, and his place in the veneration of the entire church is indicated by the ancient litanies in which he almost invariably—and most fittingly—opens the "literary processions" of martyrs.[118] As we have seen, in the Roman liturgy it is St. Stephen who conveys the mystical meaning of the liturgical oblation as an imitation of Christ's sacrifice: the *Secreta* on his feast draws that parallel between martyrdom and the devotion of the faithful of which the *corona* is the symbol. In Sant' Apollinare Nuovo the figure of the protomartyr offering Christ the crown of his martyrdom would have conveyed the second, ascetical meaning of the offertory rite as imitation of Christ's sacrifice.

The early church conceived Christ as the first martyr. The ancient sacramentaries convey this thought no less than does patristic literature.[119] And the Passion cycle of Sant' Apollinare Nuovo is but one example of the expression of this thought in art.[120] In a sense—and this idea is expressed frequently—Christ is indeed the only martyr.[121] For his imitators, the martyrs, merely partake of his Passion and resurrection; their glory would be impossible without his. Of this idea the crown of martyrdom is an expression; it is the crown with which Christ has been rewarded and which he alone may wear. Early Christian art has suggested this idea by transforming the crown of thorns into the crown of martyrdom, more frequently by placing a crown over Christ's head but also by depicting the martyrs not wearing the crown but offering it to Christ in the very gesture which Tertullian demanded.[122] The pseudo-Augustinian commentary on the Book of Revelation explains the theological significance of this gesture by pointing out that the Elders "cast their crowns" before the throne of God (4:10) in order to honor him to whom their glory is entirely due.[123] Hence the oblation of the martyr's crown indicates not only the imitative nature of the sacrifice but also the doctrine that man can accomplish nothing on his own and that, even in his sacrifice, he merely returns to God what he has received by grace.

The Transfiguration mosaic in Sant' Apollinare in Classe conveys the theology of the consecratory act; the procession mosaics in Sant' Apollinare Nuovo that of the offertory. Since the apse of this sanctuary had already collapsed when the chronicler Agnellus wrote his description, we cannot know for certain what subject was represented there. It is all the more fortunate that, in the nave of the one basilica and in the sanctuary of the other, the two compositions have survived which convey the acts of the liturgical drama to which the two parts of a church are dedicated. Between works of such quality no comparison is possible or useful. But we have to devote a few remarks to the artistic aspects of the mosaics in Sant' Apollinare Nuovo, since it is not the dignity of the subject matter alone but, above all, the mode of its expression which accounts for the beauty of a work of art.

X

The language of these mosaics is remarkable, above all, for its restraint. The processions of virgins and martyrs are completely integrated into the architecture, they follow the rhythm of the columns which support the arcades; but by doing so they transform the architecture itself into an offertory procession. The oblation of crowns is a motif of utmost simplicity, as if the basic meaning of the rhythm was not to be disturbed. The very slight variations at the head of the processions—Epiphany on the one side and what might be described as the image of Imitation on the other—are sufficient to bestow upon that simple processional pattern the full grandeur of its twofold meaning.

We have already spoken of the biblical sources of the concept of imitation. It is noteworthy that the very language of the Bible presents it under a definite physical image:[124] the Pharisees observe angrily that "the whole world *goes after* [Christ]" (John 12:19); Christ himself calls the imitation a "coming after me" (Matt. 16:24; Luke 9:23); Peter asserts that by suffering for the gospel we "follow Christ's steps," being converted to the shepherd and bishop of souls (I Pet. 2:21 and 25). The same image occurs in the Gospel of St. John. Christ is the shepherd who "goes before them, and his sheep follow him because they know his voice" (10:4). In other words, the imitation of Christ, of which the offertory is the mystical realization, appears in the language of the New Testament under the image of the same processional pattern that the liturgical rite prescribed. The procession of martyrs in Sant' Apollinare Nuovo conveys this meaning of the oblation, just as the virgins convey its eschatological significance as a pageant greeting the epiphany of the Divine King. The simplicity of this language is as admirable as is its poetic sensitivity.

The restraint of the mosaics is also due to their function as settings for the liturgical drama. They are not meant to be complete, and they reveal their full significance and their life only when the eucharistic sacrifice is being celebrated in the basilica. They have necessarily appeared dry and monotonous and awkward to the *cicerones* of the nineteenth century, who did not realize that they were gazing at the decorations of an empty stage.[125] But if one looks at these mosaics while the liturgy is being enacted, one realizes that its solemn testimony is also that of the virgins and martyrs, who suddenly seem to gain life and to unfold before us the vision of the Celestial City.

We spoke of the way in which each of these compositions addresses itself to one part of the congregation. To each of them they seem to convey that meaning of their sacrifice to which their natures must be particularly sensitive. The epiphany motif is stronger in the procession of virgins. In the beauty of their bridal garments they seem to appeal to the women of sixth-century Ravenna to follow the wise virgins who went out to meet the heavenly bridegroom. The bridal image is in the ancient liturgies particularly associated with the idea of Christ's *parousia,* his mysterious advent at the hour of the sacrifice. At the end of the Armenian liturgy there occurs the following hymn: "Mother of faith, thou shrine of holy spousals, heavenly bridechamber, home of thine immortal bridegroom who hath adorned thee forever: a marvellous second heaven art thou from glory to glory exalted, which by the laver dost regenerate us children radiant like the light, Thou that dost distribute this spotless bread and givest us to drink this pure blood. . . ." After all have partaken of communion, the chant continues: "Our God and our Lord hath appeared to us. Blessed is he that cometh in the name of the Lord."[126]

The Christian mystery, in analogy to the *hieros gamos* of the pagan mysteries, is here conceived as the wedding feast of the heavenly bridegroom, who adorns his bride, the soul, with the resplendent garment of the resurrection. The thought occurs also in the Nestorian liturgy: "O ye that have been invited by the great purpose to the living marriage feast. . . ."[127] The bridechamber where the sacred union takes place is the sanctuary of the basilica. In his exposition of the liturgical rite, Narsai describes the sanctuary "as a type of the kingdom of God which our Lord entered": "A beauteous bridechamber He has fitted on earth for a type of that which is above, that they may delight therein mystically until the end."[128]

The procession of virgin martyrs in Sant' Apollinare Nuovo presents the eschatological meaning of the liturgy as a bridal vision, inviting the women of Ravenna to approach the sanctuary as the wise virgins who go out to meet the Spouse on the Day of Judgment. This appeal to feminine experience, this divination of an insight of which perhaps only the feminine psyche is capable, occurs occasionally also in the ancient homiletical literature.[129] The mosaics in Sant' Apollinare Nuovo are the most beautiful artistic evidence of the active share which Christian worship assigned to every member of the ancient church; they also reflect a concept of man which called not only upon the intellect but upon human nature in its entirety to experience and to live the mysteries of redemption (Pl. 34).

This appeal of the mosaics is partly due to the skill with which Archbishop Agnellus made use of the older works that he found in the basilica. Our difficulty in finding the incision which separates his mosaics from those of his Arian predecessors is proof of a very great achievement on his part. Joined to the thirty-two older figures in the zone above, the procession seems to present "the society of patriarchs, prophets, apostles and martyrs" with whom Leo the Great had exhorted the faithful to behold the glory of the Epiphany. The Advent of the Magi, in turn, is as intimately linked to the procession of virgin martyrs as it is to the two christological scenes above: The bridal motif is like a reflection of the liturgy which envisages the Epiphany as the *hieros gamos* of the church and her celestial bridegroom. The Wedding at Cana and the Multiplication of the Loaves belonged likewise in the Epiphany cycle; the Gallican and Mozarabic liturgies mention these miracles along with the advent of the Magi as the mysteries of this feast, and the same thought occurs in a celebrated Epiphany hymn which is in all probability the work of St. Ambrose of Milan.[130] On the other hand, the Wedding at Cana fits beautifully into the bridal motif of the entire left wall. It is not impossible that even the mosaics that date back to the Arian epoch of the basilica take cognizance of the fact that this side of the nave was reserved for the women of the congregation: besides the Wedding at Cana, the Woman of the Issue of Blood, the Samaritan Woman, and the Widow's Mite carry a special message to the female observer. Even if this was not the original intention, however, Agnellus' procession of virgins blends beautifully into these representations.

The same is true for the opposite wall. Certainly, the contemplation of Christ's Passion, the *Imitatio Christi,* is not the concern of men only. Nevertheless, the mosaics render the Passion in what might also be called a "heroic" way, which seems to stress the virtues of courage and undaunted confession, by which that age and society would expect men rather than women to give testimony to the truth. Here, again, the procession of martyrs and the Passion cycle complement each other.

XI

The restraint, the simplicity, and the wise and sensitive adaptation of these mosaics to the existing architecture and decoration of the basilica do not yet explain entirely the secret power with which they move us. This seems to be due also to the fact that they convey the meaning of the Christian faith in terms of the elementary experience which all human beings share and in which all religious faith may originate: the experience of death. An enemy of Christianity like Emperor Julian the Apostate was not altogether wrong when he pointed to the cult of tombs as one of the main characteristics of the young faith.[131] The monuments of the ancient church remind us consistently that we can understand the message of redemption only if we can understand the meaning of death. This knowledge is conveyed by the architecture of the Christian sanctuaries as well as by the images which adorn them. Recent discoveries have shown how much not only the domed church of the East but even the Christian basilica owes to sepulchral architecture.[132] And, among the mosaics we have discussed in this essay, both those of San Vitale and those of Sant' Apollinare in Classe betray the influence of funerary imagery.[133] Even more obvious is this derivation in Sant' Apollinare Nuovo. In the christological cycles and in the procession of martyrs the use of mortuary imagery appears significant and deliberate.

Both the advent of the Magi and the processions of apostles and martyrs approaching Christ have often been represented on early Christian sarcophagi, as well as in the catacombs.[134] Of special interest for us is a number of sarcophagi in Ravenna which undoubtedly had been completed by the time that the mosaics in Sant' Apollinare Nuovo were executed.

On the front of the sarcophagus of the exarch Isaacius in San Vitale there are represented the three Magi, hurrying with their gifts into the presence of the Mother of God. The infant Christ upon her knees extends his hands to receive their offerings. As patristic exegesis indicates, the advent of the Magi may symbolize the advent of the blessed soul in heaven. The reason for this interpretation will be given presently. That this is the meaning of the scene on the sarcophagus is shown by the representations on the remaining sides; the left end shows the Raising of Lazarus, the right one, Daniel in the Lion's Den, both frequently employed in Christian mortuary art as images of resurrection. The back is adorned by the labarum between fruit-bearing palm trees and peacocks—the early Christian symbols of eternal life.¹³⁵

Processions of apostles or martyrs with the crowns of martyrdom occur frequently on Roman sarcophagi, though not on the sarcophagi of Ravenna which have survived.¹³⁶ Several of these, however, represent Christ enthroned in the center, while apostles or martyrs, some of whom carry crowns and others the cross as the scepter of their triumph, are seen approaching Christ from either side. The most interesting and beautiful of these is the so-called "Rinaldo" sarcophagus in Ravenna Cathedral.¹³⁷ Here Christ is depicted seated upon a mountain. That the scene is laid in Paradise is indicated by the four rivers emerging from the rock. The representation is in several aspects quite similar to the central mosaic in San Vitale. The Lord holds a book in his left hand (though not closed, as in San Vitale, but open), and it has justly been remarked that this motif—"the book of life of the Lamb" (Rev. 21:27) —belongs in the iconography of the Last Judgment. It seems to have its prototype, however, in the ceremonial of imperial Rome. On the Marcus column the Emperor Marcus Aurelius is depicted receiving a delegation from the East. In his left hand he holds a *volumen,* "undoubtedly the text of a treaty concluded with the barbarians."¹³⁸ With his right he seems to be distributing gifts.

It will be noticed that the apostles approaching Christ from either side incline their bodies in a gesture of reverence which resembles that with which the ambassadors receive the gifts of Marcus Aurelius and also, incidentally, that of the Three Magi. Furthermore, the barbarians receive the imperial gifts with veiled hands: the apostles carry their crowns in the same manner.¹³⁹ It is not altogether clear, however, whether these crowns are received or offered. One is at first inclined to suppose the latter. But the analogy with the mosaic in San Vitale, as well as Christ's gesture, suggests that he has just distributed the reward. The ambivalence of the representation may well arise from the ambivalence of the crown

symbolism, which is at once heavenly reward and token of man's devotion (cf. Pl. 45, *c*).

Two other features of the relief deserve consideration. The representation of Christ enthroned recalls the imperial ceremony of distribution of the *congiarium* as depicted on the Arch of Constantine. Here, too, the emperor is shown seated on a throne in the center, while on either side senators stand ready to receive his bounty in the folds of their togas.¹⁴⁰ The analogy between such secular representations and the sarcophagus, the sources of which will occupy us later, is even more marked in a representation on the base of the Emperor Theodosius' obelisk in Constantinople (*ca.* A.D. 400). Here the emperor is represented distributing victory crowns to the winners in the circus games.¹⁴¹ The eschatological content of the scene on the Rinaldo sarcophagus is indicated not only by the Book of Life and the "seat of majesty" (cf. Matt. 25:31) on which Christ is seated but also by the palm trees and the clouds behind him. According to St. Paul's eschatological vision (I Thess. 4:17), the blessed will be taken up together "in the clouds to meet Christ, into the air: and so shall we be always with the Lord." The relief, however, blends this scene with the other image which the apostle has evoked so often—the coronation with the crown of glory as a symbol of the heavenly reward. The fusion of the two motifs is, very likely, no invention of Christian art; it had already appeared in the resurrection hymn of Ephrem Syrus, which preceded the Ravenna sarcophagi by a century. This vision, no doubt, facilitated the interpretation of the advent of the Magi, so similar in most iconographical features, as a symbol of the soul's advent in heaven¹⁴² (Pls. 4, 5).

The translation of these mortuary scenes into the Christian sanctuary should not surprise us. The church, too, is a tomb: it is the Easter sepulcher not only of Christ but also of his saints and, indeed, of every Christian. "Yesterday," Gregory Nazianzen says, "I suffered with Christ on the Cross. Today I am entering into glory with him. I was buried with him yesterday, I rise again with him today. Let us be gods for his sake, he became man for ours."[143] These words refer to the celebration of Easter, but they also describe the experience which underlies the entire liturgy of the ancient church. By reminding the onlooker of this meaning of the Christian mystery, the mosaics in Sant' Apollinare Nuovo hint at the deepest meaning of Christian, perhaps of all, religious worship. In order to understand the ultimate message of these compositions, we must recall how similar the experience of death which they convey is to that which permeates the Christian rite.

The Hellenistic mysteries not only have in common the belief in redemption through imitation or impersonation of the god's myth by the initiate but also share the experience and ritual in which that redemption is represented as the initiate's death and his resurrection or rebirth. As a result we find a most noteworthy affinity between the rites of initiation and ancient funerary ceremonial.

This is perhaps most obvious in the mysteries of the Egyptian god, Osiris. The ancient religion of Egypt has justly been called a "religion of death." In no other religion is the origin of mythology and worship in the experience of death more apparent. The striking similarities between Egyptian funerary rites and the cult of Osiris have their reason in the avowed purpose of transforming the dead into another Osiris. The dead man here "impersonates" the dead god in order to participate in the god's mythical resurrection. On Egyptian tombs we read inscriptions like "I am Osiris." The Book of the Dead, the oldest of funerary liturgies, evokes this identity of the God and the dead in a language which recalls the paradigmatic prayers of the early church: ". . . who didst make Osiris to be victorious over his enemies, make thou [here follows the name of the dead] to be victorious over his enemies."[144]

One may ask whether the myth is really the source of the funerary ritual or whether the ritual has not created the myth. Is not the image of the dying and rising Osiris the objectivation of the experience of fear and hope which, since the dawn of mankind, has moved every human heart in the pres-

ence of death? However that may be, it should be borne in mind that funerary rites are life-giving rites. Enactment of the god's funeral must therefore impart new life to the dead for whom it was celebrated or even for the living, who in this funerary ceremony impersonated the god.

The Hellenistic mysteries do not conceive the redemption of the initiate as taking place only after death. As he impersonates the god's death and resurrection in the sacred drama, the divine life is bestowed upon him even while he is still on earth. But this rebirth is the result of death. The initiate dies in order to be reborn; his initiation is in some decisive aspects his burial.

The ceremony of initiation makes the novice experience the horrors of death. He may either enact the god's sacrificial death or his migration through the shadows of the underworld. But at the end of this fearful ritual he beholds the vision of eternal bliss, and it is this vision which is evidence of his transfiguration into the risen god. (This transformation through ecstatic vision, incidentally, is one of the profoundest insights of religious experience. It may be recalled that, in the *Divine Comedy*, Dante's gradual ascent from hell through purgatory to heaven is not the description of an eschatological panorama but the confession of the gradual illumination of the poet's soul, a metamorphosis not unlike that of Apuleius. The spiritual journey begins on Good Friday and ends on Easter Sunday; it is wholly related to the mystery of Christ's death and resurrection, which the church celebrates during these days.)

The Christian rite of initiation is baptism. We have already described this sacrament as a funerary rite. The catechumen is buried in the baptismal font as in a tomb. Emerging from it, he received a white robe. The white robe figures in many Hellenistic rites of initiation but seems to have its origin in funerary ritual, where its symbolic and magical meaning is certain. The dead man is buried in a white garment as a magical image of the heavenly body he is to "put on" at the time of the resurrection. In the mysteries the white robe denotes the initiate's resurrection and, more precisely, his transfiguration into the risen god. The resplendent robe which Lucius receives in Apuleius' *Golden Ass* identifies him with his god.[145] It has the same significance in the Christian baptism: "All you," writes St. Paul (Gal. 3:27), "who have been baptized in Christ, have put on Christ." The old man has died in the font, Christ has risen. The Christian has received the garment of resurrection. "Receive the white garment," the priest says in bestowing this gift upon the newly baptized, "which mayest thou wear without stain before the judgment seat of our Lord Jesus Christ, that thou mayest have life everlasting."

What renders such mortuary symbolism particularly meaningful is the fact that the newly baptized represents not only Christ's resurrection on Easter morning but his own future resurrection from the dead. This is apparent in the beautiful response from the nocturnal office of Saturday after Easter: "Isti sunt agni novelli, qui annuntiaverunt, alleluja: modo venerunt ad fontes. Repleti sunt claritate, alleluja, alleluja. In conspectu Agni amicti sunt stolis albis, et palmae in manibus eorum."

The vision, of course, is that of the great multitude described in the Book of Revelation (7:9), "clothed with white robes, and palms in their hands," whom the "Lamb has led to the fountains of life." That the neophytes are here compared to those who have washed their robes white in the blood of the lamb is significant. The Saturday after Easter, the *Sabbatum in albis,* was the last day on which the neophytes wore their white garments. The liturgy of this day emphasizes the symbolic meaning of this garb. Paul's words to the Galatians are quoted in the *Communio.* But the other liturgical texts of the day make it clear that the robe of Christ refers not only to the catechumen's resurrection from the baptismal font but also to his future resurrection from the dead. It is as if the liturgy of the day on which the insignia of resurrection are worn for the last time seeks to link this rebirth with that which the Christian expects on the Day of Judgment. Hence

the frequent parallels between baptism and resurrection:

Collect: "Grant, we beseech thee, almighty God, that we who have reverently celebrated the Easter festival, may deserve through it to arrive at eternal joys."

Secreta: "Grant us, we beseech thee, O Lord, ever to rejoice in these Paschal mysteries: that the continued work of redemption may be to us a source of perpetual joy."

This prayer *super oblata* deserves special attention. The neophyte's first participation in the eucharistic meal followed immediately upon baptism.[146] Our prayer is still an echo of the feelings with which the newly baptized, in the white robes of the risen, approached the divine meal. They could not but recall the words of the Book of Revelation: "Blessed are they that are called to the marriage supper of the Lamb" (19:9). It is no coincidence that the liturgy of the Saturday *in albis* envisages the Christian mystery as a preparation for the heavenly meal in the Kingdom of God. At the same time, however, the prayer states explicitly that the joy of the paschal mysteries and the perpetual joy that is to come are not separated by a chasm but that death and resurrection of the faithful are "continued" in the sacrificial oblation of Christ whenever the eucharistic mystery is celebrated. This rite thus becomes the confirmation of Paul's words that the Christian is "renewed day by day" (II Cor. 4:16). And we may ask whether in this sense the Mass, like baptism, is not a funerary rite, the Christian's burial and resurrection.

The time concept of the mysteries conceived the sacred events enacted as present *hic et nunc.* On Christmas and on Easter Sunday the liturgy speaks of Christ's birth and resurrection as occurring *today.* In one ancient liturgical prayer the Mass is referred to as the original act of redemption.[147] The ancient idea of imitation, furthermore, conceived these sacred events as mysteriously real in the faithful. This twofold experience established a secret correspondence between the mystery of Christ's death and the death of the faithful. It assigned to the eucharistic drama its place in the Christian funeral; and the mystery of Christ's death and resurrection became also the mystery of the resurrection of the dead.

The apocryphal Acts of Matthew have the following legend concerning the apostle's death: Having put the saint to death, the king "had a coffin made of iron and sealed it with lead, and privately put it on a ship at midnight and sank it in the sea. All night the brethren watched at the palace gate"; at dawn a voice came: commanding the bishop of the city, Plato, to take the gospel and the psalter and go to the east of the palace and sing Alleluia, and read the gospel and to "offer up the bread and the vine . . . and communicate with me, as the Lord Jesus showed us the offering that is above, on the third day after he rose. So it was done, and the chanter went up on a great stone and sang: Precious in the sight of the Lord. . . . I slept and rose up again. . . . And they answer: Shall not the sleeper awake? . . . Now will I arise, saith the Lord. Alleluia. They read the gospel and made the offering. It was about the sixth hour, and Plato looked out to sea seven stadia away, and lo, Matthew standing on the sea between two men in bright apparel. . . ."[148]

It is obvious that the recital of Christ's resurrection has here effected the resurrection of the apostle. The thought of this immediate participation of the dead in the resurrection of Christ occurs many times in the ancient liturgies.[149] A liturgical prayer in the *Apostolic Constitutions* asks that the dead be granted a part in the mystery of Christ's resurrection, that they may rise with him.[150] The Nestorian liturgy has the following passage: "Lo all the departed lay down in thine hope that in the glorious resurrection thou mightest raise them up in glory."[151] The idea is always implicit that, since Christ's resurrection is presently taking place in the mystery rite, the resurrection of the dead will also be effected at that moment. This idea has influenced both the Christian funerary rite and the eucharistic liturgy itself, or rather it led to a significant affinity between them.

The *Apostolic Constitutions,* which are no later than A.D. 400, already prescribe Masses for the dead on the third, eighth, and fortieth days after his death; counting from Christ's death, these dates correspond to his resurrection, his appearance among the disciples, and his Ascension.[152] The correspondence is undoubtedly deliberate. In the Roman rite the same thought appears both in the Mass of the dead and in the eucharistic liturgy itself. We first quote the relevant passages from the Mass of the dead.

Collect: "O God, who art ever ready to have mercy and to spare, we humbly beseech thee in behalf of the soul of thy servant . . . whom thou hast this day called out of this world, that thou wouldst not deliver him [her] into the hands of the enemy, nor forget him forever, but command the holy angels to take him and lead him to the home of paradise, that forasmuch as in thee he put his hope and trust he may not endure the pains of hell, but may come to the possession of eternal joys."

The *Lesson* gives Paul's vision of Christ's Epiphany for the resurrection of the dead with which we are already familiar. It is of interest that the lesson for All Souls' Day, which is intimately related to the liturgy of the dead, gives the other Pauline vision of the Resurrection (I Cor., chap. 15), in which the apostle predicts that man's corruptible body "must put on incorruption, and this mortal put on immortality"—again the vision of new life as the garment of immortality put on by the dead. The *Gospel* narrates the resurrection of Lazarus.

Offertory: "O Lord Jesus Christ, King of Glory, deliver the souls of all the faithful departed from the pains of hell and from the deep pit: deliver them from the mouth of the lion, that hell may not swallow them up, and they may not fall into darkness; but may the holy standard bearer Michael introduce them to the holy light: Which thou didst promise of old to Abraham and to his seed. We offer to thee, O Lord, sacrifice of praise and prayers: do thou receive them in behalf of those souls whom we commemorate this day: grant them, O Lord, to pass from death to life."

Super oblata: "Look favorably, we beseech thee, O Lord, upon the offerings we make on behalf of the soul of thy servant N., that being cleansed by heavenly remedies, it may rest in thy mercy."

Communio: "May light eternal shine upon them, O Lord, with thy saints, for ever, because thou art merciful."

Three facts are noteworthy in these texts: they invoke the image of the dead's resurrection. This resurrection is envisaged as taking place not in the future but in the hour in which the sacrifice in commemoration of the dead is being enacted. In this sacrifice the mystery of Christ's death and resurrection blends imperceptibly into the mystery of the resurrection of the deceased.

This is particularly noticeable in the offertory, which has been preserved in its ancient form. The text has caused a good many difficulties, since it seems to invoke the redemption even of those who already are in hell.[153] But we have already seen that such time concepts have no meaning in the religious experience of the ancient church: the prayer is envisaged as being offered for the dying, at a moment, as it were, in which God's judgment is still pending; it retains its character even if said after man's death.

A further explanation is suggested, however, by the mystical identification between the soul of the dead and the sacrifice offered. St. Michael, whom the canon of the eucharistic rite invokes as the angel of the sacrifice, also appears here as the *psychopompos* who conveys the soul to heaven. These two offices of the archangel are in reality one, since the soul of man partakes of Christ's resurrection, of which the sacrifice is the sacramental realization.

The dead are present not only in the Mass offered on their behalf but in every eucharistic rite. It would not be altogether incorrect to say that, like the martyrs, those who have departed in the Lord are present in the Christian mystery, with this difference, however, that, whereas the transfiguration of the saints is celebrated, that of the other dead is requested in the prayers of the eucharistic drama. In virtue of this solemn function every Mass is a funerary, or,

rather, a life-giving, rite: "with this sacrifice the priest absolves all the departed for it has the power to vanquish death."[154] The mystery of redemption transfigures all Christians, the martyrs and saints no less than the departed. Hence all are present at its enactment, all are commemorated after the sacred oblation; and hence, also, the sepulchral symbolism employed in the representations of these martyrs in the offertory mosaics in Sant' Apollinare Nuovo.[155]

The Roman Canon, like that of Milan and, in all probability, that of Ravenna, divides its martyrs into two distinct groups. The first, as we saw, is mentioned immediately after the offertory as being "in communion" with those who offer. The second group of martyrs, which includes all the virgins mentioned in the canon, appears in the "Nobis quoque," a prayer which follows after the consecration and immediately after the prayer for the dead and is, in fact, as directly related to it as the *Communicantes* is to the oblation.[156]

It is noteworthy that the later prayers of intercession follow immediately upon the solemn invocation of Christ's death and resurrection; that they ask that not only the dead but also the living members of the congregation may enjoy the communion with the martyrs; and that here, as in the *Communicantes,* this communion is envisaged as an event not of the future but of the present. The moment of the consecration realizes the Resurrection of Christ and of his faithful united in his Mystical Body; and, as the sacrifice ascends heavenward, there is unfolded the vision of the Resurrection, when not only "the dead who are in Christ" but also "we who are alive, who are left, shall be taken up together with them in the clouds to meet Christ."

The separation of the two commemorative prayers of intercession in the Roman rite has caused much speculation, all the more since these prayers form a solid chain in most of the other liturgies and since, in the Byzantine as well as in the Syro-Monophysite rites, their place is after the consecration.[157] We should like to suggest that the different arrangement in the Roman rite finds its explanation in the dramatic significance of the different acts of the mystery drama and especially in their relation to death and resurrection. Although, as we have insisted before, the liturgy conceives Christ's death and resurrection as inseparable, the offertory, as the representation of Christ's immolation, is more specifically related to his death,[158] the consecration (*transfiguratio*) to his resurrection. Quite fittingly, therefore, the vision of man's death is also evoked in offertory prayers. "Lo all the departed lay down in thine hope [the offertory of the Nestorian liturgy reads] that in the glorious resurrection thou mightest raise them up in glory."[159] Similarly in the liturgies of the West: the Gallican offertory asks that the dead, as well as the living, may partake of the resurrection of Christ.[160] The idea of death is even more pronounced in the offertory prayers of the Roman rite.

Time and again, the prayers *super oblata* in the Gregorian sacramentary ask that the faithful be purged from his frailty, that he be absolved from the chains of sin, that his body as well as his mind be sanctified. The sacrament is envisaged as a medicine; one feels that the chains of sin are also the chains of death and that these prayers over the oblation, like the offertory for the dead, is a prayer for resurrection. It is significant that the second *Secreta* during the season of Lent, which is deeply pervaded by the fear and experience of death, asks for protection from all enemies of body and soul and the glory of the future life.[161]

But, if the oblation of the sacrifice thus presents at once the death of Christ and that of the faithful, the *transfiguratio* of the sacrifice in the moment of consecration evokes the vision of the Resurrection. "In verity," Narsai says, "did the Lord of the Mystery rise from the midst of the tomb; and without doubt the Mystery acquires the power of life. On a sudden, the bread and wine acquire new life; and forgiveness of iniquity they give on a sudden to them that receive them";[162] not only forgiveness of iniquity to the living but also the glory of the resurrection to the dead: in his famous *Expositio brevis* the Pseudo-Germanus of Paris says explicitly that

the dead are commemorated at the moment of consecration because this act denotes Christ's Advent for the resurrection of the dead.[163]

This thought also appears in the Eastern liturgies. Their consecratory prayers, the so-called *epikleseis,* invoke the descent of the Holy Ghost not only over the sacrifice but over the faithful; the fact that these are usually mentioned ahead of the sacrifice suggests that the original intent of the *epiklesis* was the transfiguration of the faithful rather than of the sacrifice. It is equally significant that the descent of sanctifying grace is here visualized as the descent of the dove of the Holy Ghost upon Christ during his baptism in the River Jordan.[164] The ritual and imagery of baptism is, as we have seen, a mystery of rebirth, of resurrection. Most fittingly, then, the prayer for the resurrection of the faithful follows immediately upon the *epiklesis;* we give but one example from the liturgy of the Syrian Jacobites:

"Forasmuch then, O Lord, as thou hast the power of life and of death and art a God of mercies and of love towards mankind, vouchsafe to remember all those who have been well-pleasing unto thee since the world began, holy fathers and forefathers, prophets and apostles and John the forerunner and baptist and St. Stephen chief of deacons and first of martyrs, and the holy and glorious mother of God and ever virgin Mary and all saints: We ask of thee, O Lord great in mercies, who makest possible things impossible, unite us to the blessed church, number us with that church, give us a place through thy grace among the firstborn which are written in heaven. For for this cause we too remember them that they too while they stand before thy lofty tribunal may remember our misery and poverty and may offer unto thee with us this fearful and unbloody sacrifice for the care of them that live . . . and for the repose of all them that have fallen asleep aforetime in the *faith of the truth,* our fathers and brethren."[165]

One might say that the meaning of these Eastern prayers of intercession is clearer than that of the Roman: the living and the dead are mentioned together, and the idea of their communion with the saints in the Heavenly City is made more meaningful by the preceding vision of the *epiklesis*. The explanation for this greater intensity or concentration is obvious: the Eastern rites, which have postconsecratory prayers of intercession, date from a time—after the end of the fourth century—when the offertory procession of the laity had been abolished.[166] With this exclusion of the laity, the approximation of man's death and resurrection to the death and resurrection of Christ at the time of the offertory became less meaningful and less palpable. It was therefore only consistent to concentrate all prayers of intercession in the moment after the *epiklesis*.

In the Roman rite, on the other hand, the offertory procession of the faithful was still in practice when the liturgy received its definite shape under Gregory the Great. This fact cannot have failed to affect profoundly the selection and arrangement of the liturgical texts. To the idea of the mystical share of the faithful in the death and Passion of Christ the offertory procession lent reality and actuality. Hence it was only fitting to link the idea of intercession, of the communion of the saints, to this act.[167] But it was no less consistent to mention the dead at the moment of Christ's resurrection, i.e., after the solemn enactment and verbal commemoration of these events.[168] As the idea of the sanctification of the faithful and the sacrifice receives expression in the distinct rites of offertory and consecration (although the two sacrifices can in no sense be conceived as separate), so the two prayers of intercession in the Roman rite must be understood as intimately related. Here, too, death is swallowed up in victory. If the offertory may be described as a funerary rite, expressing the self-immolation of the faithful in imitation of the death of Christ and if the moment of consecration anticipates the resurrection of the dead for the Second Epiphany, the same reality and the same experience pervade both parts of the liturgy. Man is made to live the mystery of redemption by being reminded of the agony of death and by divining the glory which he is to inherit.

Like the liturgy, the mosaics in Sant' Apollinare Nuovo borrow mortuary imagery in order to unfold the vision of the Book of Revelation.[169] The processions of martyrs are those who have washed their robes white in the blood of the Lamb, whom the Lamb has led to the fountains of the waters of life. But they also remind the onlooker of Christ's own words: ". . . the hour cometh wherein all that are in the graves shall hear the voice of the Son of God. And they that have done good things shall come forth unto the resurrection of life. . . ." It is the secret of these mosaics that they make the tremor of death the medium through which man perceives the vision of his transfiguration, through which he is enabled to join the communion of saints even while in this life.

The spiritual and poetical message of the compositions in Sant' Apollinare Nuovo transcends the concern of any particular epoch. In their theological and liturgical language, however, they reflect a historical moment, less dramatic than that which Maximian immortalized in his artistic projects and strangely contrasting with these; but this very contrast is of great historical significance. If we compare San Vitale and Sant' Apollinare in Classe, on the one hand, and Sant' Apollinare Nuovo, on the other, the two first works are as Byzantine as the last one is Roman. To this contrast and its implications we have to devote the last chapter of the present essay.

CHAPTER SIX

East and West in Ravenna

IN THE early pages of this work we suggested that the historical importance of Ravenna is derived from the fact that the two basic patterns of Christian civilization which have come to be identified with Orient and Occident met within its walls for the last time and that within the same walls they parted. No other city has produced monuments which embody the spirit of the two worlds with equal clarity; nowhere else does the student have the opportunity to compare and contrast the two. And only in Ravenna does the clash between the two patterns of civilization appear in its full impact upon the destiny of the Christian world. To make this clear, we now proceed, finally, to a comparison of the monuments that we have studied in the preceding pages.

I

All the works of art that Maximian commissioned bear the hallmark of the one abiding purpose of his career—to draw Ravenna into the orbit of Byzantium. But the archbishop was not satisfied with imposing upon his city the political and theological concepts of the imperial capital; he sought, rather, to win the population of his see and his metropolitan province to his side by capturing their imagination, by engulfing them in the religious experience of the East, of which the patterns of state and doctrine are but manifestations. Here, and not in the dexterity and shrewdness of his political moves, lies the secret of Maximian's success and, indeed, of his genius.

He was no demagogue, no propagandist; he could not claim for his administration the democratic sanctions of an electorate. But he was aware of the deeper stratum of man's soul from which even the social fabric receives its shape and to which it must be attuned in order to remain acceptable. With the people to whom he was a stranger and at first an enemy, he shared the realm of the imagination, the reverent concern with the childlike and profound creations of what Bergson has called the *faculté fabulatrice*. This explains why the archbishop conceded to the imaginative and poetical pageant of liturgy and worship so important a function in his historical designs. His liturgical and artistic projects were to impart to the people of Ravenna the experience in which the civilization of Byzantium originated; Maximian's churches must be seen as the theaters, his mosaics as the settings, for a great dramatic vision, by the enactment of which the archbishop sought to move and to mold the mind of the Christian West. What was the essence of this vision?

Since the end of the fourth century the piety of the Christian East, but, above all, that of Byzantium, had been impregnated by the experience of the awesome majesty of God. The same Son of Man who appears so humble and so human in the Synoptic Gospels was then perceived with the trembling and fear which the divine presence instils in man. This experience had been shaped in the fire of a great struggle. Arianism had sought to strip Christ of his divinity. Had this movement won, Greek philosophy would have conquered Christian theology; it would have destroyed the mystical experience of redemption. Orthodox theology set out to defend this experience against the essentially rational approach of its opponents.

This concern had already appeared in the theology of Athanasius, the conqueror of Arius. Inasmuch as philosophy is concerned with measuring truth against human reason, the patriarch of Alexandria has no claim to the title of philosopher. His exposition of the divine nature defies Hellenic cosmology and Hellenic logic. Rapt in the contemplation of the mystery which revelation has unfolded before his eyes, he is not concerned with solving it by logical or epistemological means. The paradox of redemption does not embarrass, but confirms, him in his conviction. His reason surrenders as absolutely as does his soul.

We find the same spirit in John Chrysostom. The patriarch of Constantinople, like the patriarch of Alexandria, directed some of his greatest theological works against the Arians. In 386 he had already delivered five sermons against the followers of the Arian Aetios, whom he perceived to be perverting the community of Antioch. The orations are entitled *De incomprehensibili dei natura* ("On the Incomprehensible in God").[1] They are like a single great fugue on the theme of St. Paul (I. Cor. 13:8): Knowledge will be destroyed where the mystery of divine love is perceived. The *Anomoioi* had declared they knew God as God knows himself; to Chrysostom this assertion is the root of all malice and apostasy, and he counters with a magnificent exposition on the ineffable nature of God, which not even the angels, let alone any human being, can fathom. St. Paul has well said that God dwells in unapproachable light, and Chrysostom has only ridicule for those who seek to delimit and circumscribe God by the constructions of dialectics. Indeed, to the orator it seems a sacrilege, an insult to God, if man attempts to explore the divine substance; for not only does God's nature defy all conceptual designations, but his majesty inspires man with trembling and fear, so that not only man's mind but his whole person will not dare approach the divine majesty.[2]

These words are not the abstractions of theological speculation. Even the reader senses the personal experience which inspires Chrysostom's thought: there is a dramatic, a visionary, quality in his eloquence, as if he were preaching in the very presence of the holy. "We admire many things," he exclaims in the first of the sermons quoted, "the beauty of a portico, of paintings, of a youthful body. We also admire the vastness of the Ocean; but fear will be added to this admiration, if we perceive the abysmal depth of the sea. And it is this fearful admiration which the Psalmist experiences in contemplating the vast and immense Ocean of God's wisdom: 'I will praise thee, for thou art fearfully magnified: wonderful are thy works'" (Ps. 138:14).[3]

Chrysostom's theology and his religious experience reflect those of his contemporaries. But no individual was more responsible for the shaping of the imaginative pattern into which this experience was cast than he was.

The liturgy still in use in the Byzantine church bears the name of Chrysostom. To what extent he is really its author is uncertain; but the reflection of his spirit in this work is beyond doubt.

Liturgy is the mystery of faith realized by man's entire personality, by the perceptions of the mind, the intuitive vision of the soul, the action of the body. The theology of the Christian East is reflected in the creations of its religious imagination and in the pattern of its worship, no less than in its sacred art. If the Deity is conceived as incomprehensible to the mind, it is also unbearable to the senses; if it is unapproachable epistemologically, it is equally unapproachable ritually: emphasis upon the awesome and fearful nature of God begins in the second half of the fourth century;[4] by the end of that century the Byzantine and Syro-Monophysite churches have abolished the offertory procession of the laity and thereby the liturgical approach to God.[5] At the same time, the holy is concealed: both the altar and the most sacred act of the divine drama are hidden from the eyes of the faithful. The *Ikonostasis*—the screen shutting off the sanctuary from the nave—seems to have come into existence early in the fifth century.[6]

This twofold development affected the Eastern rite in yet another sense. The pristine liturgy had been primarily action. Under the impact of the new religious experience it was transformed into vision. The spirit of "soberness and sense," which to Edmund Bishop epitomized the ancient Roman rite, was found in the early liturgies in general. The acts performed (which only a much later age interpreted as symbolic) had, without exception, a concrete, practical, simple function. To these acts Eastern worship imparted a mysterious and awe-inspiring meaning. To touch the sacred objects, to perform the mystery of redemption, is to Chrysostom a fearful, a superhuman, undertaking. Only the priestly dignity will enable man to perform the sacramental act without being consumed by the holy as by a divine fire. Such thought must transform the entire character of the liturgy.

In the homilies of Narsai the sacrament is described as a drama, a dreadful mystery enacted by the priest before the eyes of the faithful, a heavenly vision, an object for contemplation. But Chrysostom had already compared the liturgy to a theater.[7] This notion could not have suggested itself as long as every Christian took active part in the sacred rite as actor of the mystery drama. But, with the laity excluded from such participation in the liturgy and from the sanctuary where it was enacted, the church was necessarily divided into stage and auditorium, the congregation into actors and onlookers, the drama itself into physical action and spiritual vision.[8]

The ancient liturgical writers of the Byzantine church vied with one another in describing their liturgy as a sacred theater. "When we become contemplators of the divine mysteries," says Germanos, "we praise the great mystery of the economy of the Son of God."[9] To these contemplative minds the liturgy opened up the glories of a heavenly vision. The bishop, traversing the church, ascending to the altar, and taking his seat upon his cathedra, appeared like Christ ascending into heaven and taking his place on the eternal throne.[10]

The transformation of the liturgy into vision is perhaps most noteworthy in the so-called "Great Entry." This rite is derived from the ancient oblation of gifts and corresponds to the offertory procession of the Western liturgy. But, under the impact of the new religious experience, its original character has become almost unrecognizable. Instead of the laity proceeding toward the sanctuary, it is now the celebrant and his retinue of clerics who, leaving the sanctuary by the door of the prothesis, carry the sacred offerings through the church and return to the sanctuary, where they are received by the bishop.[11] As the solemn pageant moves past them, the faithful fall down on their knees in adoration; as a physical act, the carrying of the sacred objects from, and back to, the sanctuary is without purpose. What matters is the heavenly vision which it unfolds. The Cherubic Hymn, which is chanted on this occasion, describes this vision:

"Let us who mystically represent the Cherubim and offer thrice holy hymn to the lifegiving Trinity, now put aside all earthly cares. That we may receive the King of all. Who comes invisibly attended by hosts of angels, alleluia, alleluia, alleluia!"[12]

The Great Entry has frequently been depicted in the sanctuaries of the Eastern churches: a procession of angels, dressed as deacons, carry the liturgical objects in solemn procession. Christ himself, in episcopal attire, is seen twice: blessing the procession and receiving it as it re-enters the sanctuary—just as the real bishop received the Great Entry procession in the Byzantine liturgy.[13] This explicit identification of the bishop with Christ and of the deacons with angels is profoundly characteristic of the spirit of the Eastern liturgy; as we have said, the rite is to the faithful a sacred theater in which the material things and the human beings of flesh and blood are images of the invisible glories of heaven.

Not only has this concept inspired mosaics and murals, it has also molded the monumental pattern of Byzantine architecture. It could not have been otherwise. The tangible forms and the setting in which the divine drama was being enacted appeared to Eastern piety as symbol and image. The dome and the whole nave were interpreted as an image of heaven; it became the sacred stage for the mystery drama which the faithful watched from the side aisles and galleries.[14]

To a Western observer like Liutprant of Cremona, the greatest Byzantine church, Hagia Sophia, appeared on solemn feast days as a theater.[15] His observation is born out by Eastern writers and has been confirmed by modern students of this great building. In a remarkable study Andreades[16] has described the aesthetic dichotomy which pervades Hagia Sophia. Standing in the center of the church under the great dome, the visitor is overcome by a feeling of exaltation, as if he were standing in the center of the cosmos itself. As he approaches the galleries, he seems to dwindle in size and importance, and, when he looks back through the arcades into the vast expanse, the disproportion between the insignificance of the onlooker and the magnitude of that central space has become overwhelming.

These impressions are gained by formal and aesthetic analysis only; the great church has for centuries ceased to be the setting for the Christian rite. But even the empty shell gives testimony of the living spirit that shaped it and of the religious experience which found its voice in Chrysostom and its poetical image in the liturgy of the East. From behind the arcades of the galleries the faithful watched the liturgical drama enacted under the great dome of the center and upon the sacred stage, which only the priest and the emperor were permitted to enter and in which the entire civilization had its fountainhead.

Hagia Sophia is the greatest, but not the earliest, church of the central type. San Vitale of Ravenna, though completed several years later, had been begun six years before. Its dimensions are far more modest. But the spirit of Byzantium has remained much more alive here than in the Constantinopolitan

sanctuary, which from a church was converted into a mosque and from a mosque into a museum (Pl. 48).

Even in the sixteenth century, San Vitale reminded an observer of a theater.[17] From the two stories of galleries which surround the octagonal center, one looks upon the sanctuary proper as upon the stage of a theater. The liturgy of the sixth century must have increased and implemented this theatrical effect. The mosaics attest to the extent to which the architecture of San Vitale was attuned to the liturgy.

In the sixth century the Great Entry had only begun to develop. But we know of two important features of the Eastern liturgy already in existence at that time: the abolition of the offertory procession of the faithful and the role conceded to the emperor in the sacred rite. The dedicatory mosaics reflect both developments.

In looking at these works, one realizes how completely the apotheosis, which the Byzantine liturgy bestows upon the emperor and the bishop, is in keeping with the religious experience of the East. If the holy is conceived as fearful and even deadly to man, then contact with it in the enactment of the sacred rite must bestow upon the priesthood superhuman power and dignity. Chrysostom has time and again dwelt on the power and dignity of the sacerdotal office which he calls *tremendous* and *formidable*.[18] The Transfiguration mosaic in Sant' Apollinare in Classe and the chair of Maximian are glorifications of the Christlike dignity of the bishop who, in the words of Narsai, "hovers like an eagle before the faithful, preparing the food of perfect age and depicting in his own person the dread mystery of the Passion."[19]

But a religious experience which is seized, above all, with the power and majesty of God, which surrenders to his awesome presence, will be inclined to lend the same attributes to the representative of this authority on earth and will transfer to it both the attitudes and the emotions of religious homage. It is of the greatest interest to observe how the Fathers of the East, despite their struggle with the imperial power over issues of doctrine and morals, have never denied the association of Christ and emperor. Chrysostom himself denounced his sovereign bitterly and suffered cruelly for his courage. But the patriarch's respect for the ceremonial and pageant of the imperial court is significant. He may contrast the splendor of the emperor's passing in full panoply with the coming of Christ, "who will not come in a golden chariot drawn by a yoke of mules, with dragons embroidered on his clothes and shields arrayed about him, but whose coming will be none the less infinitely more glorious and more fearful."[20] But the pious Theodosius the Great appears to Chrysostom "clad in Christ"; he has put on "the corselet of justice, the sandals of the gospel of peace, the sword of the spirit, the shield of faith, and the helmet of deliverance."[21] The image is unquestionably an allegorization of the imperial attire; and it is significant that the emperor, like the bishop, appears here in the spiritual garb of the perfect Christian, as the man who has "put on Christ," and has thus become an image of Christ himself. As such he appeared to the people in the Great Entry of the Byzantine liturgy.

II

As we pass from San Vitale to Sant' Apollinare Nuovo, we find ourselves in a different world. The contrast already appears in the architecture. The basilica is neither an invention of Christianity nor the exclusive property of the Christian Occident.[22] There are great basilicas in the East, as there are churches of the central ground plan in the West.[23] It is nevertheless true that the basilica is the proper setting for the Western liturgy, as much attuned to this rite as the domed church is to that of the East. This is clearly shown by the transformation which both types of architecture have undergone under the impact of the liturgical development. The abolition of the offertory procession rendered the basilica liturgically obsolete in the East, as a number of curiously "telescoped" examples still prove;[24] and the West never found the central church quite adaptable to its rite. The wonderful affinity between the basilica and the Western rite, on the other hand, appears in Sant' Apollinare Nuovo. This church bespeaks the spirit of Leo the Great, as San Vitale does that of John Chrysostom.

It would be meaningless to call this structure a theater. Even here the sanctuary is a stage, but the nave certainly does not suggest an auditorium. The two parts of the interior seem to be fused by the rhythm of a twofold movement, the columns proceeding toward the sanctuary in a continued procession, while the sanctuary opens into the nave, as does the source into the stream. One might hazard the remark that, even in the absence of all liturgical sources, this architecture would permit us to assume that the rite enacted within its walls required the active participation of the entire congregation and that its essence was not contemplation but action.

This language of the architecture is wonderfully clarified by the mosaics. It is worth while to compare the processions with the divine liturgy so frequently depicted in the churches of the East. The latter always adorn the sanctuary, reflecting a rite—the Great Entry—in which only the priesthood participated; the former adorn the nave, representing the offertory procession in which the entire congregation appeared as "a kingly priesthood, a holy nation, a purchased people." With all their magnificence, the mosaics of Sant' Apollinare Nuovo, like the architecture to which they are attuned, have something sober and functional about them which is unlike the supernatural splendor of Byzantine art.

It would be a mistake to stress unduly the differences between the great Christian Churches. The visionary element is not lacking in the West; the Roman liturgy conceives the basilica as an image of the Heavenly Jerusalem. But it is significant that even this vision never leaves the earth entirely behind. It has recently been argued with a good deal of conviction that the Christian basilica must be understood as the image of the classical city, that the nave, as an image of "the street of the city . . . of pure gold" which the Book of Revelation describes (21:21), reproduces ancient city streets.[25] This resemblance is particularly striking if we compare a basilica like Sant' Apollinare Nuovo with one of those sumptuous streets of late antiquity which, transformed or blended into a vast oblong court-yard, served as settings for the ritual of the mon-archy. Thus, in Diocletian's palace at Spalato, the head of the principal street is actually conceived as a peristyle leading to the monumental façade of the vestibule. Under the great central arch of this façade the emperor appeared to his assembled subjects as *deus praesens*,[26] a vision of majesty which inspired the representations of the enthroned Christ in the apses of early Christian sanctuaries (Pl. 47, *b*).

The affinities between such open courtyards and the Christian basilica are closer than may appear at first sight. There are known to have existed in early Christian times a number of *basilicae discopertae*, i.e., sanctuaries the central naves of which were uncov-ered and therefore resembled an atrium.[27] The peri-styles of the imperial palace, on the other hand, un-derwent a transformation in the direction of basilical architecture when, with the development of court ceremonial, ladies were obliged to attend functions of state not in the courtyard itself but under the ad-joining galleries, which were therefore expanded in-to regular side aisles.[28] In the sixth century, Theod-oric's great palace in Ravenna, in every respect an expression of the Gothic ruler's imperial sovereignty in Italy, contained such a peristyle with side aisles, apparently patterned after similar ceremonial struc-tures in the Sacred Palace at Constantinople (Pls. 46, 47, *a*).[29]

The courtyard in Theodoric's palace is represented in the mosaic in Sant' Apollinare Nuovo; and those who have visited this sanctuary can hardly have failed to notice the resemblance between the "golden street" of the actual nave dedicated to the cult of Christ and the representation of the open basilica— it, too, a truncated street—of ruler-worship.

These affinities are significant. We have, in this essay, repeatedly traced the interrelation between the symbolism and ritual of the imperial court and those of the Christian church. It is hardly surprising that an age which conceived the monarchical sphere

as a reflection of the celestial one should have visual-ized the Epiphany of the Savior (as evoked by the liturgical drama) after the pattern of the epiphany of the emperor and that it should have designed the sacred stage on which the manifestation of the god-head took place after the model of the ceremonial court of the imperial palace. After all, do not even the European languages attest the fact that this par-ticular architecture, more than any other symbol, had become the expression of majesty? To this day, the term "court" has remained the synonym for the monarchical establishment and its ceremonial dis-play.[30]

In the common inspiration of their architecture and imagery by monarchical symbolism, Sant' Apol-linare Nuovo and San Vitale are children of the same age.[31] Yet one cannot help reflecting upon the dis-similarity of the religious sentiments which they ex-press. In San Vitale the emphasis is upon the majesty of God, which the faithful beholds with trembling; in Sant' Apollinare Nuovo—even while the apse mosaic was intact—the dominant note must have been the joyful rite by which the Lord is greeted and acknowledged by his elect. The relation of the pro-cession mosaics to the offertory of the laity makes worship the active concern not only of the ecclesi-astical and monarchical hierarchies but of the entire congregation.

In San Vitale the political element is represented in the dedicatory portraits of the *Augusti*. It is assigned to the sanctuary, close to the altar and to the sacra-mental scenes to which the imperial dignity is mysti-cally related. Integrated into the great eschatological motif of the Second Advent, these portraits of Jus-tinian and Theodora appear as justification and apotheosis of their administration. At the same time, however, it is precisely this theological context which withdraws the political sphere from its con-tact with historical life. The *Augusti* belong not to the political but to the celestial hierarchy, their mon-archy is an image of the heavenly one, their images are those of transfigured saints.

In Sant' Apollinare Nuovo, on the other hand,

not the supreme authority of the state but the *polis* is represented: the processions of martyrs are seen to emerge from the twin cities of Ravenna and Classe. Situated at the entrance of the nave, these compositions are points of departure for the sacred road of the liturgy. They link the political and the eternal worlds; but, as our minds turn to the sanctuary proper, we leave the political world behind us.

We find a similar relation of the contemporary and historical world to the mysteries of redemption in the Roman liturgy. Until the middle of the sixth century the popes continued to improvise from year to year certain liturgical prayers; specific reference to contemporary events thus introduced the sorrows and joys and the great political movements and their meaning to the Christian into the eternal vision of revelation. And even when Gregory the Great, at the end of the century, gave to the eucharistic liturgy its definite form, his own historical experiences— the destruction of Rome, the Lombard invasions— became the vivid foil for his expectation of the world to come. The liturgy of the Byzantine church had, more than two centuries before, been withdrawn from such contact with the historical world.[32]

The mosaics in Sant' Apollinare Nuovo recall yet another vision which has molded the world view of the Christian West. As we behold the saints proceeding from the cities of the sixth century to the Heavenly Jerusalem, we are reminded of that interpretation of the course of history which Augustine gives in the *City of God*.

The bishop of Hippo describes Christianity as "the universal way of the soul's freedom," as "the king's highway that leads to the eternal, dangerless kingdom, to no temporal or transitory one";[33] and in the fifteenth book he goes on to explain the movement of universal history "from man's first offspring until he cease to beget any more" as a journey on this universal way. He perceives the "city of heavenly hope," like the "city of worldly possession," coming out "at the common gate of mortality";[34] the heavenly citizen as "by grace a pilgrim upon earth and by grace a citizen in heaven": "This is that glorious city of God, knowing and honouring Him alone: this the angels declared, inviting us to inhabit it, and become their fellow-citizens in it. They like not that we should worship them as our elected gods, but with them Him that is God to us both: nor to sacrifice to them: but with them, be a sacrifice to Him."[35] And Augustine exhorts the citizen of the heavenly city to join "all the blessed immortals . . . in sacrificing ourselves to the Adoration of the Father, the Son, and the Holy Ghost."[36]

Here, then, the apocalyptic vision of the "street of gold" appears again, but as the universal road connecting life and the movements of history with eternity. And life itself is seen as a procession, in the pattern of that imitation to which St. Paul exhorted the faithful. Augustine quotes the very passage from Romans, chapter 12, adding the admonition that "all the whole and holy society of the redeemed and sanctified city be offered unto God."[37] Here the shape of the liturgy has assumed universal significance, encompassing all human endeavor directed to the attainment of the ultimate good and compelling the movements of history as the irresistible current compels the waves of the stream.

In Sant' Apollinare Nuovo the liturgy has received a similar interpretation. This monument, however, suggests not only the moral and ascetic aspects of the religious experience of the West but also its theological side. As the domed church of the East seems to belittle man, excluding him from the divine mystery, the incomprehensible and awesome nature of which is symbolized in the vast expanses of the dome, so the pattern of the basilica attests the priestly dignity of every member of the congregation and seems to call man before the face of God. In that sense it may be suggested that the advent of the Magi symbolizes the religious "approach" of Western piety.

The mosaic in Sant' Apollinare Nuovo is the only monumental representation of this scene in Ravenna. It is worth while to compare with this work the tiny figures of the Magi with which the garment of Theodora is embroidered in her portrait in San Vitale. Here, we have suggested, the advent scene was intended as no more than an allegory of the liturgical dignity of the imperial couple. The Magi in Sant' Apollinare Nuovo represent the Epiphany of the Western church.

The Eastern rite never accepted this interpretation of the advent of the Magi. It celebrated Epiphany as the feast of Christ's baptism in the River Jordan, a scene which is depicted in the domes of Ravenna's ancient baptistries of San Giovanni in Fonte and Santa Maria in Cosmedin. Like the advent of the Magi in the Western Mass, the baptism of Christ is a mystery enacted in every eucharistic rite of the East.[37a] By their visual pattern alone the two events underscore the difference of religious experience. The baptism, visualized at the moment of the Eastern *epiklesis,* conceives the divine power as descending upon man and, as it were, overwhelming him. The advent of the Magi, visualized in the offertory procession of the Roman rite, conceives man as approaching Christ with his oblation, which is both propitiatory gift and mystical imitation of Christ's sacrifice. The baptism, we might say, conceives man as suffering the work of sanctification, the advent sees him actively co-operating with it.

This scene, finally, is also a symbol of an intellectual approach to God which found its expression in the christological doctrine formulated by Leo the Great. We saw how the pope used the advent of the Magi to illustrate both his theology and his theological method. The star, resplendent above the humble manger, manifested the union of the divine and human natures in Christ; and every believer, educated and uneducated alike, was urged to approach the mystery and, in celebrating the feast of the Magi, to enlighten his mind with the perception of the Incarnation. There is a clarity and simplicity and an epistemological confidence in this invitation to share the illumination of the Magi which, to the East, must have appeared wholly irreconcilable with the unfathomable nature of God; so Leo's christology, because of its very clarity and simplicity, has been rejected as "barren" not only by Monophy-

sites but also by Protestants like Harnack.[38] But if this doctrine lacked subtlety, it carried a conviction and palpability which alone were capable of translating the abstract idea of redemption into personal experience and moral action.

The Monophysites taught that the divine and human natures were infinitely apart and that their union had taken place only because of the absorption of human nature into the divine; this idea did not impair the dignity of the deity but made it impossible for man still living the life of human nature to experience its redemption. Leo the Great's theology, on the other hand, was based on the conviction that the Logos unites itself to every pious soul, that the mystery of His Incarnation is actively renewed in every man, even while in this life. This doctrine surely is far more than "mysticism."[39] It enabled the faithful to experience the redemption, to know themselves to be "partakers of his divinity who vouchsafed to become partaker of our humanity," as an ancient liturgical prayer phrases it; to the person this experience imparted a dignity and to the will a confidence in its ability to attain to the good which have profoundly affected Christian ethics.

As we compare the illustration of the offertory of the laity in Sant' Apollinare Nuovo with the imperial offertory in San Vitale, we cannot help reflecting also upon the political implications of the religious experience of the West. The mosaics in San Vitale demand that we revere the rulers who stand so close to the throne of God. The entire liturgy seems to revolve around the emperor, who is not only the apex of the social pyramid but also the image of Christ, the instrument of his divine will. It is in the majesty of government that Christ manifests himself in San Vitale. He appears in the apse as the heavenly emperor judging the *agon* in the arena of life. It is the same metaphor which John Chrysostom uses in depicting the Last Judgment, exhorting his listeners to keep their eyes fixed on Christ as the charioteers keep theirs fixed on the emperor[40] (Pls. 4, *5a, 5b*).

But in Sant' Apollinare Nuovo this manifestation, the epiphany of the Godhead, is conceived as the acknowledgment of Christ's kingship by his saints. In San Vitale the *ecclesia* rests on authority, in Sant' Apollinare Nuovo on freedom—there man is urged to humble himself, to recede from the majesty of God; here he is invited freely to acknowledge it and, by so doing, to partake of its glory. The political implications of this attitude are clear. The concept of God's majesty confirmed the absolute powers of the Byzantine emperor; the dignity of "a kingly priesthood, a holy nation," of which Roman theology and liturgy reminded every Christian, has also reflected upon the constitution of the ancient church: the elections of bishops, and even of the pope himself—who, as Christ's vicar, could claim at least the same divine sanctions as the Byzantine emperor—required the *consensus* of the people, because, as Leo the Great wrote, "he who is to rule over all must also be elected by all."[41]

Of this interrelation of political and theological concepts Sant' Apollinare Nuovo provides an example no less interesting than is San Vitale. The ancient city-state, strange though it may seem, received its last apotheosis in this sixth-century basilica. Not only does the nave evoke the memory of classical cities to convey the vision of the heavenly one; not only does the procession of virgins and martyrs recall the epiphany pageants of ancient citizenry; but the selection of this ceremonial for the expression of religious worship is most revealing, for that pageant bespoke not only the submission of the ancient city to a ruler but also her autonomy. In outward appearance at least, the *poleis* continued as sovereign states, and the Hellenistic kings were careful to treat them as allies rather than as subjects, even pretending that the taxes which they imposed—like the well-known "crowns"—were gifts rather than enforced levies.[42] Thus the Greek heritage—which "never knew the term of subject as legally binding"—entered into an alliance with the monarchies of late antiquity; and one feels that the peculiar blend of dignity and devotion, of freedom and assent, so noticeable in the graceful epiphany pageants, was its most lasting fruit. Has not this attitude survived in

the way in which the Christian West conceived man's relation with God? Thus curiously transformed or transfigured, the entire political legacy of the ancient world was destined to be passed on to posterity. Sant' Apollinare Nuovo is a monument to this role of Christianity as a mediator between two worlds.

III

What requires a word of explanation is the almost purely Roman inspiration most remarkable in the Arian mosaics of Sant' Apollinare Nuovo but notably enhanced by the additions of Archbishop Agnellus. These can be explained only as a gesture of reconciliation aimed, above all, at Rome but also at the pre-Byzantine past of Ravenna itself. The christological cycles, anti-Monophysite and anti-Theopaschite in their interpretation of Christ's life and death and actually "Leoninian" in their allusion to Christ's distinct natures, were left untouched. The Advent of the Magi, whether retained from an older cycle or newly commissioned by Archbishop Agnellus, is an even more explicit acknowledgment of the theology and liturgy of Rome. One may object that even Maximian, in his Transfiguration mosaic, conveyed theological concepts which have close analogies in the teachings of Leo the Great. But even though the theological language of this work was, deliberately, no doubt, couched in terms acceptable to both Rome and Byzantium, it conveys, above all, the religious experience of the East. The Epiphany scene in Sant' Apollinare, on the other hand, suggests precisely those doctrines, convictions, and sentiments which were significantly Roman and militantly anti-Byzantine.

The same spirit prevails in the processions of the saints. The selection of the martyrs and virgins certainly presents an act of deference to the churches of Rome and Milan. The reference to the offertory procession, moreover, indicates that under Archbishop Agnellus a far-reaching *rapprochement* between the rites of Ravenna and those of the other Italian sees was initiated. Here again the metropolitan seems to have proceeded with that tact which imparts special significance to the term "reconciliation" used by the chronicler to describe the work of adaptation of Arian sanctuaries to the rite of the Orthodox church: if the thirty-two figures above the processions represent, as we have suggested, the patriarchs, prophets, apostles, and evangelists, then the martyrs and virgins complete the hierarchy of saints as the ancient liturgies, Arian and Orthodox, invoked them. While the older figures remain curiously aloof, however, only the martyrs and virgins especially invoked in the diptychs of Ravenna participate directly in the liturgy: the individuality of this city is not lost sight of in the vision of the celestial one.

This union of the universal with the particular, of the eternal with the political, is underscored by the representations of Ravenna and Classe. These scenes fit so beautifully into the general composition that their preservation by Archbishop Agnellus seems natural. Nevertheless, the compositions represented, as we pointed out, the buildings of Theodoric with an exclusiveness which was bound to keep alive the king's memory as the Maecenas and benefactor of the cities. Likewise preserved was the inscription which hailed Theodoric as builder of the sanctuary. It is true, the martyrs leave the cities behind them; and, as we accompany them through the nave of the basilica and before the throne of God, the importance of the political sphere dwindles. But we are not allowed to forget entirely Ravenna's place in this magnificent vision. The sixth century conceived every historical move as projected toward the eschatological goal; it demanded that all political action be justified in terms of the transcendental values of the Christian faith. The ecclesiastical position which Ravenna had achieved under Justinian could not have been justified more magnificently than in the perspective of Christ's epiphany and of the Last Judgment. But the tribute paid to the city's past was an argument altogether different from that employed by Maximian, and one wonders if it corresponded to the wishes and aims of Justinian.

Agnellus was old enough to have known Theodoric. He had been made a deacon by Archbishop Ecclesius, a supporter of the Gothic king. In view of Agnellus' social position and perhaps his former military career, a personal acquaintance with Theodoric appears not improbable; and, as a native of Ravenna, he must have been more aware of the king's beneficial government of his city, of his long record of tolerance of the Orthodox church, than of his opposition to the political and religious schemes of Justinian. The emperor, moreover, was old when Agnellus took possession of the metropolitan see of Ravenna. He may have died before the mosaics in Sant' Apollinare Nuovo were completed. It required no extraordinary political shrewdness to realize that the Empire's threatened position in the East and the internal weaknesses of its administration must gradually weaken and perhaps ultimately cut off altogether the support it could send to its Western territories. Regardless of such political or military support, however, Ravenna, her ecclesiastical position once established, must gradually emancipate herself from the East.

The very position of leadership which the see claimed in the Christian West demanded sympathy with, and a certain receptiveness to the religious sentiments of this part of the *ecoumene*. Authority and force are meaningless in the realm of religion. Even the Emperor Justinian's theology appears to have been less an attempt to mold the religious views of his Christian subjects than a response to them. The see of Rome was equally sensitive to popular customs and traditions in matters of worship. Agnellus acted in the same spirit.

All the evidence that we have of his political and religious views suggests that, instead of continuing Maximian's endeavor to Byzantinize Ravenna, he turned toward Rome. The letters sent him by Pope Pelagius indicate both Ravenna's willingness to accede to the political wishes of the papacy and a spirit of co-operation between the two sees.[43] The same tendency seems to be reflected in the liturgy. Mgr Testi-Rasponi, the most distinguished expert on this matter, has pointed to the curiously cyclical development of the rite of Ravenna. Under Maximian it moved far away from Rome and in the direction of Byzantium.[44] His successors gradually reversed this trend. If, under Gregory the Great, the liturgical writings of Maximian were forwarded to the Eternal City, if elements of the liturgy of Ravenna were incorporated into the Roman sacramentary, Ravenna itself gradually adopted one element of the Roman rite after another, until, at the height of the Middle Ages, the last traces of her liturgical autonomy were abolished. This *rapprochement* was due less to sentiments of friendship and subordination on Ravenna's part than to the spirit of rivalry which required that she appear no less orthodox, no less in harmony with the religious sentiments of the West, than did Rome; as one watches this development, the ancient tradition of Christian Italy and the ties of geography and custom seem to reassert themselves in Ravenna, even while the see is still a Byzantine outpost. The mosaics in Sant' Apollinare Nuovo are the earliest evidence of this trend, even in regard to its political implications.

In this church, too, Justinian is depicted. The portrait of the aged emperor—his last in Ravenna—appeared at the entrance wall of the basilica. As early as the sixteenth century the work was in a state of complete deterioration, and today only the bust of Justinian remains.[45] We can say with certainty only that the work represented Justinian and Agnellus; the analogy with the mosaics in San Vitale and Sant' Apollinare in Classe has prompted the suggestion that the composition in Sant' Apollinare Nuovo also commemorated an imperial donation, i.e., the transfer of the property of the Arian church to the Orthodox community of Ravenna.[46] If so, this event is belittled rather than hailed, and we can only marvel at the contrast between this portrait of the emperor

and the earlier one. Where the dedicatory mosaic in San Vitale (like its replica in Sant' Apollinare in Classe) adorns the sanctuary and is deliberately related to the eucharistic rite, the emperor's portrait in Sant' Apollinare Nuovo remained invisible for the congregation facing the priest and seems to have had no liturgical relation whatever, for it seems impossible to attach the image to the processions of saints—the representations of Ravenna and Classe interpose an insuperable obstacle. Even if we assume that the onlooker was to relate Justinian's donation to the mystical and liturgical offertory, the impression is unavoidable that the emperor lags behind, that he has no place in this illustration of the Western rite—the same rite which dropped the emperor from its prayer of intercession (Frontispiece).[47]

The Roman aspects of the mosaics in Sant' Apollinare Nuovo are an omen of impending historical events. These works, though executed when Justinian's power in Italy was at its zenith, indicate that the entire Byzantine scheme of bringing the West back into the fold of the monarchy was doomed to fail. They betray the widening rift between East and West; and they show that this rift was not only the result of the political and intellectual crisis ominously gathering in the Orient but also, and perhaps to an even greater extent, of the overwhelming prestige of the papacy in Italy and throughout the entire Christian West. It was this prestige which forced even Ravenna to join in the movement of withdrawal from Byzantium, which so curiously anticipated the tide of Islam and enabled Christian civilization to survive it. As he leaves Sant' Apollinare Nuovo, the visitor realizes how little this survival owes to political hazard and how much to the grandeur of a vision which still challenges him in the sacred twilight of the basilica.

LIST OF ABBREVIATIONS

ASS   *Acta sanctorum.* Ed. J. BOLLANDUS. Paris, 1863 ff.

BHL   *Bibliotheca hagiographica Latina, antiquae et mediae aetatis.* Ediderunt Socii Bollandiani. Brussels, 1898–1901.

CSEL   *Corpus scriptorum ecclesiasticorum Latinorum.* Editum consilio et impensis Academiae litterarum caesareae Vindobonensis. Vienna, 1866 ff.

DACL   *Dictionnaire d'archéologie chrétienne et de liturgie.* Ed. F. CABROL and H. LECLERCQ. Paris, 1907 ff.

EL   *Ephemerides liturgicae.*

FCL   *Forschungen zur christlichen Litteratur- und Dogmengeschichte.* Ed. A. EHRHARD and J. P. KIRSCH. Mainz, 1900 ff.

FR   *Felix Ravenna.*

JL   *Jahrbuch für Liturgiewissenschaft.*

JTS   *Journal of Theological Studies.*

JWCI   *Journal of the Warburg and Courtauld Institutes.*

LQ   *Liturgiegeschichtliche Quellen und Forschungen.* Ed. K. MOHLBERG and A. RÜCKER. Münster, 1919 ff.

MEL   *Monumenta ecclesiae liturgica.* Ed. F. CABROL and H. LECLERCQ. Paris, 1900 ff.

MGH   *Monumenta Germaniae historica.* . . . Edidit societas aperiendis fontibus rerum Germanicarum medii aevi. Hannover and Berlin, 1826 ff.

MTS   *Monumenti: Tavole storiche dei mosaici di Ravenna.* Ed. C. RICCI. Rome, 1930 ff.

OC, OC², OC³ *Oriens Christianus.* First, second, and third series.

OCP   *Orientalia Christiana periodica.*

PG   *Patrologiae cursus completus . . . series Graeca.* Ed. J. P. MIGNE. Paris, 1857 ff.

PL   *Patrologiae cursus completus . . . series Latina.* Ed. J. P. MIGNE. Paris, 1844 ff.

PW   PAULY-WISSOWA. *Realencyklopädie des classischen Altertums.* Stuttgart, 1894 ff.

RB   *Revue Bénédictine.*

RG   *Rassegna Gregoriana.*

RM   *Mitteilungen des Deutschen archäologischen Instituts in Rom.*

RQ   *Römische Quartalschrift*

SAC   *Studi di antichità cristiana.*

SZ   *Stimmen der Zeit* (identical with *Stimmen aus Maria Laach*).

ZKT   *Zeitschrift für katholische Theologie.*

LIST OF WORKS CITED BY ABBREVIATIONS

Agnellus	AGNELLUS. *Liber pontificalis ecclesiae Ravennatis.* Ed. A. TESTI-RASPONI in the new edition of L. A. MURATORI, *Rerum Italicarum scriptores,* Vol. II, Part III (Bologna, 1924). Testi-Rasponi's edition, while as yet incomplete, contains all those parts of the *Liber pontificalis* to which reference is made in the present essay. I refer to the text as "Agnellus" and to Mgr Testi-Rasponi's excellent commentary as "Testi." Cf. also HOLDER-EGGER'S commentary in his edition of Agnellus in *MGH SS. rerum Langobardicarum,* pp. 265 ff.
Alföldi, *Insignien*	ALFÖLDI, A. "Insignien und Tracht der römischen Kaiser," *RM,* Vol. L (1935).
Alföldi, *Zeremoniell*	———. "Die Ausgestaltung des monarchischen Zeremoniells am römischen Kaiserhofe," *RM,* Vol. XLIX (1934).
Anon. Vales.	*Anonymi Valesiani pars posterior, MGH, Auct. antiquissimi,* Vol. IX, Part I.
Ante-Nicene Fathers	*Ante-Nicene Fathers.* Ed. A. ROBERT and J. DONALDSON. Reprint of the Edinburgh edition. New York, 1899 ff.
Aquileia	*La Basilica di Aquileia.* Bologna, 1933.
Bannister	BANNISTER, H. M. *Missale Gothicum.* ("Henry Bradshaw Society," Vols. LII and LIV.) 2 vols. London, 1917 and 1919.
Bardenhewer	BARDENHEWER, O. *Geschichte der altkirchlichen Literatur.* Freiburg, 1932.
Batiffol, *Justinien*	BATIFFOL, P. "L'Empereur Justinien et le siège apostolique," *Recherches de science religieuse,* Vol. XVI (1926).
Baumstark, *Liturgia*	BAUMSTARK, A. *Liturgia romana e liturgia dell'esarcato.* Rome, 1904.
Berlendis, *De oblat.*	BERLENDIS, F. DE. *De oblationibus ad altare.* Venice, 1743.
Bishop, *LH*	BISHOP, E. *Liturgica historica.* Oxford, 1918.
Botte, *Canon.*	BOTTE, B. *Le Canon de la messe romaine.* Louvain, 1935.
Brandi	BRANDI, K. "Ravenna und Rom," *Archiv für Urkundenforschung,* Vol. IX (1926).
Bréhier-Batiffol	BRÉHIER, L., and BATIFFOL, P. *Les Survivances du culte impérial romain.* Paris, 1920.
Brightman	BRIGHTMAN, F. E. *Liturgies Eastern and Western.* Oxford, 1896.
Cabrol, *Ravenne*	CABROL, F. "Autour de la liturgie de Ravenne," *RB,* Vol. XXIII (1906).
Casel, *Mysterium*	CASEL, O. "Mysterium und Martyrium in den römischen Sakramentarien," *JL,* Vol. II (1922).
Caspar	CASPAR, E. *Geschichte des Papsttums von den Anfängen bis zur Höhe der Weltherrschaft,* Vol. II. Tübingen, 1933.
Ciampini	CIAMPINI, J. *Vetera monimenta.* Rome, 1693.
Const. apost.	*Constitutiones apostolorum.* Ed. F. X. FUNK. Paderborn, 1905.
Cosmas	COSMAS INDICOPLEUSTES. *Topographia Christiana, PG,* Vol. LXXXVIII.
Cumont, *Mages*	CUMONT, F. "L'Adoration des mages et l'art triomphal de Rome,"*Mem. pont. accad.,* Vol. III, Ser. 3 (1932).
Cumont, *Symbolisme*	———. *Recherches sur le symbolisme funéraire chez les Romains.* Paris, 1942.
De cerim.	CONSTANTINUS PORPHYROGENETUS. *De cerimoniis aulae Byzantinae, PG,* Vol. CXII.
Delehaye	DELEHAYE, H. *Les Origines du culte des martyres.* Brussels, 1933.
Diehl, *Études*	DIEHL, C. *Études sur l'administration byzantine dans l'exarchat de Ravenne.* Paris, 1888.
Diehl, *Justinien*	———. *Justinien et la civilization byzantine au VIe siècle.* Paris, 1901.
Duchesne, *L'Église*	DUCHESNE, L. *L'Église au VIe siècle.* Paris, 1925.
Duchesne, *Origines*	———. *Origines du culte chrétien5.* Paris, 1903.
Ebner	EBNER, A. *Quellen und Forschungen zur Geschichte und Kunstgeschichte des Missale romanum im Mittelalter.* Freiburg, 1896.
Eisler	EISLER, R. "Orphisch-dionysische Mysteriengedanken in der christlichen Antike," *Vorträge der Bibliothek Warburg,* Vol. II (1922–23).
Etheria	ETHERIA. *S. Silviae peregrinatio, CSEL,* Vol. XXXIX.

Férotin V	FÉROTIN, M. *Le Liber ordinum, MEL*, Vol. V. Paris, 1904.
Férotin VI	———. *Le Liber mozarabicus sacramentorum, MEL*, Vol. VI. Paris, 1912.
Garrucci, *Storia*	GARRUCCI, R. *Storia dell'arte cristiana*. Prato, 1873–81.
Gelasianum	*Sacramentarium Gelasianum*. Ed. H. A. WILSON. Oxford, 1894.
Gerbertus	GERBERTUS, M., *Monumenta veteris liturgiae Alemannicae*. St. Blasien, 1776.
Grabar, *L'Empereur*	GRABAR, A. *L'Empereur dans l'art byzantin*. Paris, 1936.
Grabar, *Martyrium*	———. *Martyrium: Recherches sur le culte des reliques et l'art chrétien antique*. Paris, 1946.
Graevius	GRAEVIUS, J. G. *Thesaurus antiquitatum et historiarum Italiae*. Leyden, 1722.
Gregorianum	*Sacramentarium Gregorianum*. Ed. H. LIETZMANN. *LQ*, Vol. III. Münster, 1921.
Harnack	HARNACK, A. *Lehrbuch der Dogmengeschichte*[4]. Vol. II. Tübingen, 1928.
Hefele	HEFELE, H. *Conciliengeschichte*[2]. Freiburg, 1873.
Histoire	*Histoire de l'église depuis les origines jusqu'à nos jours, publiée sous la direction de Augustin Fliche et Victor Martin*, Vol. IV: *De la mort de Théodose à l'élection de Gregoire le Grand*. Ed. P. DE LABRIOLLE and others. Paris, 1937.
Hodgkin	HODGKIN, T. *Italy and Her Invaders*. Vol. IV. Oxford, 1885.
Jaffé	JAFFÉ-WATTENBACH, R. *Regesta pontificum Romanorum*. Leipzig, 1885.
James	JAMES, M. R. *The Apocryphal New Testament*. Oxford, 1926.
Jungmann	JUNGMANN, J. A. "Die Stellung Christi im liturgischen Gebet," *LQ*, Vols. VII and VIII. Münster, 1925.
Kennedy	KENNEDY, V. L. "The Saints of the Canon of the Mass," *SAC*, Vol. XIV (1938).
Kollwitz	KOLLWITZ, J. *Ostroemische Plastik der Theodosianischen Zeit*. Berlin, 1941.
Kruse	KRUSE, H. *Studien zur offiziellen Geltung des Kaiserbildes im römischen Reiche*. Paderborn, 1934.
Lanzoni, *Diocesi*	LANZONI, F., *Le Diocesi d'Italia dalle origini al principio del secolo VII* (An. 604). Faenza, 1927.
Lanzoni, *Fonti*	———. "Le Fonti della leggenda di Sant'Apollinare di Ravenna," *Atti e memorie della r. deputazione di storia patria per le provincie di Romagna*, Ser. IV, Vol. V (1915).
Lanzoni, *Reliquie*	———. "Reliquie della liturgia ravennate del sec. V secondo il *Liber pontificalis* di Agnello," *RG*, Vol. IX (1910).
Lanzoni, *Studi*	———. "Studi storico-liturgici su Sant' Apollinare Nuovo," *FR*, Suppl. II. 1916.
Le Blant	LE BLANT, E. *Études sur les sarcophages chrétiens antiques de la ville d'Arles*. Paris, 1878.
Leonianum	*Sacramentarium Leonianum*. Ed. C. L. FELTOE. Cambridge, 1896.
Lib. diurn.	*Liber diurnus Romanorum pontificum*. Ed. SICKEL. Vienna, 1889.
Lietzmann, *Messe*	LIETZMANN, H. *Messe und Herrenmahl*. Bonn, 1925–26.
Loisy	LOISY, A. *Les Mystères païens et le mystère chrétien*. Paris, 1914.
LP	*Liber pontificalis*. Ed. L. DUCHESNE. Paris, 1886–92.
Lucius	LUCIUS, E. *Die Anfänge des Heiligenkults*. Tübingen, 1904.
Mabillon	MABILLON, J. *Museum Italicum*. Paris, 1689.
Mansi	MANSI, J. D. *Sacrorum conciliorum nova et amplissima collectio*. Florence, 1752.
Martène	MARTÈNE, E. *De antiquis ecclesiae ritibus*. Antwerp, 1756.
Millet, *Iconogr.*	MILLET, G. *Recherches sur l'iconographie de l'évangile*. Paris, 1916.
Mohlberg-Baumstark	MOHLBERG, K., and BAUMSTARK, A. *Die älteste erreichbare Gestalt des Liber sacramentorum anni circuli der römischen Kirche*, *LQ*, Vols. XI and XII. Münster, 1927.
Mombritius	MOMBRIZIO, B. (MOMBRITIUS). *Sanctuarium, seu vita sanctorum*. New ed. Paris, 1910.
Morath	MORATH, G.W. *Die Maximianskathedra in Ravenna*. Freiburg, 1940.
Morey, *Art*	MOREY, C. R. *Early Christian Art*. Princeton, 1942.
Muratori, *Liturgia*	MURATORI, L. A. *Liturgia Romana vetus*. Venice, 1748.
Muratori, *Mosaici*	MURATORI, S. *Mosaici ravennati della chiese di San Vitale*. Bergamo, 1945.
Narsai	NARSAI. *The Liturgical Homilies*. Ed. R. H. CONNOLLY. Cambridge, 1909.
Peterson, *Kyrios*	PETERSON, E. "Die Einholung des Kyrios," *Zeitschrift für systematische Theologie*, Vol. VII (1929–30).
Pfeilschifter, *Kirche*	PFEILSCHIFTER, G. "Der Ostgotenkönig Theoderich der Grosse und die katholische Kirche," *Kirchengeschichtliche Studien*, Vol. III, Nos. 1 and 2 (1896).
Pfeilschifter, *Theoderich*	———. *Theoderich der Grosse*. Mainz, 1910.

Pontificale	*Pontificale Romanum summorum pontificum jussu editum a Benedicto XV et Leone XIII pontificibus maximis.* Mecheln, 1934.
Probst	PROBST, F. *Die Liturgie des vierten Jahrhunderts und deren Reform.* Münster, 1893.
Reitzenstein, *Bemerkungen*	REITZENSTEIN, R. "Bemerkungen zur Märtyrerliteratur," *Göttinger Nachrichten.* 1916.
Reitzenstein, *Mysterien*	———. *Die hellenistischen Mysterienreligionen.* Leipzig, 1920.
Roetzer	ROETZER, W. *Des Heiligen Augustinus Schriften als liturgiegeschichtliche Quelle.* München, 1930.
Rubeus	RUBEUS, H. *Italicarum et Ravennatum historiarum libri XI.* Venice, 1589.
Savio	SAVIO, F. *Gli antichi vescovi d'Italia: La Lombardia,* Part I: *Milano.* Florence, 1913.
Schermann, *Kirchenordnung*	SCHERMANN, T. *Die allgemeine Kirchenordnung.* Paderborn, 1914–16.
Schubart	SCHUBART, W. *Justinian und Theodora.* München, 1943.
Schurr	SCHURR, V. *Die Trinitätslehre des Boethius im Lichte der "skythischen" Kontroversen.* Paderborn, 1935.
Schuster	SCHUSTER, I. *The Sacramentary, Liber sacramentorum.* English trans. Vols. I and II. London, 1924–25. Vols. III, IV, V. New York, 1927–30.
Setton	SETTON, K. M. *Christian Attitude towards the Emperor in the Fourth Century.* New York, 1941.
Stefanescu	STEFANESCU, J. D. "L'Illustration des liturgies dans l'art de Byzance et de l'Orient," *Annuaire de l'Institut de philologie et d'histoire orientales,* Vols. I and II. Brussels, 1932–33.
Stornaiolo	STORNAIOLO, C. *Le Miniature della Topografia Cristiana.* Milan, 1907.
Testi	*See* AGNELLUS.
Treitinger	TREITINGER, O. *Die oströmische Kaiser- und Reichsidee nach ihrer Gestaltung im höfischen Zeremoniell.* Jena, 1938.
Van Berchem	BERCHEM, M. VAN, and CLOUZOT, E. *Mosaïques chrétiens du IVe au Xme siècle.* Geneva, 1924.
Vogt	VOGT, A. *Constantin VII Porphyrogénète: Le livre des cérémonies, commentaire,* Vol. I. Paris, 1935.
Voigt	VOIGT, K. *Staat und Kirche von Konstantin dem Grossen bis zum Ende der Karolingerzeit.* Stuttgart, 1936.
Wetter I	WETTER, G. P. *Altchristliche Liturgien: Das christliche Mysterium.* Göttingen, 1921.
Wetter II	———. *Altchristliche Liturgien,* Vol. II: *Das christliche Opfer.* Göttingen, 1922.
Wieland, *Altar*	WIELAND, F. *Altar und Altargrab der christlichen Kirchen im vierten Jahrhundert.* Leipzig, 1912.
Will	WILL, E. *Saint Apollinaire de Ravenne.* Strassburg, 1936.
Wilpert, *Katakomben*	WILPERT, J. *Die Malereien der Katakomben Roms.* Freiburg, 1903.
Wilpert, *Mosaiken*	———. *Die römischen Mosaiken und Malereien der kirchlichen Bauten.* Freiburg, 1924.
Wilpert, *Sarcofagi*	———. *Sarcofagi cristiani antichi.* Rome, 1932.
Wulff	WULFF, O. *Frühchristliche und byzantinische Kunst,* Vol. I. Berlin, 1918.
Zattoni, *Origine*	ZATTONI, G. "Origine e giurisdictione della metropoli ecclesiastica di Ravenna," *Revista di scienze storiche,* Vol. I (1904).
Zattoni, *Valore*	———. "Il Valore storico della 'Passio' di Sant' Apollinare e la fondazione dell'episcopato a Ravenna e in Romagna," *Rivista storico-critica delle scienze teologiche,* Vols. I (1905) and II (1906).

NOTES

PREFACE

1. From "Sailing to Byzantium," *The Tower* (1928), in *Collected Poems*. Copyright 1933 by the Macmillan Company and quoted with their permission.

CHAPTER ONE

1. See the description of Ravenna in Procopius *De bello Gotico* v. 1. 16 ff.; PW, *s.v.* "Ravenna." Cf. also A. Torre, "Il Porto di Ravenna," *FR*, nuovo ser., Vol. IV, Fasc. 3 (1934). For a good summary of Ravenna's early history see W. Goetz, *Ravenna*² (Leipzig, 1913).

2. On the question of Theodoric's alleged persecution of the church see Pfeilschifter, *Theoderich*, pp. 90 ff.

3. The source of this story is the famous *Pars posterior* of the *Anonymus Valesianus* xv. 94 f., p. 324. Its reliability was first questioned, with brilliant arguments, by Pfeilschifter, *Kirche*, pp. 208 ff. His thesis seems to be almost generally accepted today (see, however, *Histoire*, p. 436). The present writer, as will be seen later, believes that the author of this legend was Archbishop Maximian of Ravenna (see below, n. 71).

4. See Schurr, p. 223; see also W. Bark, "Theodoric vs. Boethius: Vindication and Apology," *American Historical Review*, Vol. XLIX (1944), and "The Legend of Boethius' Martyrdom," *Speculum*, Vol. XXI (1946).

5. As a victory monument San Vitale is also described by Muratori, *Mosaici*, p. 7. On the symbolism of the octagonal plan see R. Krautheimer, "Introduction to an 'Iconography' of Medieval Architecture," *JWCI*, Vol. V (1942).

6. See H. Grisar, *Das Missale im Lichte römischer Stadtgeschichte* (Freiburg, 1925); and J. P. Kirsch, *Die Stationskirchen des Missale romanum* (Freiburg, 1926). I have discussed the relation of this station to the liturgical texts in "Das abendländische Vermächtnis der Liturgie," *Deutsche Beiträge* (Chicago, 1947), pp. 47 f.

7. The *Passio* is printed in *ASS*, Junii IV, pp. 683 f.; Mombritius, pp. 117 ff.; and among the works of St. Ambrose in *PL*, XVII, 742. See also *BHL*, 3514. For the date and significance of the *Passio* see Savio, pp. 788 f.; and Lanzoni, *Diocesi*, pp. 725 ff.

8. See Testi, pp. 163 f.

9. *Ibid.*, p. 163.

10. *Ibid.*, pp. 162 ff.

11. The suggestion is Testi-Responi's and appears entirely convincing.

12. *De aedif.* i. 1. 65 ff.

13. W. Schubart (p. 197) describes Julianus Argentarius simply as a banker. This may have been his occupation, but it does not account for his social and political position.

14. See Reitzenstein, *Mysterien*, p. 3.

15. See Duchesne, *L'Église*, p. 82; Batiffol, *Justinien*, p. 210.

16. Mansi, VIII, 832: "Davidicae mansuetudinis et Mosaicae patientiae; et apostolicae clementiae instar in eo conspexi."

17. Chapman, *St. Benedict and the Sixth Century* (London, 1929), esp. pp. 57 ff., where the thesis is advanced that Justinian used Benedict's Holy Rule in his Code.

18. See Hodgkin, p. 562, whose translation I am using.

19. *Corpus juris* i. 27, "De officio praefecti"; see also the argument by which Justinian sought to persuade the Franks to fight the Goths (Procopius *De bello Gotico* v. 5. 8).

20. For the following see Grabar, *Martyrium*, I, 20 ff.

21. *Ibid.*, pp. 219 ff. Significant in this connection is also Grabar's comparison of Constantine's architectural projects with those of Diocletian in Spalato.

22. On the history of this musico-arithmetical concept of world harmony see the magisterial study of L. Spitzer, "Classical and Christian Ideas of World Harmony," *Traditio*, II (1944), esp. 417 ff. and 438 ff., and Vol. III (1945).

23. Grabar, *Martyrium*, I, 224, 305.

24. Agnellus xxvii. 77, p. 198.

25. *Ibid.* 70 f., pp. 188 f.

26. See Procopius *De bello Gotico* vii. 27. 5 f. and 37. 28.

27. For the arguments in favor of this date see Testi, p. 198. Muratori (*Mosaici*, p. 7), on the other hand, maintains the traditional date of 547. If we assume San Vitale to have been consecrated so soon after Maximian's appointment, it is, of course, hardly possible to assign all the mosaics to the brief period between October, 546 (cf. *DACL*, *s.v.* "Maximien") and April, 547. In that case we must assume the compositions to have been completed only after the consecration—a thesis which to me appears much more acceptable than that of their origin before 546. I have here accepted Mgr Testi-Rasponi's chronology not only because it seems to me to be borne out by the iconographical testimony of the mosaics but also, and above all, because of the weight that his arguments seem to carry. For a judicious evaluation of both sides of this chronological puzzle see Ricci, *MTS, San Vitale*, p. 1.

28. For the following see Testi, p. 144; Lanzoni, *Diocesi*, p. 743; and Brandi. Attention may be called to Schubart's recent study, *Justinian und Theodora*, which, while not presenting new material, is an excellent summary of the results of recent scholarship in this field.

29. See Hefele, Vol. II. In Dom H. Leclercq's translation and emendation of this work (III, Part I [Paris, 1909], 1 ff.) the reader will find an abundant list of relevant literature. See also Duchesne, *L'Église*, chap. v; *Histoire*, pp. 458 ff.

30. Agnellus may involuntarily provide us with a clue as to reactions to this struggle in Ravenna itself: xxii. 48, p. 142.

31. *Ibid.* xxvii. 1, p. 189.

32. *Ibid.* 79, p. 206.

33. Batiffol, *Justinien*, p. 239; Duchesne, *L'Église*, p. 188.

34. See Bardenhewer, pp. 320 ff. The *Pro defensione* is printed in *PL*, LXVII, 527 ff.

35. Duchesne, *L'Église*, p. 190.

36. "Ecce ergo et pars omnium sacerdotum inter quos ecclesia mea constituta est, id est, Galliae, Burgundiae, Spaniae, Liguriae, Aemiliae atque Venetiae contestor quia quicumque in edicta ista consenserit, superscriptarum provinciarum pontifices communicatores habere non poterit" (Mansi, IX, 154; cf. also Hefele, III, Part I, 57).

37. Mansi, IX, 147; Hefele, III, Part I, 37; *Histoire*, p. 466.

38. Agnellus xxvii. 78, p. 201. Dioscurus II ruled from 517 to 519; Timotheus II, of whom Maximian wrote "quem ego navigans orientem in sua civitate bene administrante [*sic*] vidi," from 519 to 536 (see A. Baudrillard, *Dictionnaire d'histoire et de géographie ecclésiastiques*, II [Paris, 1914], 330 f.).

39. III, 26; *MGH SS. rerum Lang. saec. VI–IX*, p. 105.

40. Agnellus xxvi. 7, p. 192: "bis in Constantinopulis se detulit." The inscription in Santo Stefano, *ibid.*; on the question of chronology see Testi, pp. 192 f.

41. Agnellus vii. 74, p. 193; cf. Testi's notes (pp. 192 f.).

42. Agnellus xxvii. 70, p. 186.

43. *Var.* xii. 22; *PL*, LXIX, 872.

44. Duchesne, *L'Église*, pp. 219 ff.

45. Testi, p. 195. Today the magnificent basilica of Santa Maria Formosa has disappeared. "Di tutto il grande complesso della basilica oggi non rimane che una piccolissima parte del muro perimetrale sinistro, circa metà delle due sagristie e la capella" (A. Morassi, "La Chiesa di Santa Maria Formosa, ò del Canneto in Pola," *Bollettino d'arte*, XVIII [1925], 11 ff.). Morassi believes this basilica to have been Maximian's first work.

46. Agnellus (XXI, 35, p. 96) mentions a monastery of SS. Gervase and Protase, which existed in the fifth century.

47. Lanzoni, *Diocesi*, p. 751.

48. On Piacenza and Reggio see *ibid.*, pp. 830 and 801, and Will, pp. 33 ff. I was unable to see A. G. Loreta, *Le Chiese di Sant' Apollinare* (Bologna, 1924).

49. See Diehl, *Études*, p. 52; Zattoni, *Origine*; Massigli, "La Création de la métropole ecclésiastique de Ravenne," *Mélanges d'archéologie et d'histoire* (1911).

50. See Testi, p. 187; Lanzoni, *Diocesi*, p. 758; Brandi, pp. 34 ff.

51. Pope Pelagius denied the authenticity of a letter, purportedly by him and defending the Three Chapters, which was circulated among the bishops of Aemilia (P. Ewald, "Die Papstbriefe der britischen Sammlung," *Neues Archiv für ältere deutsche Geschichtskunde*, V [1880], 561). The letter, whether authentic or not, was undoubtedly given such prominence because the bishops of Aemilia held the same views. Later, and because of the Pope's about-face, they seceded from his communion (see *Histoire*, p. 479).

52. Agnellus xxvii. 72, p. 191.

53. *Ibid.*

54. Agnellus (*ibid.*) enumerates relics of the following saints: Peter, Paul, Andrew, Zacharias, John the Baptist, John the Evangelist, James, Thomas, Matthew, Stephen, Vincent, Lawrence, Quirinus, Florian, Emilian, Apollinaris, Agatha, Eufemia, Agnes, and Eugenia, all of which were enshrined in Santo Stefano. It need not be assumed that all these relics were procured in Constantinople or even by Maximian; but a large part of them undoubtedly was.

55. *Ibid.* 75, p. 195.

56. Testi, pp. 195 f.

57. See the learned dissertation on the legend of St. Andrew as first bishop of Constantinople in *ASS*, Augusti I, pp. 1 ff.

58. On this church see Testi, p. 195.

59. Grabar's assertion (*Martyrium*, I, 373) that San Vitale is a *martyrion* in form only, since the church is not the sepulcher of the martyr, is not entirely correct. According to the *Passio beatorum martyrum Gervasii et Protasii*, St. Vitalis suffered martyrdom on the place on which his church was erected. And the sepulchral symbolism of this sanctuary was meant to confirm the claim of the legend. How well this language was understood is shown by Fortunatus' *Vita S. Martini*,

which Grabar himself quotes in a subsequent passage (*ibid.*, I, 408). The work refers to San Vitale as the martyr's tomb.

60. Pfeilschifter, *Theoderich*, esp. pp. 47 ff.

61. Caspar, II, 191; Voigt, pp. 172 ff.

62. The reference to the reign of Theodoric as a golden age occurs repeatedly in the writings of Ennodius. See "Libellus adversus eos qui contra synodum scribere praesumpserunt," *MGH, Auct. Antiquiss.*, VII, 67; and "Panegyricus dictus clementissimo regi Theodorico ab Ennodio dei Famulo," *ibid.*, p. 214; see also Pfeilschifter, *Kirche*, pp. 147 ff.

63. Cf. Duchesne, *L'Église*, p. 74.

64. Pfeilschifter, *Kirche*, p. 173; and *Theoderich*, p. 94; *LP*, I, 106; Caspar, II, 193.

65. Duchesne, *L'Église*, p. 95.

66. Schurr, p. 223.

67. Cf. Harnack, II, 422.

68. Agnellus XXVII. 72, pp. 91 f.; and Testi, *ibid.*

69. Agnellus xxvii. 78, p. 201; on the question of authenticity see Testi, pp. 201 ff.

70. See above, n. 38. The several volumes which Agnellus mentions seem to refer to this work only.

71. We refer to the much disputed question of the authorship of the *Pars posterior* of the *Anonymus Valesianus;* Waitz and, following him, Holder-Egger and a large number of other scholars have suggested that chaps. 79 ff. (24 ff. in Cessi's edition) of this work, with their remarkable anti-Gothic bias, are really based on the *Chronicle* of Maximian. This theory has been rejected by R. Cessi, "Studi critici preliminari" in his edition of the *Anonymus Valesianus* (in Muratori, *Rerum Italicarum scriptores*, XXIV, Part IV [Citta di Castello, 1913], clxii ff.), largely on the ground that the evidence is insufficient and—far less convincingly—on that of the date, between 527 and 533, which he assigns to these parts of the work. Testi's assertion that Maximian was not even the author of the *Chronicle* seems to provide a further difficulty. It may be observed, however, that the only safe assumption in regard to the author of the *Pars posterior* is that he was a cleric of Ravenna, writing around the middle of the sixth century; that this period coincided with the episcopate of Maximian, who was famed as a historical author; that, if the *Chronicle* is not Maximian's work, the history from which Agnellus made his excerpts certainly was; that these excerpts, as we have suggested, may reflect his ability subtly to color historical narrative; that the archbishop's position lent extraordinary weight to whatever views he expressed in his work; and that, finally, anti-Gothic bias became official policy under his administration only. If these shreds of evidence are pieced together, it is difficult to avoid the conclusion that the legend which masterfully created an anti-Theodorican myth that survived for centuries is the work of Maximian, whose genius and policy it reflects.

72. "Emendavi cautissime cum his, que Augustinus, et secundum evangelia, que beatus Ieronimus Romam misit et parentibus suis direxit, tantum ne ab idiotis vel mali scriptoribus vicientur" (Agnellus xxvii. 81, p. 208).

73. See *ibid.*, and Testi's commentary. K. Mohlberg, moreover, has sought to identify Maximian as the author or editor of the oriental section of the *Martyrologium Hieronymianum* (see *OC*[3], Vol. VII [1932]).

74. Duchesne, *Origines*, p. 187; Baumstark, *Liturgia*; Testi, p. 209; see, however, T. Schermann, "Die pseudoambrosianische Schrift *De sacramentis*," *RQ*, Vol. XVII (1903). Schermann suggests Maximus of Turin as the author and asserts that "Verfasser stand im Metropolitanverband mit Mailand wenn er nicht dort ansässig war." More recently, the *De sacramentis* has again been vindicated for St. Ambrose (see G.

Morin, "Pour l'authenticité du *De sacramentis*," *JL*, Vol. VIII [1928], with whom V. L. Kennedy [p. 19] agrees; cf. *JTS*, Vol. XLIV [1943]).

75. Cf. Schuster, II, 253, and IV, 368, where the archbishop of Ravenna is called "the real Minister of Public Worship in Italy." Cabrol, *Ravenne*, stresses the importance of Peter Chrysologus for the development of the Roman liturgy.

76. Testi, p. 210.

77. See Mohlberg-Baumstark, p. 44*.

CHAPTER TWO

1. Agnellus xxiv. 58, p. 167.

2. The inscription (*ibid.* 61, p. 172) names SS. Gervase and Protase as sons of St. Vitalis and thus betrays the influence of the *Passio*.

3. "Expensas vero in predicti martiris Vitalis eclesia, sicut in elogio sancta recordationis memorie Iuliani fundatoris invenimus, XXVI. milia aureorum expensi sunt solidorum" (Agnellus xxiv. 58, p. 167).

4. The episcopates of Ursicinus and Victor, which intervened between those of Ecclesius and Maximian, lasted only three and six years, respectively. The dearth of artistic projects within these years is nevertheless noteworthy if we recall that it took Maximian barely a year to build S. Stefano (see Agnellus' remarks: xxv. 62, p. 174; 63, p. 178; xxvi. 66, p. 181). Testi-Rasponi also concluded "che le costruzioni giulianee, intorno al 540, erano molto arretrate" (p. 178).

5. Van Berchem, p. 146. According to Agnellus (xxiv. 61, p. 173), Ecclesius' episcopate lasted only ten years and five months; hence Van Berchem's chronology is inaccurate and should read *532* instead of *534*.

6. Pfeilschifter, *Theoderich*, p. 94. Ecclesius' unreliability, from the emperor's viewpoint, may account for the large measure of authority which Julianus Argentarius assumed over the initial phases of the architectural program.

7. Swoboda, though he does not share my view as to the homogeneity of the entire program of mosaics, dates them after 539 and "wahrscheinlich nach Amtsantritt Maximians" (K. M. Swoboda, *Neue Aufgaben der Kunstgeschichte* [Brünn, 1935], pp. 33 ff.).

8. On the *Agnus Dei* in the Roman rite see Bishop, *LH*, p. 145. For the lamb symbolism in the Eastern liturgies cf. Brightman, pp. 24, 63, 73; Jungmann, pp. 229 f.

9. The idea of a Book of Life which lists the names of the elect is, of course, derived from the Book of Revelation (cf. 20: 10, etc.); on the diptychs of Ravenna see Lanzoni, *Studi*. Interesting evidence for the dependence of the portraits of SS. Gervase and Protase upon the *Passio SS. Martyrum Gervasii et Protasii* is adduced by Savio, pp. 788 ff. On the derivation of these medallion images from funerary portraits see Grabar, *Martyrium*, II, 24 ff.

10. Cf. Van Berchem, p. 152. In patristic exegesis the three angels signify, of course, the Trinity. See Cyril of Alexandria *Contra Julianum* i. 20 (*PG*, LXXVI, 532 ff.); the passage is quoted in the otherwise valueless study of J. Quitt, "Die Mosaiken von San Vitale in Ravenna: Eine Apologie des Diophysitismus," in J. Strzygowski, *Byzantinische Denkmäler*, Vol. III (Vienna, 1903).

11. *De sacramentis* iv. 6. 27 (*PL*, XVI, 464); it would seem that we can trace this prayer even farther back. The Pseudo-Augustinian *Quaestiones veteris et novi testamenti* 109. 21 (*CSEL*, L, 268) attacks the church for calling Melchizedek the "high priest" (*summus sacerdos*) instead of reserving this title for Christ only. The author of the *Quaestiones* has been identified as the converted Jew, Isaac, who wrote at Rome between 370 and 374 (see G. Morin, "L'Ambrosiaster et le juif converti Isaac," *Revue d'histoire et de littérature chrétiennes*, Vol. IV [1899], and also in *RB*, Vol. XX [1903]; Bardenhewer, III, 523 ff.; and Kennedy, p. 20).

12. The sacrifice of Melchizedek was already represented in Santa Maria Maggiore near the sanctuary and may thus be taken as an allusion to the liturgy (see Van Berchem, Fig. 15); it is noteworthy that the next scene in this cycle is again that of Abraham and the three angels. See also the following prayer from the dedication rite of a church: ". . . sicut Melchisedech Sacerdotis praecipui oblationem dignatione mirabili suscipisti, ita imposita huic novo altari munera, semper accepta ferre digneris" (*Pontificale,* "De ecclesiae dedicatione").

13. See Stornaiolo, p. 7; and the recent essay by M. Anastos, "The Alexandrian Origin of the *Christian Topography* of Cosmas Indicopleustes," *Dumbarton Oaks Papers,* Vol. III (Cambridge, 1946), where the work is assigned to the years 543–52. I was unable to use E. O. Winstedt's edition of the *Topographia Christiana* (Cambridge, 1909).

14. *PG*, LXXXVIII, 194.

15. Schuster, III, 150 ff.; Mabillon, II, 77 ff.

16. Martène, I, 34; cf. esp. 41; and *DACL, s.v.* "apertio aurium." Patristic exegesis occasionally assigns the animals to different evangelists (see J. Sauer, *Symbolik des Kirchengebäudes* [Freiburg, 1902], pp. 63 ff.).

17. On the rendering of *nomina sacra* in early inscriptions see L. Traube, *Nomina sacra* (Munich, 1907).

18. For reproductions of the works mentioned see Van Berchem, pp. 65, 84, 92, 107 f. Dr. Ernst Kitzinger calls my attention to another Roman precedent of the representation of the evangelists with their symbols in the Lateran (now destroyed) (see Ciampini, Vol. I, Pl. 75).

19. The suggestion is Testi-Rasponi's.

20. Alföldi, *Zeremoniell*, p. 70.

21. *De mundi creatione* (*PG*, LVI, 489); quoted in Kruse, pp. 79 f.

22. See Setton.

23. Bréhier-Batiffol, pp. 24 f.

24. Agnellus xviii. 25, p. 72.

25. See Alföldi, *Zeremoniell*, p. 78; Kruse, pp. 31 ff. The statue of Theodora in Constantinople (cf. Procopius *De aedif.* i. 11. 8 f.) gave monumental expression to her political role in the imperial capital.

26. A parallel to the portraits in San Vitale was the mosaic in the vestibule of the Sacred Palace, where Justinian and Theodora were shown receiving the submission of the kings of the Goths and Vandals and the "godlike honors" of the senate (cf. Procopius *De aedif.* xx. 1. 10. 10 ff.).

27. *CJ* xi. 40. 4 (ed. Paul Krueger [Berlin, 1877], p. 976).

28. *MGH Epist.*, II, 365; cf. Kruse, p. 45; Voigt, p. 88.

29. Testi, p. 197; I cannot follow the distinguished historian's assertion that the offerings depicted are merely symbolic.

30. On this ancient rite, which will be more fully discussed in a subsequent chapter, see *Ordo Romanus I* in Mabillon, II, 11. This *Ordo* is, in substance at least, almost certainly from the time of Gregory the Great (cf. J. Koesters, *Studien zu Mabillons römischen Ordines* [Münster, 1905], pp. 12 ff.); see also J. Bona, *Rerum liturgicarum libri duo* (Augustae Taurinorum, 1753), I, 198 ff.; Berlendis, *De oblat.*; J. B. Thiers, *Traités des cloches et de la sainteté de l'offrande* (Paris, 1721), pp. 173 ff.; Martène, I, 139 f. The earliest known representation of the offertory occurs in the floor mosaic of the ancient basilica of Aquileia (*ca.* A.D. 314) (see *Aquileia*, Pl. 41; also Eisler, p. 204; H. Lietzmann, "Die Entstehung der christlichen Liturgie nach den ältesten Quellen," *Vorträge der Bibl. Warburg*, 1925–26).

31. *MGH Leges*, Sec. III, *Concilia* i, p. 166.

32. T. Klauser reports an interesting example: "Liturgie der Heiligsprechung," *Heilige Überlieferung: Ildefons Herwegen zum silbernen Abtsjubiläum* (Münster, 1938).

33. See Probst, p. 178; E. Bishop in *Narsai*, p. 117.

34. Theodoretus, *Ecclesiastica historia* v. 17 (*PG*, LXXXII, 1232 f.).

35. *De cerim.* ii. 26 (*PG*, CXII, 1164); Sozomenus, *Historia ecclesiastica* vii. 25 (*PG*, LXXII, 1496).

36. *Testi*, p. 197.

37. Cf. F. Kern, "Der *Rex et Sacerdos* in bildlicher Darstellung," *Festschrift Dietrich Schaefer* (Jena, 1915), pp. 1 ff.

38. *Cosmas* 216.

39. N. Kondakoff, *Histoire de l'art byzantin* (Paris, 1886), I, 139.

40. *Vita Constantini* (*PG*, XX, 12 [926], 20 [935], 38/39 [951f.]).

41. See Treitinger, pp. 81 ff.

42. *Oratio* i ("Loeb Classical Library" ed.; Dio i, pp. 20 ff.).

43. *Cosmas* 192.

44. Eisler, p. 59.

45. See the Moses Midrash (after Isa. 63:11; Ezek. 34:12 ff.), quoted by I. Scheftelowitz, "Das Fischsymbol im Judentum und Christentum," *Archiv für Religionswissenschaft*, XIV (1911), 31 f.; Eisler, p. 53.

46. See Wulff, p. 107; Eisler, p. 54.

47. See *Mosaicarum et Romanarum legum collatio*, ed. M. Hyamson (London, 1913). According to Hyamson (p. xlviii), the work was composed between 394 and 438.

48. Cf. Alvaro d'Ors Pérez-Peix, "La Actitud legislativa del Emperador Justiniano," *OCP*, Vol. XIII (1947).

49. The most memorable expression of this conviction is *Corpus juris civilis*, "De conceptione digestorum" (ed. Krueger-Mommsen [Berlin, 1893], p. xiii). On the Moses metaphor see also Grabar, *L'Empereur*, p. 90.

50. See above, chap. i, n. 16.

51. On the Milion see J. Ebersolt, *Le grand palais de Constantinople* (Paris, 1910), p. 15; S. Salaville, "L'Iconographie des sept conciles œcuméniques," *Echoes d'Orient*, XXIX (1926), 144 ff.; Grabar, L'Empereur, pp. 90 ff.

52. Schurr, p. 167; *Histoire*, pp. 429 f.

53. *De cerim.* 238; cf. Treitinger, p. 37.

54. *De cerim.* 216.

55. *CD* x. 6 and 25 (*CSEL*, XL, Part 1, 455 and 487 ff.).

56. It is probable that this comparison was suggested by the sumptuous vessels in which the *Augusti* are seen offering the eucharistic gifts. A formula for the *benedictio calicis* in the ancient Mozarabic rite compares the liturgical vessels with the golden "dishes and bowls" which Moses was commanded to prepare for the libations (Exod. 25:29): "Deus qui Moysi famulo tuo Horeb monte seruanda populo tuo praecepta disponens, templum sanctum tuum qualiter edificaret instituisti, sacra quoque uasa que inferri altario tuo deberent ad instar uasorum celestium docuisti . . ." (Férotin V, pp. 157 f.). On Moses in the liturgies of the East see *Orate Fratres*, October 5, 1947.

57. See Ephrem Syrus, *Opp. Omn.* (Rome, 1743), VI, 298, n. 42. Grabar has already called attention to the influence of these verses upon the iconography of the Second Advent.

58. See Stornaiolo, p. 89, *Pl.* XLIX.

59. See Wetter I, pp. 20 f. The eschatological aspect of the liturgy will be more fully discussed in a subsequent chapter.

60. See below, pp. 90 ff.

61. *De cerim.* i. 60 (*PG*, CXII, 541 f.). See below, p. 119.

62. See Testi, p. 197. The story seems to originate with Rubeus, pp. 158 f. (also in Graevius, VII, Part 1, 154).

63. M. Magistretti, *La Liturgia della chiesa milanese nel secolo IV* (Milan, 1899), p. 195; Kennedy, p. 21.

64. Boniface I in his *Ep.* vii, written in A.D. 420 to the Emperor Honorius (*PL*, XX, 767); Celestine I (422–32) *Ep.* xxiii. 1 *ad Theodos. jun.* (*PL*, L, 528); both letters are quoted in R. H. Connolly, "Liturgical Prayers of Intercession. I. The Good Friday," *JTS*, Vol. XXI (1919/20).

65. See Canon 29 of the Council of Elvira (A.D. 305 or 306) in Hefele, I, 139; and Jerome *Comment. in Jerem. proph.* (*PL*, XXIV, 784); both passages are quoted by Bishop (see *Narsai*, pp. 98 ff.).

66. *PL*, XX, 551 ff. On the interpretation of the difficult passage see R. H. Connolly, "Pope Innocent I *De nominibus recitandis*," *JTS*, Vol. XX (1918/19); Kennedy (p. 23) agrees with Connolly's interpretation.

67. *Cosmas* 299.

68. The text of the liturgy of St. Mark in Brightman, p. 129; cf. Lietzmann, *Messe*, pp. 91 f. The Mozarabic prayer referred to is a *benedictio super munus quod quisque ecclesiae offert*: "Deus . . . te supplices nixis precibus exoramus, ut de sede Maiestatis tuae oblationi fidelium sanctificator accedas. Suscipe de manu famulorum tuorum Illorum munus oblatum, quod a tua clementia benedictum, in huius sanctuarii tui usum manet consecratum sint hec in conspectu tuo libenter accepta sicut quondam Abel famuli tui uel Melchisedec munera tibi placuerunt oblata" (Férotin V, p. 158). The editor stresses the relation of the prayer to the "objets offerts pour le culte et la décoration du sanctuaire"; but, if even such gifts could evoke the image of the sacrifices of Abel and Melchizedek, this must be true, a fortiori, for the oblation of the eucharistic elements.

69. John's letter in A. Thiel, *Epistolae Romanorum pontificum genuae*, (Brunsbergae, 1867), pp. 832 f. The passage in question reads as follows: "Tantum ad satisfaciendum scripsimus ut et venerabile nomen sanctae recordationis Leonis quondam facti urbis Romae archiepiscopi in sacris diptychis tempore consecrationis propter concordiam affigeretur." From this, Bishop (*Narsai*, p. 111) infers, probably correctly, that "as early as the beginning of the sixth century the diptychs were recited in the mass of Constantinople in the same place as that in which they are found in the earliest extant MSS of that liturgy and in the present rite, i.e., after the consecration." J. Pargoire (*L'Église byzantine* [Paris, 1923], p. 100), on the other hand, and, following him, L. Bréhier (*Histoire*, pp. 547 ff.) believe that even in the sixth-century version of the liturgy of Chrysostom the diptychs of the living and the dead preceded the canon. In regard to the intercession for the emperor, the two opinions do not necessarily conflict if we assume an additional prayer for the emperor at the time of the offertory, especially when he attended the sacred rite or was to be especially commemorated as donor of the church. The brief intercession at the time of the Great Entry, quoted in the text above (Brightman, p. 378), shows the possibility of two separate intercessions. It is noteworthy that the Russian rite, which also descends from that of Chrysostom, commemorates the emperor and his family in the same place (see D. Sokolow, *Darstellung des Gottesdienstes der orthodox-katholischen Kirche des Morgenlandes* [Berlin, 1893], p. 64).

70. See Berlendis, *De oblat.*, pp. 260 ff.; Ebner, p. 414; Stefanescu, II, 428.

71. Brightman, pp. 333 and 389. Prayers on behalf of the ruler originate, of course, in the exhortation of St. Paul (I Tim. 2:2). The elaborate wording and imagery of the liturgy of St. Basil is of special interest in view of the age of this rite. A letter of Peter the Deacon and other oriental monks, written about A.D. 520, attests its existence and general usage in the Christian East (*PL*, LXV, 449; cf. *DACL*, VI, Part II, 1599). The fact of the liturgy's existence at the time of Justinian does not yet prove its text to have been identical with that of the ninth century; on the contrary, there is good reason to think that the wording of the diptychs may have been varied from time to time at that early age. But I see no reason why the thought and imagery of the intercession for the emperor, as preserved in the ninth-century version of the liturgy of Basil, should not be an accurate reflection of much older prayers.

72. In the Eastern church, Justinian and Theodora are both venerated as saints (Feasts, November 14/15) (see Bréhier-Batiffol, p. 72).

CHAPTER THREE

1. Cf. also the remarks of Van Berchem, p. 163.

2. See Diehl, *Justinien*, p. 321, and *Études*, p. 321; Voigt, pp. 52, 175.

3. Diehl, *Études*, p. 321.

4. See Testi, p. 198.

5. See Hodgkin, p. 641.

6. Agnellus xxvii. 79, p. 207.

7. See, e.g., *ibid.* 75, p. 193.

8. See Testi, p. 192.

9. *Ep.* 32, in *CSEL*, XXIX, 283 f.

10. See Van Berchem, pp. 65, 106, 113.

11. The mausoleum of the empress is undoubtedly an adaptation of the cruciform *martyrion*. Though St. Gregory Nazianzen and St. Ambrose interpret this architectural form allegorically, i.e., as an allusion to the cross, the cruciform funerary monument predates Christianity (see Grabar, *Martyrium*, I, 153 ff. and 304). On the mausoleum of Galla Placidia see Van Berchem, pp. 91 ff., Ricci, *MTS Sepolcro di Galla Placidia*, esp. p. 121; and Grabar, *Martyrium, passim*.

12. Agnellus xxi. 35, p. 95, and Testi, *ibid.* The cross-staff was originally the scepter of the Christian emperor (see J. Gagé, "Σταυρὸς νικοποιός, La victoire impériale dans l'empire chrétien," *Revue d'histoire et de philosophie religieuses*, XIII (Strassburg, 1933), 382; Morath, p. 58; Grabar, *Martyrium*, II, 35.

13. See Van Berchem, p. 92.

14. *Ibid.*

15. *Ep. ad Constantinum Imp.* 4 (*PG*, XXXIII, 1170). The vision was said to have appeared above Golgotha.

16. May 3 and September 14; the reference in Van Berchem, p. 93.

17. Wickhoff, "Das Apsismosaik in der Basilika des H. Felix zu Nola," *RQ*, Vol. III (1889); on Nilus see W. Ellinger, *Die Stellung der alten Christen zu den Bildern in den ersten vier Jahrhunderten* (Leipzig, 1930), pp. 76 ff.

18. *Sermo lix: De passione domini* (*PL*, LIV, 337 ff.). For an illustration of this concept of the Passion in early Christian art see J. Wilpert. *Sarcofagi*, Vol. I, Pl. 146, No. 3; the *Via Crucis* in Sant' Apollinare Nuovo of Ravenna offers another example; see also Jerphanion, *La Voix des monuments* (Paris, 1930), pp. 138 ff.

19. *Sermo li* (*PL*, LIV, 308 ff.).

20. See Cornelius a Lapide, *Commentarius in quatuor evangelia* (Antwerp, 1660), p. 328.

21. II, 422; cf. E. Schwartz's judgment: "Dass sie [i.e., Justinian's ecclesiastical policy] eine Politik des Augenblicks war, abhängig von der jeweiligen Kamarilla, vom Praktischen abgelenkt durch die Sucht in theologischer Schriftstellerei zu dilettieren, erzwungen zugleich und gehemmt durch den unterirdischen Kampf gegen seine Gemahlin, deren Willensstärke und Schlauheit ihm überlegen war" ("Drei dogmatische Schriften Justinians," *Abhandlungen der Bayerischen Akademie der Wissenschaften, Philosophisch-historische Abteilung*, N.F., XVIII [1939], 117). I do not feel that this judgment of the distinguished historian takes sufficient account of the greater political considerations of which Justinian's theology was but a part.

22. On the Monza vials and their relation to monumental art see Morey, *Art*, p. 123, and esp. Grabar, *Martyrium*, II, 173 ff.

23. It should be pointed out, on the other hand, that in the apse mosaic in S. Stefano Rotondo (seventh century), the medallion portrait of Christ appears likewise above the cross (see Van Berchem, p.

205). Grabar (*Martyrium*, II, 194) likewise compares the composition in Classe with the representation on the vial.

24. See Testi, pp. 211 ff.

25. Millet, *Iconogr.*, Figs. 2, 3; A. Goldschmidt and K. Weitzmann, *Die byzantinischen Elfenbeinskulpturen*, II (Berlin, 1934), p. 222, Pl. 72.

26. Wickhoff, *op. cit.*, p. 173, and Van Berchem, pp. 160 f. In defense of this theory Van Berchem adduces a twelfth-century chronicle, according to which the artist had planned to depict in this space the Savior but, upon returning from his meal, discovered "hanc iconam longe mirabiliorem, quam sua, vel aliorum ingenia pingere valuissent." Van Berchem infers (*a*) that, since the present figure of St. Apollinaris is not miraculously beautiful, the chronicler's enthusiasm can be explained only by his special devotion for the saint and (*b*) that the story proves that the original intention had been to represent Christ in the place of St. Apollinaris. In point of fact, the passage does not refer to this figure at all but to the medallion portrait of Christ in the cross above (see Ricci, *MTS, S. Apollinare in Classe*, p. 13). Grabar (*Martyrium*, II, 193 ff.) maintains the integrity of the entire composition. His interpretation differs from mine by its emphasis upon the *theophany* motif, which, to me, appears too exclusive.

27. On the martyr as imitator of Christ see Reitzenstein, *Bemerkungen*, and Lucius, pp. 64 ff.; the most curious evidence of the identification of Christ and his martyr occurs on a gold glass, now in the Metropolitan Museum, where a Christ-like man carrying the cross is in all probability an image of St. Lawrence. This interpretation of Garrucci (*Vetri* [Rome, 1858], Pl. 20, No. 1) is supported by H. Vopel, *Die altchristlichen Goldgläser* (Freiburg, 1899), pp. 53 f. (Pl. 24, *a*).

28. See J. Lindblom, "Altchristliche Kreuzessymbolik," *Studia orientalia*, Vol. I (1925); on the *Orans* gesture in the ancient liturgy of Ravenna see Lanzoni, *Reliquie*; he bases his conclusions on the lost mosaic in S. Giovanni Evangelista (see Ricci, *MTS, San Giovanni Evangelista*) which we know from Agnellus' description. For the meaning of the gesture in the Roman rite see V. Thalhofer and L. Eisenhofer, *Handbuch der katholischen Liturgik* (Freiburg, 1912), II, 148 and 162; in Christian art Grabar, *Martyrium*, II, 51 f.

29. See the representation in S. Stefano Rotondo of the martyrs Primus and Felician, flanking a cross which is surmounted by a medallion with Christ's image (Van Berchem, p. 205); also the sarcophagus in Wilpert, *Sarcofagi*, III, 299. In either case the cross is, more than a symbol, the mystical token of resurrection and should be very closely related to early Christian funerary inscriptions, in which the Greek letter Tau is placed in the middle of the dead person's name (e.g., DionTysiou, KyriTllou) (see Wilpert, *Sarcofagi*, Testo, II, 323). On the cross in the iconography of martyrs see E. Schaefer, "Die Heiligen mit dem Kreuz in der christlichen Kunst," *RQ*, Vol. XLIV (1936); H. Achelis, *Die Katakomben von Neapel* (Leipzig, 1936), Pl. 36; and Grabar, *Martyrium*, II, 68 f.

30. See Loisy, p. 309.

31. James, p. 333.

32. See Wetter I, pp. 126 ff.

33. James, p. 333.

34. See the passage quoted in Wetter I, p. 124, and James, pp. 253 ff., 332 ff., 359 ff.

35. In early Christian art the same thought is expressed by juxtaposing the martyrdom of Peter and Paul with the Passion of Christ (see Wilpert, *Sarcofagi*, Testo, I, 46 ff., and Pls. I, 121, 1; 146, 1, and II, 283; more recently Grabar, *Martyrium*, II, 259).

36. *Exhort. ad mart.* 30 (*PG*, XI, 599 ff.).

37. See A. Wilmart, "Transfigurare," *Bulletin d'ancienne littérature et d'archéologie chrétiennes*, Vol. I (1911); J. Brinktrine, "Die Trans-

formatio [transfiguratio] Corporis et Sanguinis Christi in den alten abendländischen Liturgien," *Theologie und Glaube*, Vol. VIII (1916). The difference of opinion between the two authors is irrelevant for our investigation. Further material in Brinktrine, "Zur Entstehung der morgenländischen Epiklese," *ZKT*, XLII (1918), esp. 315 ff.; and Lietzmann, *Messe*, pp. 109 ff.

38. The mosaic in the monastery of St. Catherine is reproduced in V. N. Beneshevich, *Monumenta Sinaitica archeologica et paleographica* (Leningrad, 1925), Pl. II; Van Berchem, p. 183; Grabar, *Martyrium*, Pl. 41, No. 2. For other examples of the Transfiguration in early Christian art see Van Berchem, p. 222, and Grabar, *Martyrium*, Pl. 62, No. 7. For a discussion of the importance of this scene in early Christian art see Grabar, *Martyrium*, II, 193; cf. also Millet, *Iconogr.*, pp. 15 ff.

39. See Wetter II, pp. 48 ff.; Brinktrine, *op. cit.*, p. 514; and Brightman, pp. 88, 179, 329.

40. For the following see, above all, Casel, *Mysterium*; also C. A. Kneller, "Eucharistie und Martyrium," *SZ* (1894).

41. Ignatius *Rom.* 4 (*PG*, V, 807); *De mart. S. Polycarpi* (*PG*, V, 1039); Cyprian *Ep.* lvii. 3 (*CSEL*, III, Part 3, 652); cf. Cyprian, *De corona* 7.

42. This is particularly noticeable in the ancient Prefaces on the feast of a martyr; see, e.g., the *Contestatio* on the feast of St. Stephen in the *Missale Gothicum* (Bannister, I, 9; Muratori, *Liturgia*, II, 522 ff.).

43. "Dignum et justum est; aequum et salutare est; nos tibi semper agere gratias, omnipotens et misericors Deus, inter has sacramentorum epulas Martyris tui caput cum evangelica recordatione misceri; ut velut in disco metalli radiantis, ita super mensam tuae propitiationis offerre . . ." (Muratori, *Liturgia*, II, 625; Bannister, I, 110).

44. Eusebius *Hist. eccles.* v. 1 (*PG*, XX, 417 and 422).

45. *Passio SS. Martyrum Perpetuae et Felicitatis* 5 (*PL*, III, 48).

46. Note the phrase "Deus, qui hanc sacratissimam noctem veri luminis fecisti illustratione clarescere," in the first Mass of Christmas or the oration on Easter Sunday: "Deus, qui hodierna die, per Unigenitum tuum aeternitatis nobis aditum, devicta morte, reserasti. . . ."

47. See Wieland, *Altar*, p. 144. In the Orient the development was different (see *ibid.*, pp. 98 ff.; and Grabar, *Martyrium*, I, esp. 350 ff.).

48. Maximus *Sermo* lxxvii (*PL*, LVII, 689 f.).

49. Cf. chap. i, n. 6.

50. Grabar, *Martyrium*, I, 349 ff. and 386 ff. Grabar has, I think, stressed too exclusively the influence of the *martyrion* upon Byzantine architecture, at the expense of liturgical influences. The "sepulchral" ground plan of these sanctuaries and the covering dome reflect, I believe, the influence of the *epiklesis* as well as the religious sentiment of which this liturgical prayer is the expression. The *epiklesis* shares with the baptismal rite the vision of the Holy Spirit descending in the shape of a dove. Does not this fact explain the structural affinities between Eastern churches and baptistries? See below, pp. 117–19.

51. Grabar (I, 38 f. and 350) rightly stresses the fact, of great significance in this connection, that the Book of Revelation was considered canonical only in the West, not in the East.

52. See Wieland, *Altar*, p. 184; Grabar, *Martyrium*, II, 27. Reproductions of the figure in A. Venturi, *Storia dell'arte italiana* (Milan, 1901), p. 449, Fig. 407; C. Cecchelli, *S. Agnese fuori le mura e S. Costanza* (Rome, n.d.), Fig. 3; and Grabar, *Martyrium*, Pl. 32, No. 2. The liturgy offers an interesting parallel to the iconography of St. Agnes: "Beata Agnes in medio flammarum expansis manibus orabat," we read in the Office of her feast day.

53. See Van Berchem, p. 195.

54. A dedicatory inscription in the same church, apparently by a niece of Constantine the Great, reads like an explanation of the mosaic:

the sanctuary of St. Agnes announces, above all, the glory of Christ's resurrection, in which not only he but the members of his mystical body have been carried triumphantly from the night of darkness to heavenly triumph (see H. Marucchi, *Éléments d'archéologie chrétienne*, Vol. III: *Basiliques et églises de Rome* [Paris, 1902], 470).

55. Symm. *LP.* i. 263. I am gratified to see that Grabar, too (*Martyrium*, II, 60 and 106), maintains the thesis that the present mosaic reflects the iconography of an older work.

56. "Diuinum ueneranda tegunt altaria foedus
     Conpositis sacra cum cruce martyribus.
     Cuncta salutiferi coeunt martyria Christi,
     Crux corpus sanguis martyris, ipse deus.
     Namque deus semper uobis sua munera seruat;
     Atque ubi Christus, ibi spiritus et pater est.
     Sic ubi crux, et martyr ibi, quia martyris et crux,
     Martyrii sanctis quae pia causa fuit" (*Ep.* 32 [*CSEL*, XXIX, 283 f.]).

57. Diehl, *Etudes*, p. 269.

58. *Lib. diurn.*, No. 2 (also referred to in Diehl, *Études*, p. 269). "Superscriptio ad Archiepiscopum Ravennae. Reverentissimo et sanctissimo fratri ill. coepiscopo. . . ." The last word is also significant. It is not used to address other bishops, not even the patriarch of Constantinople.

59. Cf. above, pp. 21 f.

60. The *Passio* is printed in *ASS*, XXXII (Julii V), 344 ff., and in Mombritius, I, 117 ff. Cf. *BHL*, p. 623. On the political significance of the legend see Lanzoni, *Fonti*; Zattoni, *Valore*, and "La Data della 'Passio S. Apollinaris' di Ravenna," *Accademia reale delle scienze di Torino*, Vol. XXXIX (1903/4).

61. Lanzoni, *Diocesi*, pp. 740 ff. See the legend reported by Agnellus xxii. 49, p. 145, and Testi's comments (*ibid.*).

62. See below, pp. 61 ff.

63. Lanzoni, *Diocesi*, p. 740.

64. Dom G. Morin links this event to the establishment of the feast of Apollinaris in the Roman calendar and also interprets the liturgical texts in the light of the diplomatic relations between the sees of Ravenna and Rome: "Liturgie et basiliques de Rome au milieu du VIIe siècle, d'après les listes d'évangiles de Wuerzburg," *RB*, Vol. XXVIII (1911). Cf. St. Beissel, "Entstehung der Perikopen des römischen Messbuches," *SZ*, *Ergänzungsheft* 96 (Freiburg, 1907).

65. Morin sees in the gospel pericope an allusion to the *autokephalia*; it would seem more logical to assume that the honors bestowed upon St. Apollinaris were attempts to forestall this schism. On this assumption the selection of the liturgical texts must fall into the period before, rather than after, A.D. 666. See also P. Luther, *Die Beziehungen des Erzbistums Ravenna zum römischen Stuhl* (Berlin, 1889), p. 27.

66. See the gospel in its relation to the stational church and, in fact, to the entire liturgy of the first Monday of Lent.

67. See Wilpert, *Sarcofagi*, Testo, I, 129 ff.; cf. Pls. 52, No. 3, and 19, No. 6; *DACL*, XIV, Part I, 956 f.; Garrucci (*Storia*, V, 12) identifies the bearded *kriophoros* as the Good Shepherd.

68. *LP* i. 323. Cf. Will, pp. 18 ff. and 50.

69. *PL*, LII, 552; see also Cabrol, "Saint Pierre Chrysologue, a tous ses titres ajouterait celui de l'un des pères de la liturgie latine" (*Ravenna* p. 500).

70. *ASS*, Julii V, p. 339.

71. Lanzoni, *Diocesi*, p. 747.

72. See above, n. 28.

73. Gregory Nazianzen *Oratio* xxi. 29 (*PG*, XXXV, 115 f.).

74. *Const. apost.* ii. 26, p. 104.

75. *Narsai*, pp. 4 ff.

76. See Schermann, *Kirchenordnung*, II, 196 ff.

77. The third representation of this kind was commissioned by Maximian's successor, Agnellus, and seems to have adorned the back of his episcopal throne in the cathedral; it depicted the archbishop praying "manibus expanssis" (see Agnellus xxviii. 89, p. 222, and Testi's comment, *ibid.*).

78. On the mosaic see Ricci, *MTS, San Giovanni Evangelista;* Lanzoni, *Studi*. On Peter's career see Lanzoni, *Diocesi*, pp. 749 ff.

79. *Exhort. ad mart.* 30.

80. Cyprian calls the martyr "clero nostro non humana suffragatione sed divina dignatione conjunctus" (*Ep.* 39 [*CSEL*, III, Part 3, 581 f.]); see *Canon. Hippol.* 43: "Quando quis dignus est qui stet coram tribunali propter fidem et afficiatur poena propter Christum, postea autem indulgentia liber dimittitur, talis postea meretur gradum presbyterialem coram Deo, non secundum ordinationem, quae fit ab episcopo; immo confessio est ordinatio eius" (printed in Duchesne, *Origines*, p. 528; see also Lucius, pp. 64 ff.; *DACL*, X, Part II, 2471).

81. *Rom.* 4 (*PG*, V, 807); translations of this and the following passages in the text are from *Ante-Nicene Fathers*, I, 45 ff.

82. *Trall.* 7 (*PG*, V, 785); the concept of the altar as the place of mystical union between the martyr and Christ occurs also in Origen, *Exhort. ad mart.* 30; and in Cyprian(?) *De corona* 30.

83. *Philad.* 3 (*PG*, V, 820 f.).

84. *Magn.* 6 (*PG*, V, 764).

85. *Ibid.* 7.

86. *Eph.* 4 (*PG*, V, 733 f.).

87. Lanzoni, *Diocesi*, p. 746. Zattoni's attempt (*Valore*, p. 690) to deduce Apollinaris' Western origin from his name is hardly convincing. Apollinaris of Laodicea was not the only distinguished Eastern bearer of that name.

88. Peter Chrysologus, who hailed from the *territorium corneliense*, calls St. Cornelius his father (see *Sermo* clxv [*PL*, LII, 633 f.]; and Testi, p. 140).

89. The *Register* of Gregory the Great (v. 11; *MGH Epistolarum*, I, 292) provides further interesting evidence for the relation of St. Apollinaris to the ecclesiastical aspirations of Ravenna. On three great feasts was her archbishop entitled to wear the pallium, i.e., on those of John the Baptist, Peter, and Apollinaris. See Lanzoni, *Fonti*, p. 118, who points out that since the days of Maximian a solemn Mass seems to have been celebrated on St. Apollinaris' feast in Sant' Apollinare in Classe.

90. Augustine *CD* xviii. 18 (*CSEL*, XL, Part II, 289 ff.).

91. Agnellus, who refers to the defenders of the Three Chapters as Manichaeans (xxvii. 79, p. 206) may have borrowed this epithet from Maximian's historical writings.

92. Whereas the acclamation formula for the pope was "Illum papam sanctus Petrus elegit," the archbishop of Ravenna was acclaimed, in his city, with the words "Illum episcopum sanctus Apollinaris elegit" (see Testi, p. 145, and Agnellus xxii. 49, p. 145).

93. Agnellus xxviii. 85, p. 216.

94. Grabar, *Martyrium*, II, 278 ff. and 297.

95. On the mosaics in St. Demetrius see C. Diehl, *Manuel de l'art byzantin* (Paris, 1925), I, 211; and Grabar, *Martyrium*, II, 88 f. and Pl. 50. There are, of course, innumerable examples of this use of art for apotropaic and prophylactic purposes throughout and even beyond the High Middle Ages.

96. *De imag.* i. 19 ff., quoted by Grabar, *Martyrium*, II, 340.

97. On Agnellus' designation of Ravenna's bishops as "saints" see Testi, p. 21. On the other hand, the term "sanctissimus," which Agnellus uses, is quite infrequent; Ursus shares it only with Peter Chrysolo-

gus, who actually was revered as a saint; the same may have been true for Ursus.

98. For the following see Ricci, *MTS, S. Apollinare in Classe.*

99. *Ibid.;* and Van Berchem, p. 166.

100. *De sacr.* vi. 27 (*PL*, XVI, 464); Lanzoni (*Studi*) suggests that the *epiklesis* of the liturgy of Ravenna may have read: "Et petimus . . . ut hanc oblationem suscipias in sublimi altari tuo per manus angelorum tuorum." The same phrase is employed in the Liturgy of St. Peter (see Goussens, in *OC²*, III, 13).

101. *Narsai* (Homily xxi), pp. 46 ff.

102. Van Berchem, pp. 54 f., 226, 246.

103. *Pontificale*, "In dedicatione ecclesiae," p. 871; see also Cabrol, *Le Livre de la prière antique* (Paris, 1900), p. 472.

104. Férotin VI, p. 149.

CHAPTER FOUR

1. Agnellus xxvii. 77; Testi, p. 196.

2. *Ibid.* It is not even certain whether Maximian consecrated the church as Agnellus asserts; the dedication took place in 545, when the episcopal chair of Ravenna was vacant, and the dedicatory inscription makes no mention of the consecration. See also the passage from the *Codex pontificalis*, quoted by Testi, p. 196.

3. Morath, p. 14; Cecchelli, *La Cattedra di Massimiano ed altri avorii romani orientali* (Rome, 1936 ff.); Morey (*Art*, pp. 92 ff.) also accepts the identification of the monogram as *Maximianus Episcopus*, though he assigns the chair, for no convincing reasons, to an earlier date; see also his review of Morath's work in *American Journal of Archeology*, Vol. XLV (1941).

4. The relevant passages have been collected by Morath, pp. 62 ff. But I should like to call attention to a passage in the *City of God* which may indicate that St. Augustine himself was aware of the relation between Serapis and Joseph. In xviii. 4 he tells the story of Joseph in Egypt, while in the following chapter he discusses the death and cult of Serapis, "the greatest god of Egypt," as having occurred at a time when Jacob visited Joseph in Egypt.

5. This date is also suggested by Morath.

6. On the professional organization of the ivory workers and the rules of their guild in the Roman Empire see J. P. Waltzing, *Étude historique sur les corporations professionnelles chez les romains depuis les origines jusqu'à la chute de l'Empire d'Occident* (Louvain, 1895–1900), II, 316 f.; and A. Stoeckle, *Spätrömische und byzantinische Zünfte* (*Klio*, Beiheft IX [1911]), p. 60. The carefully regulated and narrowly circumscribed professional conditions under which the *eborarius* worked must be recalled if one seeks to evaluate the style of Byzantine ivories.

7. See T. Klauser, *Die Cathedra im Totenkult der heidnischen und christlichen Antike*, *LQ*, Vol. VI (Münster, 1927); and C. Hopkins' (*The Christian Church at Dura Europos* [New Haven, 1934], p. 11) remarks on the cathedra in the Christian sanctuary at Dura.

8. In this connection Cecchelli (*op. cit.*, pp. 30 ff.) calls attention to the ancient ceremony of the imposition of hands, which the bishop also performed on his throne. On this rite see Martène, I, 13; and J. Coppens, *L'Imposition des mains et les rites connexes* (Wetteren and Paris, 1925), esp. pp. 208 ff.

9. Jaffé, p. 885; already quoted by Morath, p. 71.

10. See H. Grisar, *Das Missale im Lichte römischer Stadtgeschichte* (Freiburg, 1925), p. 39.

11. "Benedico te et per Jesum Christum Filium ejus unicum, Dominum nostrum, qui te in Cana Galilaeae, signo admirabili, sua potentia convertit in vinum."

12. See M. Rostovtzeff, *Dura-Europos and Its Art* (Oxford, 1938), p. 132. On the "purely baptismal" character of the liturgy of the fourth Friday of Lent see Schuster, II, 109. The Samaritan woman, as well as the wedding at Cana, is represented in Soterus' baptistry at Naples (*saec.* V) (see Van Berchem, p. 106).

13. On the relation of this miracle to the rite of the *illuminatio* of the catechumen see Grisar, *op. cit.,* p. 39.

14. See below, chap. v, n. 31.

15. Cf. the responsory for Palm Sunday: "Ingrediente Domino in sanctam civitatem, Hebraeorum pueri resurrectionem vitae pronuntiantes, cum ramis palmarum: Hosanna clamabant, in excelsis."

16. "Et quotquot sunt infantes in hisdem locis, usque etiam qui pedibus ambulare non possunt . . . omnes ramos tenentes alii palmarum alii olivarum: et sic deducetur episcopus in eo typo quo tunc Dominus deductus est" (Etheria, p. 84). Cf. above, chap. iii, n. 73.

17. Morath, p. 70.

18. The experience here under discussion was confined neither to the early Christian era nor to the sphere of religion. In his otherwise unreliable book, *Aeschylus and Athens* ([London, 1941], p. 37), G. Thomson has shown, conclusively to my mind, the relation between the concepts of purgation in Aristotelian poetics and in Hippocratic medicine and their common religious source.

19. The references are collected in A. Harnack, "Medicinisches aus der ältesten Kirchengeschichte," *Texte und Untersuchungen zur Geschichte der altchristlichen Literatur,* Vol. VIII (1892). For a later passage see *Narsai,* p. 61. In the Roman missal innumerable vestiges of this concept have survived (see *Gregorianum,* Index, *s.vv.* "medicina," "remedium"; on the problem see also *DACL, s.v.* "médecin").

20. *Const. apost.* ii. 41 (I, 130).

21. *Haer.* 30 (*PG,* XLI, 412). See the "Hymnus ad extremam unctionem" printed in Schuster, III, 440: "Christe, caelestis medicina Patris, verus humanae medicus salutis."

22. On the feast of St. Sylvester, the Roman breviary (Lectio IV) refers to Constantine's baptism as follows: "Quem [Constantinum] . . . sacro baptismate tinxit et ab infidelitatis lepra mundavit."

23. Lanzoni, *Fonti.*

CHAPTER FIVE

1. Agnellus xxvii. 82 f., p. 210.

2. See chap. iii, n. 93.

3. See Agnellus xxviii. 84, p. 214.

4. "Rubicundam habuit faciem, plenam formam . . . pulcer in corpore" (*ibid.*).

5. Jaffé, I, 996, 1007, 1009, 1032. These communications indicate excellent relations between Agnellus and Pope Pelagius I (558–60).

6. Duchesne, *L'Église,* p. 231.

7. Agnellus xxviii. 89, p. 222.

8. The pulpit which Agnellus commissioned for the cathedral is a work of exquisite taste (see *FR,* 1912, p. 267). Other works of his are mentioned by the chronicler Agnellus (*loc. cit.*).

9. Agnellus; and Testi, pp. 216 ff.

10. See G. Tura, "A proposito dell' abside di Sant' Apollinare Nuovo," *FR,* 1915/16, pp. 367 ff. Tura suggests that the apse may not have been entirely destroyed and that the chronicler Agnellus may thus deserve credence for his assertion that the procession of saints continued in the apse, perhaps as a presentation scene depicting the saints introduced into the presence of Christ by the apostles. The theological basis for this representation, so frequent in early Christian art, is the general belief of the age that the saints, after their death, are immediately received in heaven. The vision of their reception by Christ thus antici-

pates, as it were, that of the resurrection of mankind (see J. P. Kirsch, "Die Lehre von der Gemeinschaft der Heiligen im christlichen Alterthum," *FCL,* I, Part I [1900], 68 f.).

11. "Theodoricus rex hanc eclesiam a fundamentis in nomine Domini Nostri Yhesu Christi fecit" in Agnellus' quotation (xxviii. 86, p. 219).

12. The dependence of the compositions in Sant' Apollinare Nuovo upon the murals in the catacombs was pointed out by M. Mesnil, "Sur les mosaïques de Ravenne," *Rivista di archeologia cristiana,* Vol. V (1928); Morey (*Art,* p. 162) has stressed the Latin element in these works. But the first to emphasize their Roman inspiration seems to have been St. Beissel. In his essay, "Die Mosaiken von Ravenna," *SZ,* Vol. XLVII (1894), he justly directed the attention of art historians to the patronage of Theodoric and to Cassiodorus' remarks on his sovereign's taste.

13. "Et facta veterum exclusis defectibus innovemus, et nova vetustatis gloria vestiamus" (*Var.* vii. 5. 15 [*PL,* LXIX, 711]); "Antiquorum diligentissimus imitator modernorum nobilissimus institutor" (*Var.* iv. 51 [*PL,* LXIX, 642; see also 566, 718]).

14. Pfeilschifter, *Theoderich,* p. 46.

15. "Occurrit beato Petro devotissimus ac si catholicus" (*Anon. Vales.* xii. 65, p. 324).

16. Pfeilschifter, *Theoderich,* p. 87, and *Kirche,* pp. 52, 125 ff.; and *Histoire,* pp. 355 ff. Further evidence of the close relations between the Arian and the Orthodox churches at the time is provided by a manuscript in the Chapter Library at Verona. This manuscript contains an Arian sermon copied in the sixth century by a scribe of the Orthodox church at Verona who was unaware that he was actually copying what from his viewpoint was a heretical treatise (see H. Turner, "An Arian Sermon from a Ms. in the Chapter Library at Verona," *JTS,* XIII [1911–12], 20).

17. Pfeilschifter, *Theoderich,* pp. 72 f. On the king's tolerance see *Var.* ii. 27 and iv. 17 (*PL,* LXIX, 561 and 622); on his protection of the Catholic church see his *Edictum* 125 (*MGH, Leges* [quarto ed.], V, 165). In regard to the political effects of Theodoric's policy see the remark of the *Anonymus Valesianus* (p. 322): "Sic gubernavit duas gentes in uno Romanorum et Gothorum, dum ipse quidem Arianae sectae esset, tamen nihil contra religionem catholicam temptans." See *ibid.,* p. 324, and *Histoire,* p. 342, on the king's reception in Rome, the event which profoundly impressed St. Fulgentius of Ruspa, who happened to be in the Eternal City just then (cf. *S. Fulgentii Episcopi Ruspensi vita,* probably by the Carthaginian Deacon Ferrandus, *PL,* LXVI, 130 f.).

18. Testi, p. 220.

19. Contemporary with the mosaics in Sant' Apollinare Nuovo was the christological cycle in St. Sergius at Gaza (see the description by Choricius of Gaza, *Choricii Gazaei orationes declamationes fragmenta,* ed. J. F. Boissonade [Paris, 1846], pp. 91 ff.; cf. also J. Reil, *Die altchristlichen Bilderzyklen des Lebens Jesu* [Leipzig, 1910], pp. 109 ff.). Somewhat later, from about the middle of the sixth century (according to Heisenberg), were the christological mosaics in the Church of the Apostles in Constantinople (see A. Heisenberg, *Grabeskirche und Apostelkirche* [Leipzig, 1908], II, 166 ff.; and, for comment on Heisenberg's thesis, O.Wulff's *Bibliographisch-kritischer Nachtrag* [Berlin, 1935], p. 56).

20. One exception to be noted is the beardless Christ in the Prediction of Peter's Denial.

Curiously enough, the theological significance of the two distinct iconographies of Christ in one and the same building has been denied by such eminent scholars as De Jerphanion (*La Voix des monuments* [Paris, 1930], pp. 90 ff.) and L. Bréhier (*L'Art chrétien* [Paris, 1928], p. 73), who, like Ricci (*MTS S. Apollinare Nuovo,* pp. 33 f.), reversed his earlier opinions in favor of an unlikely theory of two different schools. But these scholars make no mention of the theological controversy to which we are referring in the following paragraphs and which makes it inconceivable that the cycles in Sant' Apollinare, at the time of their completion, should not have stirred up dogmatic speculations. It is also interesting to compare these cycles with those in the Church of the Apostles in Constantinople. According to Heisenberg, these mosaics were executed at just about the time of the struggle over the Three Chapters and stress the divinity of Christ at the expense of his humanity, a fact which is clearly shown by a glance at the subjects selected.

21. See Harnack, II, 343 f.

22. Mansi, VI, 962 f., chap. iii.

23. *Ibid.* VIII, 817 ff.

24. Morey, *Art*, p. 112.

25. Baumstark, "I Mosaici di Sant' Apollinare Nuovo e l'antico anno liturgico ravennate," *RG*, IX (1910), 32 ff.

26. See *DACL*, I, Part II, 2820: "Les ariens n'eurent pas de liturgie particulière ... il paraît donc assez vraisemblable que les évêques ariens ... s'attachèrent plutôt à faire oublier leur origine, qu'à bouleverser les habitudes chrétiennes." The same opinion is voiced in *Histoire*, p. 371; and by J. Zeiller, "Étude sur l'arianisme en Italie," *École française de Rome, mélanges d'archéologie et d'histoire*, XXV (1905), 131 f. This study is not in all regards reliable.

27. Agnellus x. 8. 24, p. 71. See Lanzoni, *Diocesi*, p. 736; and L. Bréhier, "Les Colonies orientaux en Occident," *Byzantinische Zeitschrift*, XII (1903), 9 ff.; and, for a noteworthy parallel, the recent essay by U. Monneret de Villard, on the close relations between Antioch and Milan during the sixth century and the reflections of Antiochene influences in the architecture and liturgy of Milan: "Antiochia e Milano nel VI secolo," *OCP*, Vol. XII (1946).

28. Schurr, p. 205.

29. The humorous character of Sidonius' observations by no means abolishes their historical value, as W. B. Anderson in his edition of Sidonius ([Cambridge, 1936], p. 382) and, following him, Professor Morey (*Art*, p. 220) seem to believe. Equally unnecessary seems Anderson's suggestion that the "Syrians" referred to were really "bankers and moneylenders."

30. Morey (*Art*, p. 160) calls this scene "Christ and the Adulteress," possibly because a representation of this episode in St. Sergius of Gaza is mentioned by Choricius (*loc. cit*). But the mosaic in Sant' Apollinare Nuovo undoubtedly depicts the *Haemorroissa*, as is apparent not only from the context of the other miracle scenes but also from the iconography of this composition, which we can trace to early Christian art (see Ricci, *MTS, S. Apollinare Nuovo*, p. 24; Wilpert, *Mosaiken*, II, 816 ff.; Grabar, *Martyrium*, II, 252, n. 5).

31. In regard to the liturgical use of the miracle of the loaves and fishes see the final prayer in the Nestorian liturgy: "Ipsa manus dextera quae elevata est super quinque panes, ex quibus satiati sunt homines quinque mille..." (*Liturgicarum orientalium collectio*, ed. Renaudot [Paris, 1716], I, 636 ff.; quoted by Wetter II, p. 27, and Lietzmann, *Messe*, p. 245). For the Roman rite see above, p. 68.

32. Lietzmann, *Messe*, p. 46.

33. *PL*, LII, 622; see also Ambrose (or perhaps Liberius) *De virginibus* iii. 1 (*PL*, XVI, 321).

34. E.g., the door of Santa Sabina (Morey, *Art*, Fig. 149); the chair of Maximian, and the Sarcophagi in Wilpert, I, Pls. 96, 98, 115, 158, No. 3; etc. For further examples see Grabar, *Martyrium*, II, 148, 245.

35. I cannot follow Baumstark (*RG*), who seeks to explain the inversion with the liturgical arrangement of the episodes; in the liturgy this arrangement has a meaning which it could not have in the basilica.

36. Etheria, p. 92. As to the eucharistic symbolism of the Miracle of

Cana see Berlendis *De oblat.*, p. 112. With reference to a silver *amula* for the oblation of the eucharistic wine adorned with a representation of that miracle, Berlendis quotes an oration from the Epiphany liturgy of the *Missale Gothicum*: "Ut qui tunc aquas in vina mutavit, nunc in sanguinem suum oblationem vina convertat" (Bannister, I, 26, 12–14, 33–36). Cf. Cyril of Jerusalem *Catechesis* 22, *Mystagogia* 4. 2 (*PG*, XXXIII, 1098 f.).

37. Wilpert, *Katakomben*, pp. 843 and 264.

38. *Ep.* 55. 1 and 2 (*CSEL*, XXXIV, Part II, 170 f.), quoted by Roetzer, pp. 22 f. The reference to all believers as other Christs in Augustine, *CD* xx. 10 (*CSEL*, XL, Part II, 455): "Sicut omnes christos dicimus. . . ."

39. "Vere digne qui non solum pro salute mundi persecutionem sustinuit impiorum sed fidelibus suis etiam haec dona concessit ut eius fierent aut passione aut confessione consortes per" (*Leonianum*, pp. 348 f., quoted by Casel, *Mysterium*). Also relevant in this connection is the fact that, in order to discourage the excessive worship of martyrs, some early Christian communities sought to reserve the title of martyr for Christ only (Eusebius *Hist. eccles.* v. 2. 2, 3 [*PG*, XX, 433 f.]; see also Wetter I, p. 141). On Christ as the first martyr see *PG*, XL, 324 f.

40. The widow's mite may also have a liturgical meaning (see the commemoration of this scene in the Nestorian liturgy, Brightman, pp. 285 f.). On the significance of Peter's denial and its iconography see also Grabar, *Martyrium*, II, 266.

41. Agnellus xix. 30, pp. 81 f.; the story that Agnellus tells of the death of Peter Chrysologus (xxii. 52, pp. 152 ff.) may likewise be inspired by the saint's image in San Giovanni in Fonte.

42. The best-known group of these prayers goes under the name of St. Cyprian (see *Opp.* [*CSEL*, III, 144]); Le Blant (p. xxi) has added many similar prayers that are found in the ancient sacramentaries. See also Baumstark, "Paradigmengebete ostsyrischer Kirchendichtung," *OC²*, Vols. X/XI (1923). The *Pontificale Romanum* (pp. 1032 ff.) preserves a paradigmatic prayer in which the deceased is compared to Lazarus (*De officio solemni post missam pro defunctis. Responsorium Modus IV*).

43. See K. Michel, *Gebet und Bild in frühchristlicher Zeit* (Leipzig, 1901); Wulff, p. 69; Wetter I, pp. 155 ff.; Grabar, *Martyrium*, II, 8 ff.; and F. Gerke, "Das Grab—der Ursprung der christlichen Kunst," *Kunst und Kirche*, Vol. XV (1938).

44. The narrative character of early Christian sepulchral art has been asserted by P. Styger, *Die altchristliche Grabeskunst* (München, 1927); his thesis is supported by Morey, *Art*, p. 61, who quotes Le Blant, pp. xv ff., on the Daniel scene, though the French scholar's argument is by no means a defense of Styger's thesis.

45. For parallels of such "visual litanies" in Coptic art see Grabar, *Martyrium*, II, 296 ff. The author's attempt to dissociate this pictorial invocation of saints from the liturgy appears to me untenable. He insists (*ibid.*, p. 306) that in two cases these images were inspired by the Apocalypse rather than by the liturgy. But, as we have seen time and again, the ancient liturgies themselves are often patterned after the vision of the Book of Revelation. The Litanies of Ravenna in Graevius, Vol. VIII, Part I.

46. Morey (*Art*, p. 162), in his critique of this hypothesis, fails to include the patriarchs in his enumeration and counts four evangelists in addition to the twelve apostles, though the litanies mention as evangelists only the two not yet enumerated among the apostles. The same mistake was made by Kraus and Richter, whose views Morey opposes. Grabar (*Martyrium*, II, 124 ff.) calls these figures prophets, patriarchs, and apostles.

47. See Cyril of Jerusalem *Catech. myst.* v. 9 (*PG*, XXXIII, 1116). Quoted by Kirsch, *FCL*, I, Part I (1900), 184 and 198.

48. See *DACL*, I, Part II, 2820. The mosaics were executed after A.D. 459 and adorned the apse. Christ seems to have appeared in the center with six apostles on either side of him (see Ciampini, Vol. I, Pl. 77, p. 250).

49. Agnellus xxviii. 88, p. 220; and Testi, *ibid.*

50. *Anon. Vales.* xii. 71, p. 324.

51. See Morey, *Art*, p. 164.

52. See the phrase "Digne arrianorum non subiacuit feritate" (*sic!*) or "Digne ei Arianorum subiacuit feritas" in the *Immolacio* on St. Martin's feast day in the *Missale Gothicum* (Bannister, I, 129, and II, 103).

53. Van Berchem (p. xlix) points out that the white cloak, the *pallium,* gradually came to replace, with the Christians, the Roman toga. It is noteworthy, however, that the term *togatus,* like the more eloquent *candidatus,* denoted in Christian language the martyr and the saint (see Feltoe, "Toga and Togatus," *JTS*, Vol. XXIII [1921]).

54. On the influence of this passage on the eucharistic liturgy see Schermann, *Kirchenordnung*, II, 260 (396).

55. On the *loros* see R. Delbrueck, "Der spätantike Kaiserornat," *Antike*, Vol. VIII (1932).

56. "On aura remarqué combien, dans l'hagiographie de cette ville byzantine, l'élément oriental est faiblement représenté" (Delehaye, p. 328).

57. Agnellus (i. 2, p. 25) knew of an ancient sanctuary of St. Demetrius near Ravenna, close to the place where St. Apollinaris was taken prisoner. This fact may point to an ancient cult of Demetrius in Ravenna. On the cult of Vincentius see Leo Magnus *Sermo* xiii, *in Natali S. Vincentii martyris* (*PL*, LIV, 501); cf. also Lanzoni, *Diocesi*, pp. 773 f. On the order of saints in the canons of Milan and Rome see Baumstark, "Das Communicantes und seine Heiligenliste," *JL*, Vol. I (1921). Lanzoni (*Studi*) was the first to suggest that the mosaics in Sant' Apollinare Nuovo may represent the canon of Ravenna and may thus point to close liturgical ties between this city, Rome, and Milan at the time of Archbishop Agnellus.

58. They share the same feast, September 16.

59. Lanzoni, *Diocesi*, p. 725.

60. Lanzoni, *Reliquie*.

61. Baumstark, *Liturgia*, pp. 158 ff.

62. *L'Église*, p. 202.

63. Testi, pp. 23 and 191; Agnellus i. 1.

64. See the essay by Monneret de Villard quoted above (n. 27).

65. Lanzoni, *Diocesi*, pp. 347 f.

66. See the discussion in Delehaye, p. 320, and Lanzoni, *Diocesi*, pp. 535 ff.

67. Delehaye (p. 327) assigns Sabina to Vindena near Terni; Savio (pp. 935 f.) is dubious in view of the Acts of SS. Nabor and Felix, in which St. Sabina appears as a pious matron burying the corpses of the two martyrs of Milan. Lanzoni (*Diocesi*, p. 105) claims her for Rome.

68. The meaning and reference of the term *communicantes* presents some difficulties (see Botte, *Canon*, p. 55). Our interpretation appears justified, however, in view of the passage in Optatus of Mileve ii. 4 (*CSEL*, XXVI, 38): "Quam [cathedram Petri] nescio si uel oculis nouit et ad cuius memoriam non accedit quasi scismaticus contra apostolum faciens qui ait: memoriis sanctorum communicantes. Ecce praesentes sunt ibi duorum memoriae apostolorum. Dicite si ad has ingredi potuit aut obtulit illic ubi sanctorum memorias esse constat."

69. See Origen *Contra Celsum* i. 60 (*PG*, XI, 771); Irenaeus *Contra haereses* iii. 9. 2 (*PG*, VII, 870 f.); Ambrose *Expos. evang. sec. Luc.* ii. 44 (*PL*, XVI, 557).

70. Agnellus xxviii. 88, p. 221; see also A. Rücker, "Zwei Nestorianische Hymnen über die Magier," *OC²*, X/XI (1923), 45 f.

Archbishop Agnellus may have had a special devotion for the Magi. See the chronicler's description of the altar cloth (*endothim*) in the cathedral, a work begun under Maximian, which his successor "Ex quorum [viz., 'Magorum'] amore," "magorum istoriam perfecte ornavit," adding his own image ("et sua effigies mechanico opere aculis inserta est").

71. *Sermones* xxxi–xxxviii, *In solemnitate Epiphaniae Domini nostri Jesu Christi* (*PL*, LIV, 234 ff.). The reference to the presents of the Magi occurs in *Sermo* xxxvi (*PL*, LIV, 254).

72. *Sermo* xxxiv (*PL*, LIV, 247).

73. See Augustine *Sermo* cci. 1. 1 (*PL*, XXXVIII, 1026 ff.); it is worth while to compare this rather insignificant sermon with those of Leo the Great, in order to realize the extraordinarily increased importance that the Epiphany acquired in the fifth century. St. Ambrose's idea of Epiphany is less certain than that of St. Augustine. For us it hinges upon the question of whether or not Ambrose, as the Maurists believed (see *PL*, LXX, 538 f.), is the author of the celebrated hymn, *Inluminans altissimus* (*PL*, XVI, 1474), where the advent of the Magi is commemorated as one of the Epiphany mysteries along with Christ's baptism, the miracle at Cana, and the multiplication of the loaves. Dom Botte (*Les Origines de la Noël et de l'Épiphanie* [Louvain, 1932], p. 42) doubts Ambrose's authorship. See, however, H. Frank, "Zur Geschichte von Weihnachten und Epiphanie," *JL*, XII–XIII (1932/33), 147; and E. Flicoteaux, "L'Épiphanie du Seigneur," *EL*, Vol. XLIX (1935). Dom Anselm Strittmatter ("Christmas and Epiphany: Origins and Antecedents," *Thought*, XVII [1942], 608) accepts Frank's argument as convincing. There seems to be no fourth-century testimony for the identification of the advent of the Magi with the Epiphany in the East. The passage in Chrysostom's sermon *De baptismo Christi* (*PG*, XLIX, 363), which his editor in the Migne series (*ibid.*, 362) takes for an allusion to that event, does not seem to be clear enough to allow such conclusions.

74. The ancient hymn in its entirety is printed in T. Michels and A. Wintersig, *Heilige Gabe* (Berlin, 1927), "In Epiphania Domini."

75. This is the main thesis of Wetter (see *DACL*, *s.v.* "offertoire").

76. Loisy, pp. 30, 46. The view that the believer, by partaking of the sacred repast, is united to the nature of Christ, is clearly expressed by Gelasius: ". . . per eadem [viz., 'sacramenta'] divinae efficimur consortes naturae" (*Tract.* iii. 14 in Thiel [cf. above, chap. ii, n. 69], p. 541). A striking example for the dual identification of the sacrifice with the donor and the deity in the Christian mystery occurs in the liturgy of Easter Sunday. The lesson on this day is taken from St. Paul, I. Cor. 5:7: "Brethren: purge out the old leaven, that you may be a new paste, as you are unleavened; for Christ, our Pasch, is sacrificed. Therefore let us feast not with the old leaven, not with the leaven of malice and wickedness, but with the unleavened bread of sincerity and truth." These words are specifically addressed to the neophytes who, on Easter Sunday, partook for the first time of the sacred repast; the "leaven" metaphor refers at once to the eucharistic bread and to the faithful and hence identifies these with Christ.

77. *Contra haer.* iv. 17. 5 (*PG*, VII, 1023 f.).

78. Quotations in Lietzmann, *Messe*, pp. 186 ff.

79. See O. Casel "Actio in liturgischer Verwendung," *JL*, Vol. I (1921); also H. Usener, "Heilige Handlung," *Kleine Schriften*, Vol. IV.

80. See above, chap. ii, n. 30.

81. See *Aquileia*, pp. 255 ff. From what has been said above, there seems to be no reason why we should not assume the offertory procession to have originated in the apostolic age. The earliest mention of the offertory, that of Justinus Martyr (*Apol.* i. 67 [*PG*, VI, 450]), does not mention the *Opfergang* of the faithful. But his description of the eucharistic rite of his time is not meant to be complete and does not allow us

conclusions *ex silentio*. The regulations of the Christian rite in the Roman *Ordines* are in no sense inventions but rather official sanctions and ultimate formulations of practices that had gradually developed and long existed, often outside Rome. "Nihil innovatur, nisi quod traditum est," is an axiom of Roman conservatism which the historian of the liturgy must always bear in mind.

82. See Augustine *Sermo* lxxxii. 3. 5 (*PL*, XXXVIII, 508 f.); Ambrose *Comment. in I ad Timoth.* (*PL*, XVII, 497).

83. Augustine *Sermo* ccxxvii *In die paschae* 4 (*PL*, XXXVIII, 1099 f.); Gregor. *Dial.* iv. 59 (*PL*, LXXVII, 428). Even an early age saw eloquent and profound symbols of the faithful in the bread and wine offered. See J. R. Geiselmann, "Zur frühmittelalterl. Lehre vom Sakrament der Eucharistie," *Theologische Quartalschrift*, CXVI (1935), 330; see also W. Goetzmann, *Das eucharistische Opfer* (Freiburg, 1901), pp. 26 ff.; N. Gihr, *Das heilige Messopfer*, II, 44; J. Coppens, "L'Offrande des fidèles dans la liturgie eucharistique ancienne," *Cours et conférences des semaines liturgiques*, Vol. V (Louvain, 1926); Dom B. Capelle, "L'Offertoire," Dom B. Botte, "Les Origines de l'eucharistie," and Dom L. Beauduin, "L'Offertoire jadis et aujourd'hui"—all three in *Les Questions liturgiques et paroissiales*, Vols. XVII (1932), XVI (1931), and VI (1921), respectively. On the mystical identity of the offerer with his gift and of this offering with Christ see Albertus Magnus (quoted by Dom Beauduin): "Dominus vobiscum, ut oblato sacrificio incorporemini. Dominus enim vobiscum est, quando sibi vos oblatos suscipit . . . quando vos sibi unum facit et unit." Cf. also G. Ellard, "Bread in the Form of a Penny," *Theological Studies*, Vol. IV (1943).

84. Brightman, p. 73. For further references to Romans, chap. 12, in the Eastern liturgies, see *ibid.*, pp. 126, 163, 283, 322, 329.

85. ". . . quia oblatio sibi et suis magnum remedium est animarum" (*MGH, Leges* III, *Concilia* II, 1, p. 21).

86. *Sermo* xxxvi (*PL*, LIV, 253 f.); cf. Augustine *Ep.* 55. 1. 2 (*CSEL* XLIII, Part II, 170), quoted by Roetzer, p. 22; Chrysost. *De sancta pentecoste* (*PG*, L, 454 ff.).

87. See Wetter, I, p. 11. Wetter points out that the invocation *Apost. const.* viii. 13. 13 (p. 516) incorporates the eschatological passage from Ps. 117: 27, with its reference to the epiphany of the Lord. Cf. *Apost. const.* vii. 26. 5 (p. 414).

88. "Amore rerum deficientium ad incorruptibilia transferatur, et ad sublimia vocatus animus coelestibus delectetur. Confirmate amicitias cum sanctis angelis; intrate in civitatem Dei, cujus nobis spondetur inhabitatio, et patriarchis, prophetis, apostolis, martyribusque sociamini. Unde illi gaudent, inde gaudete. Horum divitias concupiscite, et per bonam aemulationem ipsorum ambite suffragia. Cum quibus enim nobis fuerit consortium devotionis erit et communio dignitatis. . . .' The passage is also an important clue to the meaning of the *Communicantes* in the Roman Canon and confirms our interpretation of this prayer.

89. See W. Bousset, *Kyrios Christos* (Göttingen, 1913), pp. 293 ff.: "Die Vorstellung von dem offenbar gewordenen Gott beherrscht den Regentenkult. Der Regent ist der auf Erden erschienene, der greifbare und sichtbare Gott." See also the article "Epiphanie" in PW, Suppl. IV (Stuttgart, 1924), esp. pp. 305 ff.

90. See Cumont, *Mages*; T. Klauser, *Reallexikon für Antike und Christentum* (Leipzig, 1939), *s.v.* "Aurum coronarium"; Peterson, *Kyrios*; Kollwitz, pp. 63 ff.

91. See Wilpert, *Sarcofagi*, Pls. 105, No. 1; 204, Nos. 2, 3; 222, Nos. 6, 7.

92. *Dial.* iv. 55 (*PL*, LXXVII, 417): "duas secum oblationum coronas detulit"; cf. also Mabillon, p. xlv.

93. *PL*, LIV, 254: "Aurum etenim de thesauro animi sui promit, qui Christum regem universitatis agnoscit; myrrham offert, qui Unigenitum Dei credit veram sibi hominis uniise naturam; et quodam eum thure veneratur qui in nullo ipsum paternae majestati imparem confitetur."

94. Lanzoni, *Diocesi*, p. 724; Labriolle, "Martyr et confessor," *Bulletin d'ancienne littérature et d'archéologie chrétiennes*, Vol. I (1911).

95. See, e.g., Wilpert, *Katakomben*, Pl. 231 and pp. 190 ff., Fig. 16; also *Sarcofagi*, I, Pl. 73, No. 2; and A. Katzenellenbogen, "The Sarcophagus in S. Ambrogio and St. Ambrose," *Art Bulletin*, XXIX (1947), Fig. 2. Styger's interpretation of this juxtaposition of the Three Magi and the Three Children is inadequate. Alföldi (p. 75), Kruse (pp. 86 ff.), and Setton (p. 206) have rightly called attention to the political significance of the scene (see above, p. 31). But this meaning can be no more than secondary in view of the funerary function of the works of art. The Three Children already appear as martyrs in the Daniel commentary of Hippolytus (ii. 30) (see Kirsch, *FCL*, I, Part I [1900], 90; also Cornelius a Lapide, *Commentaria in quattuor prophetas maiores* [Antwerp, 1654], pp. 1284 f.). On the mortuary symbolism of the Three Magi cf. Grabar, *Martyrium*, II, 249 f.

96. *PL*, LIV, 253.

97. *IIa IIae* 82 : 1. For the following see A. Daniels, "Deuotio," *JL*, Vol. I (1921).

98. The text of the *Secreta* in *Gregorianum* 13.

99. *Sermones* cviii and cix (*PL*, LII, 499 ff.).

100. This prayer was inserted into the Roman missal during the Middle Ages but had already occurred in the Mozarabic liturgy (*PL*, LXXXV, 112 f.).

101. *In Joan. evang. tr.* 84. 1 (*PL*, XXXV, 1847).

102. *Peristephanon, hymnus in hon. XVIII martyrum Caesar Augustanorum* (*PL*, LX, 962).

103. See Origen *De orat.* xxxi. 5, quoted by Kirsch, *FCL*, I, Part I (1900), 46.

104. Duchesne, *Origines*, 413.

105. *Liber de laude sanctorum* (*PL*, XX, 443 ff.); see Wieland, *Altar*, p. 174; and Grabar, *Martyrium*, II, 61. The latter points out the connection between the vision of Victricius and the procession mosaics in Sant' Apollinare Nuovo, but he does not notice the relation of these compositions to the eucharistic rite.

106. *De aleatoribus* 11 (*CSEL*, III, Parts I and II, 103): ". . . pecuniam tuam adsidente Christo, spectantibus angelis et martyribus praesentibus super mensam dominicam sparge."

107. In the early Christian basilica, the place of the altar was frequently at the end of the nave and in front of the apse. The famous sepulchral mosaic of Tabarka offers a good example (see *SAC*, XVI [1940], 170).

108. Agnellus xxviii. 88, pp. 220 f.; see also Testi, p. 66; *DACL*, *s.v.* "orientation."

109. *Carmen* 28. 20 ff. (*CSEL*, XXX, 292); R. C. Goldschmidt (*Paulinus' Churches in Nola* [Amsterdam, 1940], pp. 70 f. and 167 ff.) believes that these representations were in two recesses in the cloisters.

110. The following New Testament passages are important for the Christian crown symbolism: I. Cor. 9:25; II Tim. 4:25; II Tim. 4:7; I Pet. 5:2 ff.; Rev. 2:1 ff. and 4:4; see also the liturgically important passage in Ps. 20:4. Cf. also F. X. Kraus, *Realencyclopädie der christlichen Altertümer* (Freiburg, 1880), I, 333 ff.; E. R. Goodenough, "The Crown of Victory in Judaism," *Art Bulletin*, Vol. XXVIII (1946); *DACL*, X, Part II, 2491. On the crown in the mysteries of Demeter, of Isis, and of Mithra see Loisy, pp. 63, 155, 178; cf. also Cumont, *Symbolisme*, p. 475. I was unable to see K. Baus, *Der Kranz in Antike und Christentum* (1940).

111. Minutius Felix, *Octavius* 38 (*PL*, III, 370); Tertullian, *De corona* 15 (*PL*, II, 112). The translation is that of *Ante-Nicene Fathers*, Vol. III.

112. See Peterson, *Kyrios*.

113. *Ibid.*

114. Van Berchem, pp. 99, 174, 120.

115. *LP*, I, 235. On the relation of Mary to the martyrs in early Christian art see Grabar, *Martyrium,* II, 96 ff. and 292 ff.

116. The scepter in Christ's hands is modern. The original attribute was more likely the Book of Life.

117. Giovan Francesco da Carpi, *Croniche della provincia di Bologna de' frati osservanti di San Francesco* (Bologna, 1580), pp. 178 ff.; quoted by S. Muratori, "Di alcuni restauri fatti e da farsi nei mosaici di Sant' Apollinare Nuovo," *FR*, Suppl. II (1916), pp. 56 ff.

118. The most important instances in our present context are the ancient Greek litanies of Ravenna (see above, n. 45). But see also the litanies published by M. Coens, "Anciennes litanies des saints," *Analecta Bollandiana,* Vol. LIV (1936/37), and the Litany of All Saints in the Roman missal. For further evidence on St. Stephen's place in Christian worship see Brightman, p. 276, and E. Kantorowicz, "Ivories and Litanies," *JWCI,* Vol. V (1942). The construction of the basilica of S. Stefano and the translation of the protomartyr's relics to Ravenna by Maximian is further evidence of the saint's cult in this city.

119. See above, n. 39. That the sacrifice of Christ and his martyr is one, that the blood of the latter shares in the propitiatory power of Christ's sacrifice, is a thought which occurs innumerable times in patristic literature (see Wieland, *Altar*, pp. 163 ff.).

120. See above, n. 39.

121. See above, chap. iii, n. 35; and Grabar, *Martyrium,* II, 57 and 71 ff.

122. H. Achelis (*Die Katakomben von Neapel* [Leipzig, 1936], Pl. 40) reproduces an interesting painting from San Gennaro in which St. Peter seems to be shown rejecting a crown offered him by a youthful saint. St. Lawrence is depicted similarly (Pl. 41).

123. "Ipsi tribuentes omne quod vicerat" (*PL*, XXXV, 2423). It must be pointed out, however, that the crown is a symbol not only of martyrdom but also of virginity (see Cyril *Catech.* xii. 33, *De Christo incarnato* [*PG*, XXXIII, 767]; Prudentius, *Perist.* xiv. 1 [*PL*, LX, 581]; Cyprian *Ep.* 9). Garrucci (*Vetri* [Rome, 1859], Pl. XXII, No. 1) reproduces a glass with an image of St. Agnes, to whom two doves bring the two crowns of virginity and martyrdom. See also Cumont, *Symbolisme*, pp. 483 and *passim*.

124. For the following see E. G. Gulin, "Die Nachfolge Gottes," *Studia orientalia,* Vol. I (1925); also J. M. Nielen, "Die Kultsprache der Nachfolge und Nachahmung Gottes," *Heilige Überlieferung: Ildefons Herwegen zum silbernen Abtsjubiläum* (Münster, 1938).

125. See the judgment of H. Taine, *Voyage en Italie*, II (Paris, 1889), 211 f.: "De copie en copie, leur main machinale repète servilement des contours que leur esprit a cessé de comprendre et que leur imitation maladroite va fausser. D'artistes, ils sont devenus ouvriers, et, dans cette chute chaque jour plus profonde, ils ont oublié la moitie de leur art. Ils n'aperçoivent plus les diversités de l'homme, ils repètent vingt fois de suite le même geste, et le même vêtement; leurs vierges ne savent toutes que porter une couronne et s'avancer d'un air immobile. ... En effet, il n'y a pas un de ces personnages qui ne soit un idiot hébété, aplati, malade." Burckhardt's judgment is hardly less negative ("Cicerone," *Gesamtausgabe*, IV [Basel, 1933], 133). Grabar, on the other hand, has shown admirably that this stiff and curiously impassive attitude expresses the ideal of immutable fortitude and heroic indifference to suffering to which both the emperors of the age and the early Christians

aspired and which is, of course, particularly fitting for the image of the martyr (see *Martyrium*, II, 63).

126. Brightman, p. 452.

127. *Ibid.*, p. 257; cf. also Wetter I, p. 74.

128. *Narsai,* p. 54; see also p. 3: "The king saw a man not clad in the garments of glory, and he commanded and they bound him and cast him forth in outer darkness. So the Church scans her congregations at the time of the Mysteries, and everyone that is not adorned with a clean garment she casts forth without." For a variation of the "bridal" motif in early Christian art and its possible relation to baptism see Grabar's remarks with reference to the Resurrection scene at Dura (*Martyrium*, II, 261 f.).

129. See the beautiful sermon preached by either Liberius or St. Ambrose on the occasion when Marcellina, Ambrose's sister, took the veil (*PL*, XVI, 231).

130. See in the Roman breviary the antiphon for the *benedictus* at Laudes (feast of the Epiphany): "Hodie caelesti Sponso/ Juncta est Ecclesia,/ Quoniam in Jordane lavit/ Christus ejus crimina;/ Currunt cum muneribus/ Magi ad regales nuptias/ Et ex aqua facto vino/ Laetantur convivae." Cf. above, n. 73.

131. See the celebrated passage in Cyril of Alexandria *Contra Julianum* x. 335 (*PG*, LXXVI, 1015 ff.).

132. See E. Dyggve, "Probleme des altchristlichen Kultbaus," *Zeitschrift für Kirchengeschichte,* Vol. LIX (1940); also "Basilica Discoperta, un nouveau type d'édifice cultuel paléochrétien," *SAC*, Vols. XVI/ XVII (1940/41); and Grabar, *Martyrium,* Vol. I, esp. chap. ii.

133. Grabar links the medallion portraits of saints in San Vitale and elsewhere to the funerary portraiture of early Christian art (see *Martyrium*, II, 24 ff.); on the mosaic in Sant' Apollinare in Classe see *ibid.,* pp. 28 and 75.

134. Examples of the advent of the Magi in funerary art have been mentioned above (n. 95). For the procession of apostles with crowns on sarcophagi see Wilpert, *Sarcofagi,* Pls. 284, No. 5, and 286, No. 10; see also Wilpert, *Mosaiken*, Text, I, 504.

135. The sarcophagi of Ravenna have recently been discussed by Marion Lawrence, *The Sarcophagi of Ravenna* ("Monographs on Archeology and Fine Arts Sponsored by the Archeological Institute of America and the College Art Association of America," Vol. II [1945]). The author assigns the sarcophagi of the so-called "Rinaldo workshop" to the first half of the fifth century. This date appears entirely acceptable, even though Miss Lawrence's evidence—the iconographical relation to the marble casket of SS. Quirico and Giulitta in San Giovanni Battista —is not too convincing in view of the frequency of the three scenes in the funerary art of an earlier period.

136. We have already called attention to the frequency of presentations of this scene in churches from the fourth century onward (see Van Berchem, pp. 99, 120, 174, 190, 194, 200).

137. Lawrence, Figs. 1, 4, 7, 8. Other examples in Ravenna: Figs. 220, 223, 225.

138. Cumont, *Mages;* Pl. VI, No. 2; see also M. Wegner, "Die kunstgeschichtliche Stellung der Marcussäule," *Jahrbuch des deutschen archäologischen Instituts,* Vol. XLVI (1931).

139. For literature on the *manus velatae* see Morath, p. 48; and Cumont, *Mages*.

140. H. P. L'Orange and A. von Gerkan, *Der spätantike Bildschmuck des Konstantinsbogens* (Berlin, 1939), pp. 93 ff. The texts refer but once to the locality where *congiaria* took place: "Adhuc in praetexta puerili congiarium dedit [Commodus] atque ipse in Basilica Traiani praesedit" (*Script. hist. aug., Commodus.*, quoted *ibid.*). Cf. Rodenwaldt, "Eine spätantike Kunstströmung in Rom," *RM*, Vol. XXXVI

(1921/22); and Cumont, *Mages*, Pl. VI, No. 4. On the *congiarium* see PW, IV, 875 ff.; on its relation to the imperial triumph see Kollwitz, pp. 63 ff.

141. Grabar, *L'Empereur*, pp. 65 ff. and *passim*; G. Bruns, *Der Obelisk und seine Basis auf dem Hippodrom zu Konstantinopel* (Istanbul, 1935), pp. 61 ff.; and Kollwitz, *passim*.

142. On Ephrem see above, p. 35; cf. also Peterson, *Kyrios*.

143. *Oratio I in sanct. pascha* (*PG*, XXXV, 598); I am quoting from the fine translation in *Orate Fratres*, XIX (1945), 193 ff.

144. See E. A. W. Budge, *The Book of the Dead* (Chicago and London, 1901), esp. Vol. II, chap. lxix, p. 234. On the mysteries of Osiris see Loisy, pp. 123 ff.

145. *Metam.* xi. 24. See Reitzenstein, *Mysterien*, p. 32; Cumont, *Symbolisme*, pp. 379, 476.

146. The prayers quoted in *Gregorianum*, pp. 54 f. (pp. 65 f.). On the neophytes' proceeding from baptism to first communion see Augustine *Ep.* clxxxvi. 8. 30 (*CSEL*, LVII, 4, p. 69); Ambrosius *De myst.* 8 (*PL*, XVI, 420), with a description of the solemn procession. Dionys. Areop. *De eccles. Hier.* (*PG*, III, 404); *Narsai*, p. 54; cf. also the *oratio ad populum* (*Gelasianum*, p. 519) in Casel, *Mysterium*. See also Schermann, *Kirchenordnung*, II, 326: "Wie früh der Taufe unmittelbar die Teilnahme an der Eucharistie folgte, zeigt fernerhin Paulus . . ." (I Cor. 10:15). Schermann thinks that Rev. 7:16 f. may be a further allusion to this procession.

147. "Familia tua deus et ad celebranda principia suae redemptionis occurrat (*Gelasianum*, p. 100, quoted by Casel, *Mysterium*).

148. James, pp. 461 f.

149. See Wetter I, p. 82.

150. viii. 8 (I, 484).

151. Brightman, p. 268

152. Thiers (cf. above, chap. ii, n. 30), p. 207.

153. See G. Beran, "L'Offertorio 'Domine Jesu Christe' della Messa per i defunti" (*EL*, L [1936], 140 ff.).

154. The passage which occurs in the hymn on the Mass for the dead by the Syrian Bishop James of Batnae in Sarug (A.D. 451-521) is of the greatest interest in our present context. Above all, because the poem is an eloquent plea in favor of the restoration of the offertory of the laity and thus shows that, when the mosaics in Sant' Apollinare Nuovo were executed, the ancient rite had ardent and powerful supporters even in the non-Monophysite East. The bishop reminds his readers of Melchizedek and Moses, who offered their own sacrifice; of Abraham, who served the angels with his own hands and did not suffer his offering to be presented by others (we notice here again the same biblical offerers whom we know from the mosaics in San Vitale). The oblation of the faithful, moreover, is here specifically related to the redemption of the departed, a thought which confirms our interpretation of the offertory as a sepulchral rite (see the German translation of the hymn in P. S. Landersdorfer, *Ausgewählte Schriften der syrischen Dichter* ["Bibliothek der Kirchenväter" (München and Kempten, 1913)], pp. 304 ff.).

155. The ancient liturgies made no distinction between the commemoration of the saints and that of the dead (see, e.g., Cyril of Jerusalem [*PG*, XXXIII, 1116]). Augustine's remark that the prayer *to* the saints should not be mistaken for a prayer *for* the saints points to the existence of misunderstandings which eventually made necessary the distinctions in the wordings of these commemorative prayers (*PL*, XXXV, 1847); but the ancient sacramentaries contain a number of prayers for the souls of saints: see, e.g., the prayer for SS. Sylvester and Simplicius in the *Leonianum* (p. 148): ". . . ut . . . illum [i.e., Silvestrum] beatitudo sempiterna glorificet. . . . Maiestatem tuam Domine supplices exoramus, ut anima famuli tui Simplicii . . . in sanctorum cen-

seatur sorte pastorum." This and other examples are quoted by Casel (*Mysterium*), whose profound remarks are basic to our understanding of the experience of the liturgical mystery as the moment of redemption of all believers. It is of interest to note that as late as the ninth century the missal of Andechs contains on the feast of St. Gregory the Great a prayer "ut animae famuli tui Gregorii prosit oblatio"; liturgical experience transcends here the boundaries of theology (see G. Morin, "D'où provient le missel d'Andechs?" *Historisches Jahrbuch der Görresgesellschaft*, Vol. XLI [1921]).

156. Following are the postconsecratory prayers of the Roman Canon:

"Wherefore O Lord, we thy servants, as also thy holy people, calling to mind the blessed Passion of the same Christ thy Son our Lord, and also his rising up from hell, and his glorious ascension into heaven, do offer unto thy most excellent majesty, of thine own gifts bestowed upon us, a pure victim, a holy victim, a spotless victim, the holy Bread of eternal life, and the Chalice of everlasting salvation.

"Upon which do thou vouchsafe to look with a propitious and serene countenance, and to accept them, as thou were graciously pleased to accept the gifts of thy just servant Abel, and the sacrifice of our patriarch Abraham, and that which thy high priest Melchizedek offered to thee, a holy sacrifice, a spotless victim. We most humbly beseech thee, almighty God, to command that these things be borne by the hands of thy holy angel to thine altar on high, in the sight of thy divine majesty, that as many of us as, at this altar, shall partake of and receive the most holy Body and Blood of thy Son, may be filled with every heavenly blessing and grace. Through the same Christ our Lord.

"Be mindful, O Lord, of thy servants and handmaids N. and N., who are gone before us with the sign of faith and sleep in the sleep of peace. To these O Lord, and to all that rest in Christ, we beseech thee, grant a place of refreshment, light, and peace.

"To us sinners also, thy servants, hoping in the multitude of thy mercies, vouchsafe to grant some part and fellowship with the holy apostles and martyrs: with John, Stephen, Matthias, Barnabas, Ignatius, Alexander, Marcellinus, Peter, Felicity, Perpetua, Agatha, Lucia, Agnes, Caecilia, Anastasia, and with all the saints, into whose company we pray thee admit us, not considering our merit, but of thine own free pardon. . . ."

157. Brightman, pp. 21, 466, 474, 387, 389, 483, 492, 529; cf. also Dionys. Areop.; *De eccles hierarch.* iii. 8 and 9 (*PG*, III, 437).

158. This was still remembered in the High Middle Ages, when explanations of the Mass described the offertory as the representation of the Passion.

159. Brightman, p. 268; see the commemoration of the dead in the group of Gallican offertory prayers quoted by Wetter II, p. 62; also the *Secreta* in the Mass for a recently baptized deceased (*Gelasianum*, p. 304); and the following prayer (Gerbertus, III, 318): "Annue nobis, Dne., ut animae famuli tui haec prosit oblatio, quam immolando totius mundi tribuisti relaxari delicta."

160. Wetter II, p. 62.

161. "Exaudi nos, Deus, salutaris noster: ut, per hujus sacramenti virtutem, a cunctis nos mentis et corporis hostibus tuearis; gratiam tribuens in praesenti et gloriam in futuro" (cf. *Gregorianum*, p. 31 [36]). See the following Secrets in the *Gregorianum*: "Oblata domine munera noua unigeniti tui natiuitate sanctifica nosque a peccatorum nostrorum maculis emunda (*Gregorianum*, p. 11 [10]); "Concede quaesumus omnipotens deus, ut huius sacrificii munus oblatum fragilitatem nostram ab omni malo purget semper et muniat" (*ibid.*, p. 36 [42]); "Oblatum tibi domine sacrificium uiuificet nos semper et muniat" (*ibid.*, p. 36 [45]); "Haec hostia domine quaesumus emundet nostra delicta et

sacrificium celebrandum subditorum tibi corpora mentesque sanctificet" (*ibid.*, p. 6 [357]); "Supplices domine te rogamus, ut his sacrificiis peccata nostra mundentur, quia tunc ueram nobis tribuis et mentis et corporis sanitatem" (*ibid.*, p. 37 [45]); "Haec munera domine quaesumus et uincula nostrae prauitatis absoluant et tuae nobis misericordiae dona concilient" (*ibid.*, p. 39 [48]).

162. *Narsai*, p. 59.

163. "Nomina defunctorum ideo hora illa recitantur qua palleo tolletur [the author interprets this cloth as a symbol of the shroud in which Christ was buried] quia tunc erit resurrectio mortuorum quando adveniente Christo caelum sicut liber plicabitur" (*PL*, LXXII, 93; *Expositio antiquae liturgiae Gallicanae Germano Parisiensi ascripta*, ed. J. Quasten ["Opuscula et textus, series liturgica," Fasc. III (Münster, 1934)]; cf. also *DACL*, VI, Part I, 1083 f.).

164. ". . . Send upon us and upon these gifts set before thee thine Holy Spirit . . . who descended in the likeness of a dove upon our Lord Jesus Christ in the river Jordan" (liturgy of the Syrian Jacobites [Brightman, p. 83; cf. also p. 53]). For *epikleseis* mentioning the faithful ahead of the sacrifice see *ibid.*, pp. 179, 406; and *Const. apost.* viii. 12, 41 (I, 510).

165. Brightman, p. 93; cf. also p. 287.

166. See above, n. 156.

167. One interesting example for this interrelation of oblation and intercession in the Roman rite is suggested by a Gallican version of the *Hanc igitur* of the canon published by Ebner (p. 417) after a tenth-century manuscript in Rouen: "We therefore beseech thee, O Lord, to be appeased and to receive this offering of our bounden duty, as also of thy whole household . . . "; so far the text is identical with that of the Roman *Hanc igitur;* the Gallican prayer continues as a regular prayer of intercession for the church, the clergy, the kings, the brethren, the poor, and the dead, whereas the Roman text asks but briefly for peace and salvation from eternal damnation on behalf of God's family. But the inference is warranted that, by implication at least, the prayer is similar in intention to its Gallican sister.

168. The question of the introduction of the prayers for the dead into the Roman rite presents some difficulties. Bishop (*Narsai*, p. 114) had originally suggested that they were introduced "with much other Byzantine or Eastern church practice in the course of the sixth and seventh centuries." Later on (*LH*, p. 113) he argued as follows: "Up to the fourth century any mention of the dead was comprised in that long prayer 'for all sorts and conditions of men' said at the beginning of the Mass of the Faithful. This prayer was at a later date transferred to the Eucharistic prayer, of which it was made the concluding section; and this is now called by the liturgical experts 'The Great Intercession.' . . . This transfer was already effected by the middle of the fourth century in that great center of liturgical novelty, the Church of Jerusalem. . . . From this center the new devotion spread . . . throughout the Eastern Empire." It was adapted in the churches of Gaul and Spain. "The Church of Rome, however, taking [as individual churches did in those days] its own line, instituted the practice of mentioning the names of 'offerers' at the early point in the Eucharistic prayer [i.e., the canon] at which the offerings were mentioned. As to mention of the dead in the liturgy of Rome, we know nothing as to whether their names were recited at all in the public masses; though it must be said that from analogy it is not impossible, perhaps not improbable, that they were mentioned in the prayer 'for all sorts and conditions' in the early part of the Mass of the Faithful, just as in Gaul and Spain. Throughout the West, at some period unknown, a clean sweep was made of this great prayer 'for all sorts and conditions.' But in the liturgy of Gaul and Spain a reminiscence of it was preserved, namely in the so-called 'post nomina'

prayers of those liturgies, which occur precisely at that point in the service at which the old prayer 'for all sorts and conditions' had been said. The 'post nomina' prayer is quite brief; the object of it is first the 'offerers' [i.e., those of the congregation who have offered bread and wine for the sacrifice] and then very particularly the dead whose names had just been publicly read out. In Rome, the prayer for the 'offerers' had been long since provided for with the recital of their names in the early part of the Eucharistic prayer, namely as in the present Roman Canon. . . . This being so, and the abolition of the old prayer 'for all sorts and conditions' being absolute and complete in Rome, it is evident that . . . some special place would have to be found for this commemoration [viz., of the dead]. That is one alternative. But there is another, namely the letting fall altogether of this recital and prayer for the dead in public masses." And Bishop thinks that this second alternative was adopted, "the commemoration of the dead in the Canon being relegated to the special masses for the dead, as shewn in the *Gregorianum*." He also believes that this special memento became an integral part of the canon only by the end of the seventh century and under Franco-Gallic and Irish influence. As against this theory, Botte (*Canon*, p. 68) has called attention to the ancient character of the language, to the failure to insert the memento for the dead after that for the living, and to the striking parallel of thought in the liturgy of St. Mark (Brightman, p. 129). One may add that the *mysterium* character of the ancient liturgy makes an omission of any mention of the dead in approximation to the death of Christ extremely difficult to conceive.

169. The relation of this symbolism to death is clearly suggested in the apocalyptic imagery employed in the ancient *Commendationes animae defuncti*. See, e.g., the oration *Ad lavandum corpus* in Gerbertus (III, 313): "Suscipe, Domine, animam servi tui ill. revertentem ad te: vestem coelestem indue eam, & lava eam sancto fonte vitae aeternae; & inter gaudentes gaudeat, & inter sapientes sapiat, & inter Martyres coronata consedeat; & inter Patriarchas & Prophetas proficiat; & inter Apostolos Christum sequi studeat, & inter Angelos & Archangelos claritatem Dei semper videat, & inter paradisi rutulos [ed. *rutilos*] lapides gaudium possideat, & notitiam ministeriorum [ed. *mysteriorum*] Dei agnoscat, & inter Cherubim & Seraphim claritatem Dei inveniat; & inter viginti quatuor Seniores cantica canticorum audiat, & inter lavantes stolas in fonte luminis vestem lavet, & inter pulsantes depulsans [ed. *pulsans*] portas apertas coelestis Hierusalem reperiat; & inter videntes Deum facie ad faciem videat, & inter canentes canticum novum cantet, & inter audientes auditum coelestis soni audiat. Suscipe, Domine, servum tuum in aeternum in bonum habitaculum, & da ei requiem, & regnum, id est Hierusalem coelestem."

CHAPTER SIX

1. *PG*, XLVIII, 701 ff. No discussion of these orations could be complete without reference to the memorable pages in which Rudolf Otto called attention to their significance (*The Idea of the Holy* [Oxford, 1923], pp. 183 ff.).

2. *PG*, XLVIII, 712 and 721.

3. *Ibid.*, p. 705.

4. See Bishop in *Narsai*, pp. 92 ff.; Jungmann, *ZKT*, Vol. LIII (1929); Stefanescu, I, 28 ff.

5. Besides the literature quoted earlier, see J. A. Jungmann, *Die Stellung Christi im liturgischen Gebet* (Münster, 1925), pp. 219 f., who stresses the anti-Arian element in this development.

6. See Bishop, *LH*, pp. 23 ff.; *Narsai*, esp. p. 91; K. Holl, "Die Entstehung der Bilderwand in der griechischen Kirche," *Gesammelte Aufsätze zur Kirchengeschichte* (Tübingen, 1928), Vol. II; and, more recently, S. G. Xydis, "The Chancel Barrier, Solea, and Ambo of Hagia

Sophia," *Art Bulletin*, Vol. XXIX (1947). Xydis points out that "the independent type of chancel barrier was already generally known throughout the Empire during the fifth century," admits its relation to the Great and Little Entrances of the Eastern rite, and sees in the presence of these liturgical objects in Hagia Sophia confirmation of "the preponderant role in art which Constantinople begins to play in the sixth century."

7. θέατρον ἄπλαστον καὶ πνευματικόν, quoted by Andreades, "Die Sophienkathedrale von Konstantinopel," *Kunstwissenschaftliche Studien*, I (1934), 60.

8. The idea that the faithful may only contemplate the sacred symbols shown to them by the priests originates in the mysticism of the Pseudo-Areopagite. From here it is only a step to the definition of the sacred rite as an ἄγαλμα, an "image," which has so profoundly affected the development of the religious thought and art of the Christian East (see H. Koch, "Pseudo-Dionysius Areopagita in seinen Beziehungen zum Neuplatonismus und Mysterienwesen," *FCL*, I, Parts II and III [Mainz, 1900], 217 f.; and Grabar, *Martyrium*, II, 340).

9. Quoted by W. Gass, *Symbolik der griechischen Kirche* (Berlin, 1872), p. 155.

10. Andreades, *op. cit.*, pp. 58 ff.; Gass, *op. cit.*, 299; and, more recently, Grabar, *Martyrium*, II, 339 ff.

11. My use of the term "celebrant," as Dom Strittmatter points out, is misleading, since the rite described is a pontifical Mass in which the bishop himself is celebrant. The priest, therefore, should be referred to as "concelebrant."

12. On the Great Entry as an image of the Second Advent of Christ see F. Heiler, *Urkirche und Ostkirche* (München, 1927), p. 320. The author's main thesis is, of course, the affinity between *Urkirche* and *Ostkirche*. But it is difficult to reconcile his emphasis on the vast distance separating the liturgies of Chrysostom and Basil from the oldest liturgies of the East ("ein Abstand, der in gewisser Hinsicht noch grösser ist als der Abstand der heutigen römischen Messe von der alten abendländischen Liturgie") with his assertion that the Orthodox liturgy "in its actions and prayers has faithfully preserved the primitive and early Christian attitude" (p. 334).

13. See G. Millet, *Monuments de l'Athos*, Vol. I: *Les Peintures* (Paris, 1927), Pls. 118, Nos. 2, 3; 256, No. 2; 257, No. 2; also *Monuments byzantins de Mistra*, Pl. 114, No. 1; see also J. D. Stefanescu, Vol. I (1932/33), Pls. XXVI, XXVIII, XXX, and p. 72.

14. See the brilliant analysis of Andreades, *op. cit.*, and Gass, *op. cit.*

15. Quoted by Andreades, *op. cit.*, pp. 58 f.

16. *Ibid.*

17. Rubeus, pp. 158 f.

18. *De sacerdotio* (*PG*, XLVIII, 639 ff.).

19. *Narsai*, p. 55.

20. *PG*, LXIV, 80; quoted in Setton, p. 187.

21. *PG*, LXIII, 491; quoted in Setton, p. 189.

22. On the history of the basilica see L. Bréhier, "Les Origines de la basilique chrétienne," *Bulletin monumental*, Vol. LXXXVI (1927).

23. On the liturgical aspects and symbolism of the basilica see P. Sarnelli, *Antica basilicografia* (Naples, 1686); *DACL*, *s.v.* "Basilique"; W. M. Whitehill, "Liturgical Influences on Pre-Romanesque Apses in Spain," *Art Studies*, V (1927), 151 ff.; K. Liesenberg, *Der Einfluss der Liturgie auf die frühchristliche Basilika* (Neustadt, 1928). The final and comprehensive study of this important problem remains to be written.

24. See Liesenberg, *op. cit.*, pp. 100 ff., 128 f., 158, 181 ff.; and H. C. Butler, *Early Christian Churches in Syria* (Princeton, 1929).

25. See the interesting study of L. Kitschelt, *Die frühchristliche Ba-*

silika als Darstellung des himmlischen Jerusalem (München, 1938), where the thesis is defended that "mit der frühchristlichen Basilika . . . realistisch, nicht symbolisch, die Himmelsstadt, das Himmlische Jerusalem zur Darstellung gebracht [ist]." See also on this problem E. Peterson, *Das Buch von den Engeln* (Leipzig, 1935), pp. 14 ff.

26. On transformations of streets into courtyards in imperial Rome see P. H. von Blanckenhagen, *Flavische Architektur und ihre Dekoration* (Berlin, 1940), pp. 147 ff.; on the great peristyle in Spalato see G. Niemann, *Der Palast Diokletians in Spalato* (Wien, 1910), p. 4 and Pl. 15; on the courtyards in the imperial palace at Constantinople see Vogt, pp. 51 f.; Dyggve (see below, n. 28), p. 44, and recently *The Great Palace of the Byzantine Emperors: Being a First Report on the Excavations Carried Out in Istanbul on Behalf of the Walker Trust* (*University of St. Andrews, 1935–1938*) (Oxford, 1947); in regard to the function of these great peristyles as settings for the imperial liturgy see Grabar, *Martyrium*, I, 122 ff.; Alföldi, *Insignien*, p. 132.

27. See E. Dyggve, "La Basilica discoperta: Un nouveau type d'édifice cultuel paléochrétien," *SAC*, XVI/XVII (1940/41), 415 ff., and "Probleme des altchristlichen Kultbaus," *Zeitschrift für Kirchengeschichte*, Vol. LIX (1940).

28. Dyggve, "Ravennatum Palatium Sacrum: La basilica ipetrale per cerimonie," *Det Kgl. Danske Videnskabernes Selskab. Archaeologiskkunsthistoriske Meddelelser*, Vol. III, No. 2 (Copenhagen, 1941).

29. Dyggve (*ibid.*) was the first to interpret the representation of the *Palatium* in Sant' Apollinare Nuovo correctly. There is represented not a façade of nine arcades but a planimetrical projection of the three sides of a peristyle surrounding an open courtyard. The same manner of architectural projection occurs earlier on the Arch of Constantine (see H. P. L'Orange and A. von Gerkan, *Der spätantike Bildschmuck des Konstantinsbogens* [Berlin, 1939]).

30. On the linguistic problem see the remarks of Dyggve, "Ravennatum Palatium Sacrum . . . ," p. 53. See his reconstructions of the Palace of Ravenna (Pls. X, XI, XII).

31. It is noteworthy that the internal structure of San Vitale resembled closely the *Chrysotriclinos* of the Sacred Palace in Constantinople, constructed or completed by Justinus II, Justinian's immediate successor. This great octagon served as throneroom and gradually became the heart of the imperial palace. As Vogt (pp. 8 f.) points out, the throne stood here in the place which the altar occupied in San Vitale. In the vault a celebrated mosaic showed Christ enthroned as Pantorator. In this case, the secular structure may even have been inspired by the religious one: to that age the two spheres were inseparable.

32. See *Leonianum*, pp. 26, 47, 79; Mohlberg-Baumstark, p. 42*; H. Lietzmann, *Petrus und Paulus in Rom* (Berlin, 1927), p. 33; A. Baumstark, *Missale Romanum* (Eindhoven, 1929), pp. 26 ff.

33. *CD* x. 32 (*CSEL*, XL, Part I, 507).

34. xv. 21 (*ibid.*, Part II, pp. 106 f.).

35. xv. 1 (*ibid.*, pp. 58 ff.).

36. x. 25 (*ibid.*, Part I, pp. 483 ff.).

37. x. 6 (*ibid.*, Part II, p. 434).

37a. See above, chap. v, p. 109, and n. 164.

38. See Harnack, II, 397.

39. This is the qualification used by Harnack (*ibid.*).

40. *In Cap. I Gen. hom.* 5 (*PG*, LIII, 54).

41. "Teneatur subscriptio clericorum, honoratorum testimonium ordinis consensus et plebis; qui praefecturus est omnibus, ab omnibus eligatur" (quoted by H. Usener, "Das Verhältnis des römischen Senats zur Kirche in der Ostgotenzeit," *Kleine Schriften*, IV, 142); the same principle prevailed for papal elections (see *Lib. diurn.*, p. 51). A curious reflection of this democratic concept of consent in the sphere of the

liturgy is suggested by a passage of Innocent I's letter to Bishop Decentius (4): ". . . pax sit necessario indicenda, per quam constat populum ad omnia, quae in mysteriis aguntur atque in ecclesia celebrantur
praebuisse consensum" (cf. Probst, p. 272).

42. A. Heuss, *Stadt und Herrscher des Hellenismus* (*Klio,* Beiheft
XXXIX [Leipzig, 1937]), p. 253: "Es ist ein entscheidendes Element
für die Beurteilung der hellenistischen Monarchie, dass sie . . . auf die
Seite der rein griechischen Auffassung trat, welche keinen juristischen
bündigen Untertanenbegriff kennt"; on the "crown" tribute, see *ibid.,*
p. 111.

43. See above, chap. v, n. 5.

44. Testi, p. 210.

45. Rubeus, p. 164.

46. Agnellus xxviii. 86, p. 219: "In ipsius fronte intrinsecus, si as-
pexeritis, Iustiniani Augusti effigiem reperietis et Agnelli pontificis
auratis decoratam tesselis." F. von Lorentz ("Theoderich—nicht Justinian," *RM,* Vol. L [1935]) has attempted to identify the portrait as an
image of Theodoric; his argument is unconvincing. He detects similarities between the mosaic and Theodoric's portrait on gold coins; but
even more striking is the similarity between the mosaic and Justinian's
famed gold medallion (see Schubart, p. 101).

47. Cf. the remarks of Testi, pp. 209 f.

INDEX

(References to the notes are only occasionally included.)

ILLUSTRATIONS

PLATE 1

SAN VITALE

Anderson

PLATE 2

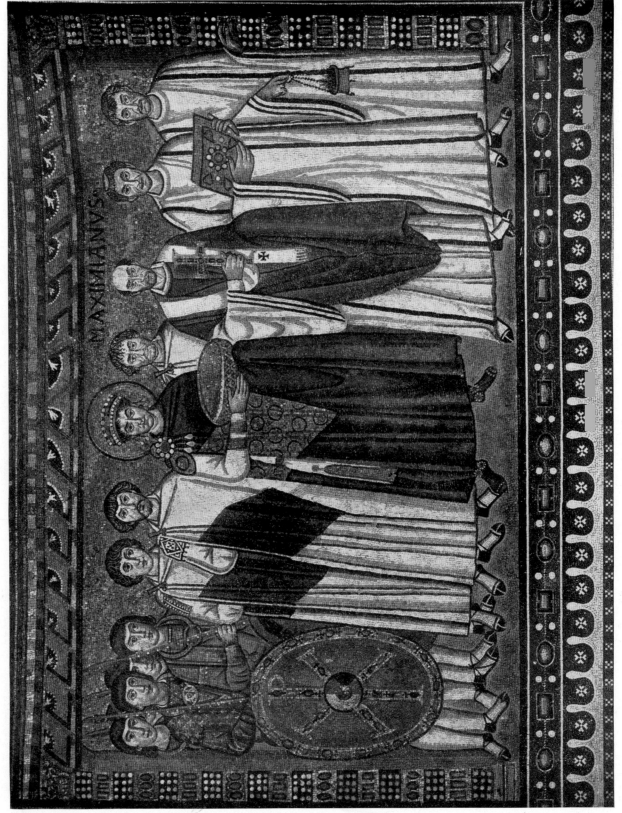

Justinian, Julianus Argentarius, and Maximian. San Vitale

PLATE 3

Belisarius (?), Justinian, and Julianus Argentarius. San Vitale

PLATE 4

SAN VITALE. THE SANCTUARY

Alinari

PLATE 5

a) THE LAST JUDGMENT. MINIATURE FROM THE *Topographia Christiana* OF COSMAS INDICOPLEUSTES (*Vatican. Gr. 699*)

b) THE EMPEROR PRESIDING AT THE CIRCUS GAMES; BASE OF THE OBELISK OF THEODOSIUS, CONSTANTINOPLE. EAST SIDE

PLATE 6

SAN VITALE. INTERIOR

PLATE 7

SAN VITALE. THE UPPER GALLERIES

Anderson

PLATE 8

THE LAMB OF GOD. MOSAIC IN THE VAULT OF SAN VITALE

PLATE 9

SAN VITALE. THE MOSAICS OF THE VAULT. DETAIL

PLATE 10

SAN VITALE. THE MOSAICS OF THE SANCTUARY

PLATE 11

The Title Saint and the Donor Presented to Christ. Apse Mosaic in San Vitale

PLATE 12

San Vitale. View of the Altar and Mosaics

PLATE 13

SAN VITALE. TWO EVANGELISTS

PLATE 14

ABRAHAM AND THE ANGELS, AND THE SACRIFICE OF ISAAC. SAN VITALE

PLATE 15

ABEL AND MELCHIZEDEK. SAN VITALE

PLATE 16

ST. MARC. SAN VITALE

Alinari

PLATE 17

a) Melchizedek; Miniature from the *Topographia Christiana* of Cosmas Indicopleustes (*Vatican. Gr. 699*)

b) Moses; Miniature from the *Topographia Christiana* of Cosmas Indicopleustes (*Vatican. Gr. 699*)

PLATE 18

THE EMPRESS THEODORA WITH HER RETINUE. SAN VITALE

PLATE 19

THE EMPRESS THEODORA. SAN VITALE. DETAIL

PLATE 20

SAN VITALE. DETAIL

Anderson

PLATE 21

SANT' APOLLINARE IN CLASSE. THE SANCTUARY

Alinari

PLATE 22

THE TRANSFIGURATION AND THE MARTYR. SANT' APOLLINARE IN CLASSE

PLATE 23

THE VISION OF THE CROSS. SANT' APOLLINARE IN CLASSE

Alinari

PLATE 24

Courtesy of the Metropolitan Museum of Art

a) St. Lawrence as the Imitator of Christ. Early Christian Gold Glass

b) The Passion of Christ and the Martyrdom of St. Peter. From an Early Christian Sarcophagus, Rome, Basilica Apostolorum

c) St. Agnes. Sculpture from Her Tomb in Sant' Agnese, Rome

PLATE 25

St. Agnes. Apse Mosaic in Sant' Agnese, Rome

PLATE 26

Alinari

The Symbolic Sacrifices. Sant' Apollinare in Classe

PLATE 27

THE GRANTING OF THE *Autokephalia*. SANT' APOLLINARE IN CLASSE

Alinari

PLATE 28

The Chair of Maximian

PLATE 29

Joseph Immersed in the Well. From the Chair of Maximian

PLATE 30

CHRIST AND THE PROCESSION OF MARTYRS. SANT' APOLLINARE NUOVO

PLATE 31

JERUSALEM AND BETHLEHEM. MOSAIC IN THE APSIDAL ARCH, SAN VITALE

PLATE 32

a) Peter's Betrayal. Early Christian Sarcophagus Rome, Lateran

b) Peter's Betrayal. Sant' Apollinare Nuovo

c) The Healing of the Blind. Sant' Apollinare Nuovo

d) The Raising of Lazarus. Sant' Apollinare Nuovo

e) Christ before Caiaphas. Sant' Apollinare Nuovo

f) The Carrying of the Cross. Sant' Apollinare Nuovo

PLATE 33

Alinari

The Last Supper (*above*); Patriarchs, Prophets, and Apostles. Sant' Apollinare Nuovo

PLATE 34

Alinari

THE EPIPHANY. SANT'APOLLINARE NUOVO

PLATE 35

The Port and City of Classe. Sant' Apollinare Nuovo

PLATE 36

PALATIVM

Theodoric's Palace in Ravenna. Mosaic in Sant' Apollinare Nuovo. Detail

PLATE 37

THEODORIC'S PALACE IN RAVENNA. MOSAIC IN SANT' APOLLINARE NUOVO. DETAIL

PLATE 38

THE PROCESSION OF MARTYRS. SANT' APOLLINARE NUOVO

PLATE 39

The Procession of Virgins. Sant' Apollinare Nuovo

PLATE 40

Alinari

FIGURE OF A SAINT. SANT' APOLLINARE NUOVO

PLATE 41

Alinari

Christ Enthroned. From the Mosaic in Sant' Apollinare Nuovo

PLATE 42

The Procession of Virgins. Sant' Apollinare Nuovo

PLATE 43

THE PROCESSION OF VIRGINS. SANT' APOLLINARE NUOVO. DETAIL

PLATE 44

St. Martin and Martyrs. Sant' Apollinare Nuovo

Alinari

PLATE 45

a) The Offertory. From the Floor
Mosaic in the Constantinian
Basilica of Aquileia

b) The Homage of a Conquered Barbarian. From the
Triumphal Arch of Lucius Verus (?)
Rome

c) Saints Offering the Crown of Martyrdom. From an Early Christian Sarcophagus (*After Wilpert*)

d) The Advent of the Magi. From an Early Christian Sarcophagus, Rome, Lateran

PLATE 46

THEODORIC'S PALACE IN RAVENNA (*Reconstruction by Dyggve*)

PLATE 47

a) THE OPEN BASILICA AT SALONA (*Reconstruction by Dyggve*)

b) DIOCLETIAN'S PALACE IN SPALATO. THE COURTYARD (*After R. Adam*)

PLATE 48

SAN VITALE. VIEW FROM THE UPPER GALLERY

Anderson

IN RAVENNA today no signs mark the fact that Julius Caesar once was here, gathering his forces before crossing the Rubicon. Dante died here after completing the *Divine Comedy*, and time has left no more mark of the great Christian poet than it has of Caesar. But between the visits of Caesar and Dante, almost in the middle of the span of fourteen hundred years, lies the epoch which not only linked Ravenna indissolubly to the history of the Roman Empire but made the city the setting of a great political and spiritual drama.

Through a unique stroke of historical good fortune, the stage of this drama has not been destroyed. Three great artistic monuments—the churches of San Apollinare in Classe, San Apollinare Nuovo, and San Vitale—served as the setting for the enactment of this drama. The dramatis personae were Justinian, the Archbishop Maximian, and Julianus Argentarius—the mysterious artist-builder.

Theological doctrine and mystical experience had a daily meaning to the inhabitants of Ravenna in the sixth century. Religious feelings found their expression in the action of the holy drama of the Christian rite. This liturgy, in turn, molded the state as well as society. The mosaics of the churches in Ravenna are addressed to the people of this age.

Mr. Von Simson fuses his deep understanding of political action, art, and liturgical rites of the early Middle Ages to interpret the architecture of the churches of Ravenna as monumental expositions of Byzantine theology—a theol-

(Continued on back flap)